THE TYPEWRITER AND THE GUILLOTINE

THE TYPEWRITER AND THE GUILLOTINE

AN AMERICAN JOURNALIST, A GERMAN SERIAL KILLER, AND PARIS ON THE EVE OF WWII

MARK BRAUDE

New York Boston

Grand Central Publishing

Hachette Book Group
1290 Avenue of the Americas, New York, NY 10104
grandcentralpublishing.com
@grandcentralpub

First Edition: January 2026

Grand Central Publishing is a division of Hachette Book Group, Inc.
The Grand Central Publishing name and logo is a registered trademark of Hachette Book Group, Inc.

Print book design by Jeff Stiefel

Library of Congress Cataloging-in-Publication Data
Names: Braude, Mark, author.
Title: The typewriter and the guillotine : an American journalist, a German serial killer, and Paris on the eve of WWII / Mark Braude.
Description: First edition. | New York : GCP, 2026. | Includes bibliographical references.
Identifiers: LCCN 2025033371 | ISBN 9781538767115 hardcover | ISBN 9781538767139 ebook
Subjects: LCSH: Murder—Press coverage—France—Paris. | Paris (France)—Social conditions—20th century. | Serial murderers—France—Paris. | Women journalists—France—Paris. | Flanner, Janet, 1892-1978. | Weidmann, Eugen, 1908-1939.
Classification: LCC HV6535.F8 P335 2926
LC record available at https://lccn.loc.gov/2025033371

ISBNs: 978-1-5387-6711-5 (hardcover), 978-1-5387-6713-9 (ebook)

Printed in the United States of America

LSC-C

Printing 1, 2025

For my mom, Elcanor

CONTENTS

AUTHOR'S NOTE

What follows is the story of two outsiders whose lives intersected in and around Paris in the dark, desperate years before the Second World War.

Both were foreigners in France, having gone there to escape their pasts and secure their futures. Both adapted quickly to their new surroundings, helped by their ability to seduce strangers in several languages, by their physical grace and magnetism, and by their shared gift for paying attention. Both longed for beauty and sought transcendence through great works of music and literature.

One was a journalist, a representative of American self-invention, American wit, and American love for democracy, who discovered that she did her best work outside of America. The other was a German confidence man and killer, a man so misshapen that when the Nazis occupied Paris they tried to destroy all record of his crimes to avoid being tainted by association.

By telling the stories of these two outsiders in tandem, I hope to capture both the brutality of the era in which their lives briefly touched and the strength people summoned to survive it, as they fought to maintain some measure of civility while watching civilization fold in on itself.

Janet Flanner

Eugen Weidmann

THE TYPEWRITER AND THE GUILLOTINE

THE LAST PUBLIC EXECUTION IN FRANCE

Versailles, June 16–17, 1939

Aren't you going to kiss me goodnight?" the German asked the warden locking his cell. Once again, he'd refused his dinner.

The night was hot, and the guards had opened a window at the end of the hall. He heard the crowd gathering outside. His decapitation would take place at three thirty in the morning on the sidewalk fronting the Saint-Pierre prison in whose basement he'd been housed for the past year and a half. The time and place had been publicized by newspaper and radio. Soldiers had been sent to keep order.

A horse-drawn flatbed carried two disassembled guillotines to the prison gates. Workmen unloaded the equipment and got to work building one of the machines by the light of a kerosene lantern and a few electric torches. They stacked the parts for the backup guillotine against the prison's high stone wall.

The state's executioner, known as the "Monsieur de Paris," a nickname dating back centuries, gave quiet instruction. It was only his fourth execution, and he was nervous. The former Monsieur de

Paris, his uncle and mentor, had recently died of an embolism, ending a forty-five-year career in which he'd claimed nearly four hundred heads. Hoping to simplify the setup, the current Monsieur de Paris had his assistants assemble the guillotine at street level rather than first erecting a platform, an alteration that would have struck his uncle as amateurish. And still the work went too slowly. The sidewalk had a slight but bedevilling tilt, throwing off the equilibrium. A test run left him unsatisfied with the speed of the blade. He had his assistants take the whole works apart to regrease each piece.

The police commissioner looked on, worried that they wouldn't make the appointed starting time. Noise from behind alerted him to a party underway in one of the higher apartments facing the prison, the people gathered there as if for a prizefight. He had an officer park a van in the middle of the street to block their view.

The photographer in the apartment above the one hosting the party would have his plans spoiled, too. He'd been squeezed for a huge amount to rent the place for the night and was already doubting he'd get a sellable shot in the darkness. The cloudy sky wasn't helping. And now the van had obscured his angle. He heard muffled noises through the ceiling. A few of the partiers had taken to the roof for a better vantage point. He went up to join them.

Below beamed the lights of a few nearby cafés that had been allowed to stay open all night. Their staffs had spent hours preparing hundreds of sausage sandwiches and readying potatoes for the fryers. One of the cafés stood a few steps from the prison gates. American music blared from its radio.

Around midnight came the first street fights. The crowds pushed against the barricades that had been placed 150 feet from the prison walls. People strained to see the simple assemblage of wood and steel and cord not much wider than a torso, and the open box beside it, angled so that the body, with a posthumous push, could roll in neatly while a basket collected the severed head. The soldiers held their ground.

In his cell the German had a long talk with the lawyer he liked best out of the four who'd defended him. She was the only woman among them and spoke his language. He was telling her about the spirituals he'd heard one night in Canada more than a decade earlier, whose tunes had haunted him since. He sang her some in a sweet baritone. "Nobody knows the trouble I've seen. Nobody knows but Jesus." He reeled off some lines he said were from Whitman, which had appeared to him from nowhere.

They embraced. He gave her a thickly packed envelope, asking to be buried with it. His last words to her were "I'm ready. And I'm listening to the bistro's radio."

Stars cut through the clearing sky. The mother of one of his victims muscled her way to the front of the crowd demanding to talk to someone in charge. She wanted to see the killing up close. Nearby another woman fainted in the crush and was nearly trampled before being dragged to safety. One observer later swore that he'd seen children in the street that night, and that they'd shouted their hatred for the monster as loudly as any adult. It was like a scene from the Middle Ages, he said.

A woman tried to slip behind the police cordon to take her place among the 160 invited guests who stood in a semicircle a dozen feet from the guillotine. She'd disguised herself as a man, as no woman, aside from the German's favorite lawyer, had been invited into this inner sanctum of spectators. She was found and arrested.

Another woman, immaculately dressed, approached the cemetery official charged with transporting the body. She pushed a handful of bills into his hands. She wanted to buy the dead man's head. She was also arrested.

The Monsieur de Paris ducked into the prison to tell the warden they would have to push things back an hour. Rather than in darkness, as planned, the event would take place in the light of dawn.

The German changed from his prison uniform into dark blue pants and a white shirt. A guard cut his long hair and with the same scissors sliced off the top of his garment, exposing his broad chest and shoulders, pale from confinement. Such precautions ensured that the blade would make a clean cut.

A telegram arrived from New York and a translator had to be found, adding further delay. The parents of one of the victims wanted to know if before strangling her the German had raped their daughter. "No," he said. "I didn't touch her."

He took communion. He refused the customary cigarette and shot of rum. He signed some documents: He had to be officially released from the prison before he could be killed outside its walls. After signing for his freedom he was bound from head to toe. His favorite lawyer removed her gloves and touched him on the shoulder.

Two of the executioner's assistants led him out the heavy green doors. His final sights would be of a few police vans; some thin trees; a horse roped to a flatbed; a newsstand; an ornately curved streetlamp, unlit; soldiers manning some low temporary fences against the shaking crowd; the half ring of invited spectators; and the executioner and his accomplices wearing dark suits and fedoras, looking like bankers pulled from their offices to perform this somber task.

He buckled when they pushed him toward the guillotine and then shut his eyes and kept them shut. His favorite lawyer shut her eyes, too, but a senior colleague told her to keep them open. She bit her lip hard to keep from fainting.

He'd been so tightly bound he could walk only in short paces. When they laid him down, his head facing the ground, his hands behind his back, he jerked against his constraints, once, before going limp. The executioner judged the blade to be misaligned. Instead of taking the time to readjust the blade, he told an assistant to reposition the head to a more favorable angle, which the man did by pulling it toward him by the ears. The German shook loose and the assistant repositioned him again, grabbing him now by the hair. The executioner pulled the cord release. It was four thirty-two in the morning.

From the apartment's roof they pelted the parked police van with champagne corks. Nearby, officers loaded the body into another of the vans, which sped off for the cemetery, though not before the dead man's favorite lawyer had glimpsed her client's bloodied head in the basket.

Guards splashed the sidewalks with buckets of water as a few women dipped the hems of their dresses in the red, believers in the centuries-old myth that a condemned man's blood increased fertility. The spent guillotine was disassembled and carted away.

A French senator, one of the nation's wealthiest citizens, described the event as having been as lively as any costume ball, and more than worth the early rise.

The dead man's senior lawyer spoke to the gathered reporters. "Everything was contradictory in this unhappy person. His crimes are monstrous; his death, saintly. All of us on his defense will remain profoundly convinced that we have just put to death an abnormal being. I've never felt such an emotion."

It took her a month to write again about the German. There was so much ground for her to cover in those last summer weeks before the war.

"He met his end bravely," she cabled New York. "That is to say, he shut his eyes when he saw the guillotine and walked to his death like a somnambulist."

She'd been pulled so far from where she'd wanted to be. She hadn't come there to write about decapitated murderers. But nor had she come there to write about Spanish refugees so desperate for food they crossed back into their former country to steal sheep, risking death by machine gun. She hadn't come to write about goose-stepping soldiers seen from her front-row seat in Nuremberg as an honored guest of the Third Reich. She hadn't come to write about Frenchmen clubbing and stabbing and shooting each other in the ash-covered streets, steps from the neon parade of the Champs-Élysées. She hadn't come to write about the bombing of children.

Why had she come to Paris?

To write, she said, about "Beauty, with a capital B."

1

IT IS ALL I HAVE, DARLING

In June 1925, Janet Flanner got a letter that set the course for the next fifty years of her life. Her friend Jane Grant, a reporter for *The New York Times*, had written to tell her about a magazine she and her husband, Harold Ross, were "giving birth to." They'd published the first issue four months earlier, with an illustrated cover graced by a top-hatted dandy, shoulders back, nose in the air, considering a wispy pink butterfly through his monocle. They'd called it *The New Yorker.*

Grant enjoyed the letters Flanner had been sending her from Paris since moving there from New York three years earlier. They gave Grant a sense of what real life felt like in that so heavily glamorized city and always came packed with news of the latest dramas among the insular and hard-drinking set of Americans who'd settled there after the war. Even more than the glamour and the gossip, Grant liked Flanner's style. Whatever people were wearing as they strolled through the Tuileries Gardens, whatever they were hearing in the nightclubs of Montparnasse, or seeing at the Louvre, or debating over wine outside the Deux Magots, Flanner would have some punchy and unexpected take on it. The letters were just "so gay and attractive," wrote Grant years later. She couldn't wait to read each one to her husband as it arrived.

Harold Ross in his quarter century at the helm of *The New Yorker* would display a rare gift for spotting talent so raw or somehow misdirected that others mistook it for ineptitude. Among his first finds, with his wife's help, was Janet Flanner. He'd tasked Grant with convincing Flanner to keep sending those letters from Paris, but now for print in their magazine.

"He wants anecdotal and incidental stuff in places familiar to Americans and on people of note," Grant told Flanner. And "dope on fields of the arts and a little on fashion, perhaps, although he doesn't want the latter treated technically; there should be lots of chat about people...and in it all he wants a definite personality injected. In fact, any of your letters would be just the thing."

Ross had suggested a weekly letter of roughly a thousand words, and he would pay forty dollars apiece. At that time in Paris you could find a good steak dinner for around three.

The money was enticing. Ever since Flanner had sailed with her lover, Solita Solano, from New York Harbor in the last days of 1921, her mother, Mary, had tried to get her back home. The elder Flanner told her daughter how much she worried about her being abroad without a steady source of income. Surely it would be easier for Janet to come live with her in Berkeley, to which she'd moved from their native Indianapolis along with Janet's younger sister Hildegarde. Surely Janet would prefer the California weather and home-cooked meals to another year of needless struggle, an ocean away from her family and oldest friends.

Flanner couldn't argue with her mother's logic. She was thirty-three and had no job. On paper she still had a husband legally bound to protect her, but she wasn't about to ask him for help. She had a bit of money of her own from her father's estate, but really it was Solano—brilliant, ambitious, resourceful Solano—who kept them both afloat.

Now this opportunity with *The New Yorker* was offering her a way to prove herself to her mother while also getting on a more equal footing to the woman she loved and lived with. And if the magazine fizzled out after a few months of naïve enthusiasm, like so many of these literary ventures, at least she could say she'd tried.

Still, she was cautious about committing herself. She was no journalist. And she hardly felt like an expert on France.

Flanner once said that she'd moved to Paris out of "pure aesthetic selfishness. If I had been born in a prettier part of the country than I was born in, which was flat and cornland, I probably wouldn't have been so eager to appreciate the beauties of Europe." And for her no country in Europe offered more beauty than France and no city more than its capital.

America, by contrast, offered her only heartache and death. She'd grown up well-versed in both. Her father, Francis, co-owned Indianapolis's preeminent mortuary, Flanner and Buchanan, with a brother-in-law. They offered the state's only crematorium and an ambulance service. It was in the office of his mortuary on a Saturday morning in February 1912 that Francis Flanner downed a cup of morphine, strychnine, and carbolic and prussic acid. "Business things," was how Flanner would explain her father's suicide. "And he felt somehow inappropriate, melancholic...The middle years. That is the mortal age. That is when an American man can no longer face life."

She quit Indianapolis soon after to take up studies at the University of Chicago. But all she wanted to do in the wake of her father's death was to live as wildly as possible. Nights she went out dancing to ragtime, mornings she slept late. She withdrew from her second year. "I was too old, you see," she told the writer Mary McCarthy decades later. At only twenty-one, she already had "no patience." To some people she would say that she'd quit school of her own accord. To others, she claimed that she "was requested to leave" for being "lawless" and a "rebellious influence," privately telling one confidante that she'd been forced out after getting involved with a female professor.

Her mother, a beautiful, imperious woman, pushed her to become an actress, wanting to see her own stifled dreams of the theater fulfilled. Janet pushed back. She told her mother that "with this nose I'd be playing Juliet's nurse, or Juliet's nurse's nurse, and never Juliet." While she did have an unusually large nose, for many who met her this only added to her charm, though Flanner disagreed. "I suffered so at the sight of my nose. I just shuddered at this beak. I was born to be old-looking. I looked my best when I turned gray [at thirty] and then I began looking like my own portrait. I was better off. Youthful, I was rather terrifying."

Her looks weren't the issue. She'd never wanted to be an actor. She wanted to write. After briefly teaching in a Philadelphia girls' reformatory run by Quakers, a job she said she took only because she found crime a fascinating subject to study, she moved back home in 1916 and talked her way into writing an arts column for *The Indianapolis Star.* There she also served as one of America's first movie critics, a role she invented for herself. Much to her mother's embarrassment she reported on the city's burlesque scene, too, even though as an unaccompanied woman she was barred from viewing any performance's second act, which would be racier than the first. "That's where I saw the funniest things in the world…the Jewish and Irish comedians. Behind the chorus girls." She was hunting for whatever cultural experiences were available to her in hidebound Indianapolis. She was teaching herself to see.

She knew she would love only women. She also knew that Indianapolis was too small for her ambitions and that it was time to look for a way out. In 1918 she married William Lane "Rube" Rehm, an unassuming New Yorker she'd met at college. It happened quickly, a slapdash ceremony in the Flanner home announced only two days before taking place. The prospect of military service might have played some part in hastening the union, stemming from the belief that a married man would endure less public shame for failing to volunteer than an unmarried one. In any case they needn't have bothered. When Rehm reported for assessment he was deemed unfit to serve in any branch of the military.

After the wedding Flanner joined her husband in New York, where he had a job editing a financial journal and planned to go into banking. She started writing short theater and gallery reviews for some of the small papers, alongside experimental fiction she showed no one.

Not long after moving to the city she met Solita Solano, three years her senior and then working as the *New York Tribune*'s drama editor while freelancing for *National Geographic*. Born Sarah Wilkinson, she'd eloped at sixteen with a family friend who'd become an engineer in charge of public works in Manila, transplanted from her quiet street in upstate New York to playing the role of company wife in a colonial society. She was soon fluent in Spanish, Italian, and three Malay languages, and running with a high-flying group that included Theodore Roosevelt's daughter. She traveled through Asia helping her husband with translations and mapmaking. He abused her, and she escaped her marriage by climbing out of her bedroom window one night in Manila and reinventing herself first as an actress in New York ("a very bad actress," according to Flanner) and then as a drama critic and eventually drama editor in Boston at the *Herald-Traveler*, the first woman in America to hold that title at a major daily. And then she'd returned to New York and secured her job at the *Tribune*. She abandoned Sarah Wilkinson and became Solita Solano, saying she took the name from a Spanish grandmother, though no family record exists to confirm her claim.

The two women met up often but only in the privacy of Solano's apartment on Ninth Street, a short walk from Flanner and Rehm's Greenwich Village home on Washington Place. Recalling those years of concealment, Flanner said she "was very...criminal. Not very good to my husband." Around this time Flanner became pregnant, after which she either miscarried or had an abortion.

More than a half century later Flanner would describe to another lover the sadness of finding herself so "at sea" in her marriage, somehow disappointed in herself for her failure to love her own husband the way she'd loved any woman. She'd found herself dominated by her "emotional push toward my lesbic [*sic*] approach to all life," as she put it. "How strange that I was turned in that direction, the way the branch of a young tree is turned and twisted without pressure from anything outside of its own inclination, acting like a rope or a chain though none exists—no constraint, no pressure from any element except the shaping of my erotic emotions within me which were like an emotional nearness, constantly pressing me into the company of some woman who excited and charmed me and when her influence waned, another took her place. But it was always a woman, never a male."

She stood in awe of Solano, who'd slipped off her provincial past like an old dress, who earned her own way, who'd already published some short fiction. And yet Solano felt just as untethered and unsatisfied as she did.

They weren't the only ones among their cohort to feel vaguely disappointed even in the midst of the country's postwar prosperity, their lives comfortable and safe but somehow lacking in depth. America, in their view, had with its superpower status degenerated into a cultural wasteland whose denizens cared only for productivity, profit, status, consumption, and dominance. The prohibition of alcohol, though in practice only a minor annoyance, epitomized the puritanical and conformist thinking they longed to escape. And though women had won the right to vote, in the streets of New York you could still get pestered by the police and labeled a prostitute simply for standing alone, smoking a cigarette. The bohemian Village was no less immune to sexism than anywhere else.

They had questions about life and how it should best be lived, and were finding no answers at home. "Feeling like aliens in the commercial world" of postwar America, they found comfort in "the idea of salvation by exile," as the writer Malcolm Cowley put it. "They do things better in Europe: let's go there."

When in 1921 *National Geographic* assigned Solano to write about Greece and Constantinople, the two women saw a chance to quit their American lives for good. Solano had been the first to push for the move but met resistance from Flanner, who worried about how it would affect her husband. She said later that Solano had been necessarily "brutal" in convincing her of the rightness of their decision.

There were no big scenes. Flanner cared for her husband, and he'd always been decent and kind. Her mother adored him. They'd tried their best to understand one another. They'd been young. She felt bad about hurting him and would continue to feel that way for years. "Nothing you could have done, honestly and in good faith to your own good self, could have altered that relationship," Rehm's brother told her three decades after the break. "And you must NOT permit any afterthought...Your life was mapped well in advance, you have clung to it and done so nobly."

She sold off all her furniture, including pieces with family history and of solid Quaker craftsmanship. She kept this fire sale from her mother and sisters. Nor did she tell them of her plans to leave. She just went.

They stretched Solano's assignment into a European tour. First came three months in Greece, remembered by Flanner as "my first great adventure in illumination," and then on to Constantinople, Rome, Florence, Vienna, Berlin. Solano filed her pieces for *Geographic* and then placed a few others at rival magazines. Flanner took some awful stabs at lyric poetry. And finally there was Paris.

They had a false start at a cheap pension near the Jardin des Plantes, whose menagerie had inspired Henri Rousseau to dream up his jungle scenes. Nearby, workers were laying the foundation for the Grande Mosquée de Paris, the country's first proper and permanent mosque, built to honor the hundreds of thousands of Muslims who'd fought for France in the Great War. After a year of construction noise and the arrival of an aspiring pianist down the hall, they'd had enough.

Just before the end of 1923 they moved to the Hotel Napoleon Bonaparte in the Left Bank neighborhood of Saint-Germain-des-Prés, having no idea that it would be their home for the better part of two decades.

Their rooms at no. 36 of the narrow Rue Bonaparte put them steps from everything they'd wanted to wring from Paris. The Café de Flore and Les Deux Magots stood a block from their door, their wide, inviting terrasses heated in winter by charcoal braziers. Across from these on the southern side of the Boulevard Saint-Germain, the main thoroughfare and shopping street, stood the Brasserie Lipp, serving *choucroute garnie* (dressed sauerkraut) at all hours. There was music in the streets. Cellar nightclubs beckoned at every turn. They heard students under their windows, teasing one another and arguing. And they woke to the songs of blackbirds nesting in the trees around the church of Saint-Germain-des-Prés, the oldest in Paris and the anchor of their quartier.

They took two rooms on the fourth of the walk-up's five floors. (One of their friends would remember the stairwell forever echoing with the sounds of "girlish laughter.") Officially no. 15 was Flanner's and 16 Solano's. Neither one had a kitchen, as the hotel forbade cooking, but they offered the luxury of steam heating, had big windows that soaked up the morning sun, and gave access to the building's lone bathroom. For twenty cents the hotel's garçon would draw the water and lay out a towel. Solano recalled that these garçons changed over constantly—usually following some small scandal, as when one of them stole her jewelry—and that all members of this revolving cast shared the name Jean and hailed from the same coal-region of Auvergne, like the hotel's proprietors: the affable Louis Doré, a neighborhood hero for getting wounded on the last day of the Great War; and his wife, Mélanie, who lived with their well-fed cat on the ground floor behind a glass door at the end of the lone hallway. For as long as they knew them Flanner and Solano insisted on addressing them as Monsieur Louis and Madame Mélanie.

The Bonaparte was "our ideal, all-purpose hotel," said Solano. "No domesticity, privacy for work and study, all delights free and within walking distance." When wanting to see more of the city they had only to wait downstairs for one of the bright green buses shuttling from Gare Montparnasse to the Opéra and Gare Saint-Lazare and back, their roofs painted with ads for the tony Galeries Lafayette department store. They would splurge on taxis if a relative or an editor came to town. Not long after moving in they went to see Oscar Wilde in the Père-Lachaise cemetery. Flanner brought a single black iris for his grave.

They could see, roughly, the shape they wanted their lives to take. Now they had only to figure out how to keep themselves fed. They'd arrived with the little money Solano had saved up from working, and Flanner's small inheritance. (Solano's father had also died, but she'd been disinherited for marrying without permission, the one stipulation regarding her in his will.) While the exchange rate tipped heavily to their side, they lacked enough to live on.

They planned to take on just enough freelance writing and editing work to get by while devoting most of their time to their respective debut novels. Works they hoped would make their names and if not their fortunes then at least keep them afloat. "I wanted to be Miss Henry James," said Flanner; or if not him then "Sterne or any of the Brontës." Despite their shaky finances they wanted to be careful about the assignments they accepted, to protect themselves against neglecting their true callings. They felt they had options. As a large, liberal, and modern city, Paris housed the staffs of many European editions of English-language papers and served as the main hub for North American correspondents covering the Continent, which meant lots of writers seeking editorial help.

"I can live here without hack work," Flanner wrote her mother in reply to yet another letter asking her to come home. "Do not like California because of the absence of art, which I really hunger for. Can't live in New York without extra working. My novel is my life work, then another and another. It is all I have, darling."

By the time she got Grant's letter, after three years of navigating the many mundane and vexing realities of this noisy, crowded city around which her fantasies had so long revolved, Flanner had little to show for her time abroad.

Solano had emerged as the more fluid writer of fiction. In 1924 she published her first novel, a gritty marital drama, *The Uncertain Feast*, to strong reviews. American critics judged it "an elegant book," as "ruthless" in its realism as anything by Theodore Dreiser or Ben Hecht. The prominent French writer Eugene Jolas called Solano the most naturally gifted of the American writers in Paris. While Solano's book didn't sell well, the publishing advance had been large enough to pay for her and Flanner to travel for more than six months through southern France and Italy. Flanner had taken along some pages of her own novel, still unfinished, which she'd titled *The Cubical City*. Solano had by then already completed chapters of her next book, to be titled *The Happy Failure*.

Flanner acted as if she had far more interest in watching the days unfold from her perch at the Deux Magots than in sitting at her desk, even as she wanted more than anything to write a book so solid it would stay known for generations. Solano reminded her of her talent and assured her family of that talent as well. "Janet's book is racing," she told Mary Flanner, when in fact Janet was working slowly and deliberately and hating herself for her glacial pace. "It's going to be beautifully written and I'm sure the first publisher that sees it will snap it up. I know of no one who writes more lovely prose than she; and the imagination and imagery she gives to her writing is extraordinary and unique." Flanner for her part evaded her mother's sometimes spiky questions about her progress. She told her that she wanted to focus more on prose than on plot and promised that whatever the book became it wouldn't be "cheap."

She comforted herself with long, solitary walks, procrastinating, sure, but also taking the time necessary to look at everything carefully, to develop new ways of seeing, to learn a new visual language in accord with her new surroundings. "I thought Paris was quite *it*," she recalled. "The color of the gray stone, the carvings, and the fancifulness of many of the buildings…The way the roof was made. The way the windows are put in…those round windows, specifically for looking out." She would watch the schoolchildren in their "black aprons with fresh white collars wrapped around their small necks," rushing home in their wood-soled boots for the typical schoolchild's snack of bread and chocolate. Her favorite views were from the bridges, where "one's eyes became the eyes of a painter, because the sight itself approximated art, with the narrow, pallid facades of the buildings lining the river; with the tall trees growing down by the water's edge; with, behind them, the vast chiaroscuro of the palatial Louvre, lightened by the luminous lemon color of the Paris sunset off toward the west; with the great square, pale stone silhouette of Notre-Dame to the east." She reveled in the absence of skyscrapers.

And then, just before Christmas 1924, George Putnam of G. P. Putnam's Sons wrote to tell her that he would publish *The Cubical City*. He'd done so with some hesitation. He thought Flanner showed promise but that the sections she'd sent him were overwritten. Solano, a friend of Putnam's, had put in a good word. He offered no advance. While encouraging Flanner to continue exploring her characters and their paths, he also warned her that her sentences could be "a little precious." He wanted to wait until the fall of 1926 to publish. The manuscript needed a lot of work.

Agreeing to write for *The New Yorker* would mean forfeiting time that could be spent getting *The Cubical City* to where it needed to be. On the other hand, the job might be a welcome distraction, a productive way to channel her quicksilver energy. The stakes of dashing off disposable reports from Paris weren't as high as writing the book that was meant to change her life, but the weekly letter form could give her a new target on which to practice, and it was a task easily performed while carrying out her greater mission as a novelist. And there was something soothing in maintaining a link to New York.

The promise of forty dollars a week didn't hurt, either. Monsieur Louis had just raised the rent on their rooms.

"Is your magazine any good?" Flanner wrote back to Grant.

"No," came the answer. "But it's going to be."

2

THE DIAGNOSIS

Dr. Furstenberg delivered his diagnosis. The young man was a "degenerate." Hiding objects from his parents for no reason, pickpocketing visiting relatives, teaching schoolmates to steal for him, and now this latest theft of a friend's wristwatch from the bathhouse where they both worked, which had gotten him sent to a reformatory: These weren't isolated acts or youthful pranks but only the most easily seen symptoms of a deep and troubling inner disturbance.

The doctor had never encountered a patient like Eugen Weidmann. At only eighteen he could rattle off full pages from Goethe as if he'd pulled them from the air. He showed no physical signs of abnormality, was strong and well made. He seemed immune to all forms of hypnosis. And he was so clearly bent on unsettling anyone who observed him that he'd made a riddle out of every question he'd been asked. He seemed to seek out pain, to want to poke around at the edge of death. He would need to be watched closely.

For Eugen's parents, Frederick and Fanny, the doctor's assessment carried the mark of shame and the potential for danger, even in their quiet corner of Frankfurt.

Fanny sometimes read in the paper—more and more often, it seemed—about some fringe theorist or scientist calling for a culling of the nation's deviant elements. They said unhealthy bloodlines offered no future value to Germany. Some preached the cleansing benefits that would come only through the forced sterilization of alcoholics, prostitutes, shirkers, and thieves. Some, twisting Darwin to serve their logic, suggested that childhood illnesses should be left untreated, leaving only the strong to survive. Some wondered if it wouldn't be best for Germany to simply "eliminate" anyone deemed physically or mentally unfit. This could be done rationally, with cases judged by a panel of doctors, the killings carried out mercifully through chemical injection or electrocution.

The Weidmanns brought Eugen back to their tidy two-story home near the left bank of the river Main. They worried about their strange, bookish boy, their only child. How would he survive in a world where the strong stood so eager and ready to eat the weak?

But the doctor had shown them a way forward.

3

AN OVERSIZED MINNOW LEARNING HOW TO SWIM

By agreeing to try writing a weekly column titled "Letter from Paris," Flanner became the closest thing *The New Yorker* had to a foreign correspondent among its growing cast. She signed on knowing little about the magazine's inner workings, including that she hadn't been the first choice for the job.

She'd first met Harold Ross and Jane Grant through the illustrator Neysa McMein, one of those "magical" people, as Flanner called her, who seemed to know everyone. Her Fifty-Seventh Street studio teemed with comedians, dancers, and writers talking into the night about art and music and sex. McMein and her husband had an open marriage. "It was all very giddy and guffy," said Flanner, admitting that she sometimes felt like a bumpkin among all those carefree bohemians, amid "all that glamour and loneliness," as F. Scott Fitzgerald wrote of his own New York life at that time.

When in 1921 Grant cofounded the Lucy Stone League, an

organization to guide women through the legal steps of keeping their birth names after marriage, Flanner and McMein became charter members. Grant refused to take her husband's name as much to leave her byline intact as to counter what she saw as a chauvinistic practice. Flanner had done the same. Solano, another Lucy Stoner, had the group's respect for having invented an entirely new name for herself, rejecting her husband and parents at once.

While Flanner grew close to Grant, she didn't immediately connect with Ross. She later said that it was because he socialized with a "gambling group," while cards bored her. She knew a lot of the people in Ross's literary troop, the Algonquin Round Table, but tried to avoid its tangle of rivalries and alliances. Still, even from her relative distance, she saw that Ross had outsized talent and ambition: a hyperliterate outsider who'd transformed himself from a "big boned westerner," as she put it, into the ultimate Manhattanite, even while keeping his country twang.

They'd been born a few months apart in 1892, he in Aspen. A dropout at thirteen, he'd tramped on the railroads and worked as an itinerant reporter everywhere from Panama City to New Orleans to California farm country. When America entered the war Ross had volunteered for an army railway unit, lured by a poster reading "First to France, First to Fight." Instead of fighting he served as an editor of *Stars and Stripes*, the newspaper for soldiers. He later claimed he went AWOL from his unit to travel 150 miles to the newspaper's office in Paris to talk his way into getting taken on. In Paris he met the Missouri-born Grant, who'd paused her reporting career to entertain troops at the YMCA's European canteens, drawing on her training as a classical singer. When the war ended she persuaded him to settle in New York, a city he'd considered "a terrible place" of which he wanted "no part." They married and set up in Hell's Kitchen. By the time

Flanner met him Ross had a job editing *The Home Sector*, a magazine for American veterans.

Ross and Grant wanted *The New Yorker* to play a role similar to that which *Stars and Stripes* had played for enlisted men. Now it would be savvy New Yorkers writing for others like themselves rather than soldiers writing for soldiers. They wanted readers younger and sharper than those targeted by bigger publications, especially Condé Nast's *Vogue* and *Vanity Fair*. They planned to hook readers with casual, humorous reporting on subjects that spoke to cultivated members of the upwardly mobile middle class, done by writers unafraid to buck convention. Ross wanted *The New Yorker* to be smart but not heavy. He had little regard for avant-garde art or "serious" literature. He once asked in an editorial note, "Is Moby Dick the man or the whale?"

Ross and Grant got a twenty-five-thousand-dollar investment from Raoul Fleischmann, who was related to the makers of Fleischmann's Yeast and ran his family's General Baking Company. Ross knew him from their weekend card game, an extension of the famous poker nights he'd hosted back in Paris with his *Stars and Stripes* comrade Alexander Woollcott, now back to working as the *Times*' drama critic. Many of the players from that card game, including Harpo Marx, the shrewdest gambler in the group, had some connection with the Algonquin Round Table, and when Ross pitched Fleischmann on the idea of what he called "a fifteen-cent comic paper" focused on New York life, he'd pointed to some of the Algonquin crew—Woollcott, Dorothy Parker, Robert Benchley—as potential contributors and advisors.

Fleischmann knew nothing about magazines but desperately wanted to escape the family business. A friend in publishing told him if he wanted to lose money so badly, it would be easier just to throw his twenty-five thousand off the side of the Staten Island Ferry.

To add to Fleischmann's stake, Ross and Grant borrowed twenty thousand dollars from friends and family. And then, disastrously, Ross tried gambling his way into getting the magazine more funding, adding another thirty thousand dollars to the couple's debts in a single drunken night. They briefly contemplated a double suicide. Fleischmann convinced the people involved to forgive some of the debt and then paid off much of the rest himself.

Launching the magazine was a risky venture, hampered by people's tendency to misread Ross, coarse and clumsy, eccentrically maned, not yet thirty, as an unschooled rube with little to offer discerning readers. But Ross and Grant had good timing. Feeling expansive amid their postwar boom, Americans were looking for new and meaningful cultural experiences. And they wanted to laugh. Comic writers such as Parker, Ring Lardner, and Will Rogers (at that time a syndicated columnist as well as a performer) were becoming national figures. Meanwhile printing and postage costs kept falling as the technologies involved in both kept improving.

Manhattan buzzed with publishing activity. The piano salesman Richard Simon and editor Max Schuster founded their publishing house the same year as *The New Yorker*'s debut, a year behind W. W. Norton and three years before Random House. When Ross took office space at 25 West Forty-Fifth Street, owned by the Fleischmann family, Henry Luce's recently launched *Time* had the office below. (The genteel Luce and scruffy Ross developed a rivalry that ended only with the latter's death; Ross in those first years could at least claim the upper hand when it came to real estate—he paid no rent so long as *The New Yorker* advertised Fleischmann's Yeast.)

With the rise of a national consumer market connected by mass media, Ross saw an opening. A devoted readership of tasteful New Yorkers of his generation, while a thin segment of the population, could attract the city's high-end business owners, who were either wasting money in national magazines advertising to people hundreds of miles away, or getting insufficient return on their advertising in the local papers, whose readers couldn't all afford what they were selling. Ross figured that his New York–focused magazine could still reach a national or even an international audience without alienating its core readership, since there had to be all sorts of people who shared what he called a "metropolitan interest" no matter where they lived.

And he wagered that he could do all of this without having to play to the tastes of "the old lady in Dubuque," as he put it in a prospectus for potential subscribers, investors, and advertisers in the fall of 1924—the "old lady" being Ross's stand-in for a reader who liked things broad and easy to digest. *The New Yorker* would "not be concerned with what she is thinking about." (He added that he meant no disrespect.) Instead, it would offer "a reflection in word and picture of metropolitan life...Its general tenor will be one of gaiety, wit, and satire, but it will be more than a jester. It will not be what is called radical or highbrow. It will be what is commonly called sophisticated, in that it will assume a reasonable degree of enlightenment on the part of its readers. It will hate bunk."

To be "enlightened" in Ross's storybook version of New York, one had to care about what was happening in Paris. He thought any urbane American should be a Francophile, which could be partly attributed to nostalgia, his memories of nights huddled in *métro* stations alongside Parisians as the Germans bombarded the city with long guns. But he was also looking to capitalize on the long-running mutual affinity between the great cultural capital of the nineteenth century and the American metropolis vying for that title in the twentieth. He understood that a link to Paris, then the world center of art and fashion, would appeal to female readers. If *Vogue* and *Vanity Fair* shared a Paris office, *The New Yorker* should at least have a Paris correspondent.

Before having the idea to ask Flanner, Ross had already solicited a few Paris Letters from another source, a writer whose name has been lost as the pieces ran unsigned. *New Yorker* contributors from that time regularly appeared under pseudonyms, usually gender neutral, or used initials, or with no byline at all. Ross wanted to attract readers on the strength of the magazine's concept and house style rather than for any star writers, which in any case he didn't yet have. Anonymity also kept otherwise-employed contributors out of trouble for moonlighting for another publication. And Ross just thought pseudonyms were the height of literary chic.

The unsigned writer's first attempts at a Paris Letter showed no feel for the city and had left Ross unimpressed. Grant had admitted as much when approaching Flanner. "I am looking to you as my great white hope. Certainly you know your Paris, better than anyonc I can think of, and while I know it is difficult to make long distance arrangements, I feel sure you can get the idea if anyone can."

The Paris Letter wasn't the only section that needed tweaking. The first issues had been disastrous: fizzy and smug, more self-amused than amusing, the tone erratic. The writing was as feeble as the circulation was low: fifteen hundred copies sold for the entire first summer. No one wanted to advertise. Page counts shrank. The future *New Yorker* star James Thurber, author of "The Secret Life of Walter Mitty" and other classic short pieces, called the magazine's debut "the outstanding flop of 1925, a year of memorable successes in literature, music, and entertainment, and the only flop that kept on going."

The magazine suffered through many wrong turns as Ross cast about for formats that might spark. Flanner would be one of nearly three hundred different writers to publish pieces in *The New Yorker*'s first ten months. Ross soon burned through the initial stake, forcing Fleischmann to draw on his wife's own family wealth to keep the magazine going. He gave Ross until the end of the year to show he had a viable business or he would cut off all funding, and he brought in a cutthroat publishing expert to get proper advertising and management systems in place, in exchange for a 10 percent stake.

Despite the pressure, Ross refused to let anything guide him more powerfully than his own curiosity, not wanting to press too hard or quickly on unsettled clay. He knew only that he preferred reaching the right audience to reaching a huge one. (Many years later he would get nervous when circulation passed the three-hundred-thousand mark. "Too many people," he said. "We must be doing something wrong.")

Flanner hated the first issues she read, finding them "frail." She called *The New Yorker* in that first year "an oversized minnow learning how to swim."

Her first Letter ran in the October 10, 1925, issue. She'd tried mimicking the biting style of the Algonquin Circle and sent it to Ross. He'd then reworked it to sound more like the earlier Paris Letters to avoid jarring any regular readers with an abrupt shift of style. The result was that Flanner's first public audition ended up echoing the previous writer's shortcomings. Her Letter's main point was to declare the whole of Paris still away on summer vacation and that "anyone who thinks anyone of consequence is back in town yet is a yokel."

Her early Letters would be filled with these kinds of high-handed pronouncements on how to conduct oneself in Paris, if always done playfully, poking fun both at her own arrogant pose and the Parisian smart set whose rituals she was investigating for American enjoyment. But even as she satirized herself on the page, she remained fixed on the idea that Ernest Hemingway would express so seductively in his books: that there existed an ideal way to live, having nothing to do with money or power or lineage but attainable only through one's deep understanding, earned through experience, of what was right to do and see and eat and drink in any situation and what wasn't.

And for Flanner, no one lived better than the French. They exercised "critical judgment," which wasn't "a question of whether this is so much better than that, [but] a question of *why*, and what makes it so...Choosing is a form of creation...Not because a thing is advertised...but because it is appropriate to your taste and preference. That is the great civilization of France—choice. Taste, based upon nothing else. In America, buying just what is advertised—that is not taste. That's opportunity."

When she saw her first Letter in print, Flanner discovered that Ross had given her a pseudonym: "Genet." She would never know why. She asked him once, he avoided answering, and she dropped it. She guessed maybe he'd thought it a Frenchified version of Janet, or wanted to pay homage to Citizen Genêt, who'd served as the French envoy to America and gained fame for his letters about the French Revolution. In any case, she thought "flâneuse," the feminine form of flâneur, the French man-of-the-crowd, would have been more fitting. She did point out that Ross had failed to put the accent circumflex over the second *e*, for "Genêt," as written in French, which was soon fixed.

The first few Letters from Paris did little to set Genêt apart from any other society columnist. But here and there they showed signs of someone happily intoxicated by language, and revealed Flanner's acid humor, in raw form, as well as her uncanny ability to find and amplify the most telling and absurd details in any situation.

Announcing that Sir Arthur Conan Doyle—who along with being the creator of the world's greatest deductive reasoner, also happened to be fascinated by the spirit world and the occult—was giving a lecture at a Parisian research center, she wrote: "The French can't pronounce his name but they mutter something, buy a ticket, and rush into the Sociétés Savantes determined to see photographs of ghosts and get ectoplasm poured all over them." On the annual St. Hubert's Hunt, a grand tradition among French bluebloods, which she underplayed as "the social event of the fortnight," she wrote: "Thousands of Parisians not noble enough to be invited to chase the stag, chased the meet in automobiles, watching what was visible of the old historic ceremonies attending the hunt—the blessing of the two hounds and scarlet huntsmen at the altar of the chateau church, the blessing and distribution of sacred bread to the members at the stable gates, the benediction of the baying pack and the kill at sunset."

Grant told Flanner she liked the first Letters. They were "chatty and instructive" and "angled for the prospective tourist." Flanner loathed them. But she loved that she'd written *something.*

Ross had changed his mind by the fall of 1925 and now wanted Letters not once a week, but every two weeks, and he cut her rate from forty dollars to thirty-five. She felt lucky to be paid at all. She promised to send her mother a portion of whatever she earned. "Hardly any of us has been really happy in life and I am happy now," she told her. She would spend half of her days at the new job while getting *The Cubical City* ready for publication.

Mary still worried that her daughter lacked direction, but she was wrong. "We knew where we were heading," Flanner later said about those years.

She and Solano had freed themselves of virtually all responsibilities—"leeches" in Flanner's words—and they could travel how, and when, and wherever they pleased, funds permitting. They were starting to feel as if they belonged in Saint-Germain-des-Prés. They spoke of "our *quartier*, our church, our river." And they knew that with enough time they would walk among the giants of fiction, realizing their shared dream in Paris, to be separated from each other only by death. All they needed to do was keep writing.

4

A YOUNG MAN ALONE ON A MOUNTAINTOP

Eugen had learned to gut and scale a fish in preparation for sale. It was cold and simple work. When he came home to bedsheets starched so nicely by his mother it felt a shame to climb in stinking of brine.

She always had so many questions. Had he stopped anywhere on his way home? Had he talked to anyone? Had he kept himself clean? The same questions she'd asked him as a boy, when she'd barely let him out of her sight.

The doctor had told his parents that a steady job was vital to his rehabilitation. But where was the reward in working for a fishmonger? Inflation had climbed so quickly that money had been twisted into some kind of cruel joke. At one point a single American dollar could buy you a trillion German marks. Where was the reward in working for anyone at all? And yet he wasn't about to go stand with those pathetic souls in the soup kitchen lines, which seemed to be growing longer by the day. His mother had warned him not to get too close to such people, they carried tuberculosis.

He would keep the job for his mother. He would put his head down and do it.

He had bigger plans for his life than being a fishmonger's assistant. But he couldn't yet name what he wanted. To be fabulously wealthy, yes, but how?

He would wait and he would work.

At night he listened to his Wagner recordings. Wagner showed him how to think himself toward the highest peak, how to release himself from this troglodyte world of small-minded men and empty transactions. He had his books. Nietzsche's words showed him how to stand alone, beyond good and evil, in revolt against all. If, unlike his father, he had no war through which to test his mettle, he would have to find other ways to prove his superiority.

Meanwhile the newspapers dealt him good stories. There was the Cannibal of Münsterberg, Karl Denke. How many beggars had he killed? There was the Berlin Butcher, George Karl Grossman. Had he really served sausages made from little girls? And now the latest, the Vampire of Hanover, Fritz Haarmann. They said he would bite his prey in the jugular.

It seemed that all the while as they marched through their empty pleasant days—working, smiling, cleaning, shopping—the people all around him harbored an inexhaustible hunger for stories of murder and rape and chaos. His own pious parents. His quiet Catholic neighbors. You didn't even need a novel or a film, although you could find plenty of blood there, too. You needed only to walk to the kiosk and buy a copy of the evening edition.

He did his exercises. Hours and hours of push-ups and sit-ups until, finally, he could sleep.

5

HOTEL BONAPARTE

By crossing the Atlantic, Flanner had finally escaped her family's gaze, though she still hung a picture of her mother over her bed. Mary knew that her daughter and Solano lived side by side in a residential hotel. She didn't ask about Janet's romantic life and Janet didn't elaborate. "We don't want to be intimate enough with our family even to think of passion, for another, in their presence; it seems indecent," Flanner would later tell another lover. "That's why, in longing, one can long freely only away from them and best among strangers."

The couple asked Flanner's mother and sister Hildegarde to come visit, and even made noises about all of them living together permanently in Paris. While Janet was apparently disappointed when her mother rejected these invitations, it's unclear if she really wanted her company. She might have known that Mary wouldn't want to come confirm an upsetting arrangement she suspected from afar, or to have Hildegarde see that relationship up close. In any case, Mary never visited her daughter in Paris.

Flanner further cut herself off from her old life by finally getting a divorce. Her husband came to Paris to sort it out. She'd been anxious about his arrival but in the end they worked together to come up with reasonable grounds for the official paperwork. They figured out that because Rehm had changed addresses in New York, they could use that to argue for desertion by the husband, raising no eyebrows and keeping things simple. He was doing well as an investment banker and offered to help manage Flanner's finances from New York.

Only once settled in Paris could she "begin anew," Flanner told an interviewer, decades later. She and Solano went out often to the city's lesbian bars and dance halls and both enjoyed flings with other women. Flanner was the more dedicated pleasure-seeker of the pair. "Hedonism, in its proper sense—that's what I was after," she once said. One friend recalled that Flanner "went out to parties and socialized while Solita stayed home and wrote."

Around the corner from their apartment, on Rue Jacob, they would drop in for tea at the wealthy American writer Natalie Barney's literary salon, a nexus of the city's lesbian community. Notoriously seductive, Barney "did not collect modern art; she collected people," wrote Solano, "and you could be sure of being dazzled" by who you saw at her regular Friday gatherings: duchesses, art dealers, and dancers trading bon mots with Gertrude Stein or Colette. For all of its serious discussion, the atmosphere at Barney's was free and open and sexual. The scene could bewilder and occasionally enrage male visitors, such as William Carlos Williams, who wrote of women "sneaking off together into a side room while casting surreptitious glances about them...I went out and stood up to take a good piss." He added a story about a minor politician who, after seeing women dancing with one another at Barney's "undid his pants buttons, took out his tool and, shaking it right and left, yelled out in a rage, 'Have you never seen one of these?'"

Novelist Djuna Barnes often graced Barney's salons, and she, Flanner, and Solano grew close. One writer recalled seeing the trio on the Café de Flore's terrace sitting in a row "like three Fates" in matching black tailored suits with white satin scarves, boldly going hatless. "Three pairs of white gloves and three martinis were on the marble-topped table before them. It was like seeing in triplicate the sophisticated chic that only years in Paris could produce." Solano said that Barnes sometimes slept in one of their rooms, usually "when in trouble."

For all the progressiveness they saw in their patch of Paris, however, Flanner and Solano knew that most people in their adopted country would have been appalled by the idea of two independent women living and working and enjoying themselves together as they did. This was a country where women couldn't vote, where wives couldn't engage in legal matters without authorization from their husbands. In the villages some people still believed the touch of a menstruating woman could cause meat to spoil. Low birth rates were a constant concern after such tremendous loss of life in the war, and the state alongside the Catholic Church pressured women to marry and have children. Abortion was illegal; both the pregnant woman and whoever caused her to miscarry could be imprisoned.

Flanner and Solano were cautious when discussing one another in print. But in their daily lives within the magic circle of the Left Bank the two women felt free to live as they wanted. Attitudes there toward sexuality were largely laissez-faire. As Gertrude Stein put it: "I like all the people who produce and Alice does too and what that they do in bed is their business and what we do is not theirs." And as one Montparnasse bartender recalled, if a café's manager got too uptight about an unaccompanied woman smoking or going hatless in his establishment, she could just find a more accepting place nearby and take "the entire Anglo-American colony" with her.

Flanner and Solano both drew admirers easily. Flanner was "magnetically handsome," said Solano, with her big brown eyes and immoderate nose. She moved confidently with "a dancer's small body" in which "she took more than a modest pride." She was proud, too, of her wavy smoke-colored hair, worn at ear length. And in her smooth, deep voice she could answer any question put to her with an "impromptu, polished oral essay," as one observer wrote. Her "diction and delivery were those of an actress in the grand manner," said *The New Yorker* editor William Shawn. "When she walked into a room, she made an entrance; the lights went up, and drama ensued."

Solano also knew how to make an entrance, always superbly dressed, her thick brown hair cut short and blunt. Flanner wrote of her "lovely little figure," dark complexion, fine white teeth, and "large swimming eyes of an intense blue which at times contained an expression of sadness, while observing everything minutely and accurately, from a dozen dictionaries to the evening *joie de vivre*."

Most often that "joie de vivre" revolved around food and drink. Flanner said the French taught her how to eat, made her see it as more than just quenching hunger but as something you were meant to feel with your whole body, "the sensual satisfaction" of mixing a bit of tender meat with a hard crust of bread in your mouth chased by a sharp bite of cold wine.

They adopted a simple routine. First they would share a leisurely breakfast, usually at Les Deux Magots, talking over their respective projects, sometimes splurging on brioche. Flanner also liked a bistro called La Quatrième République whose owner claimed that he'd named the place in advance so that he wouldn't have to pay for a new sign, since the France they knew, now in its Third Republic, was bound to fall and be reborn soon enough. For the equivalent of an American quarter they served "a plate full of hors d'oeuvres including a slice of

Jura paté, flavored with wild thyme, and as the main dish, a succulent stew or an escallop of veal and a salad with goat's cheese, plus a small carafe of the onionskin [wine from the Jura] and, of course, a demitasse of black French coffee which tasted like death." This came served by Yvonne, dubbed Yvonne the Terrible despite being excellent at her job.

They wrote at home in the afternoons. Evenings were for the book-stalls of the quais along the Seine, the sprawling flea markets on the outskirts of town in search of visual novelty, the galleries and muse-ums. Nights were for couscous and mint tea in the covered stalls, for drinking, and for dancing.

They trekked across the river to a concert hall at the base of the hill of Montmartre, peeking in to its restaurant, one of James Joyce's favorites, to see the great man "being served royally." Or they popped down to the "brazen, gay and licentious" nightclubs of Montparnasse. They would watch Kiki de Montparnasse fill the tiny Jockey with her unusual energy, seducing the crowds with her eroticized obscenities. Or they dashed off to drink at the neighborhood hotspots—Le Dome, Le Select, La Rotonde—though Flanner found their regulars a bit young and rowdy for her taste.

They were as mad as everyone else for *le jazz*, as the French called it, brought to France by Black GIs and touring groups in the last years of the war. Flanner and Solano sought it out in the "noisy and eco-nomical" dance halls, which "offered little room for anything but dancing. The tables where one sat for drinking were pushed against the wall; the crowd was too young and too inexperienced to drink much anyway...the java was passionately popular, and *le fox*—the foxtrot, a recent importation from America—was beginning to catch on." They went to hear the *biguine* bands at the Bal Nègre, a single big hall adjoining a tobacco shop west of Montparnasse, a joyful gather-ing place for the city's French Antillean communities.

They sometimes treated themselves to a night at the sumptuous Opéra Garnier. Flanner discovered the two most valuable among the cheapest seats in the building, in the upper gallery and way off to the side, where "if you leaned against a pillar, you had comfort and a wonderful view of the stage, far away."

If mornings often began at Les Deux Magots, nights usually ended across the street at the Café de Flore, Flanner in her trademark seal coat trimmed in skunk. There they mixed among a crowd that "had its own *mores*, its private ideology," as Simone de Beauvoir wrote about "the little band of regulars who met there daily" in those years, its members "neither wholly Bohemian nor wholly bourgeois...They lived on unspecified private incomes, from hand to mouth, or on their expectations."

With each passing day Flanner and Solano could hear familiar accents cutting more clearly through the café chatter, as if some unseen hand was steadily turning up a dial marked "American." Like Flanner's, an unusually large portion of these accents reflected youths misspent in the Midwest. Would-be writers and artists who'd been first drawn to New York found there that most everyone was dreaming about some other place where things were surely more exciting. And France, in the rush of its postwar rebuilding efforts and with its vast empire, was welcoming more foreigners than anywhere else on earth. More than three million immigrants would arrive in Paris and its suburbs that decade, making up close to 10 percent of the population, higher than in any other city in Europe. (Foreigners also constituted a quarter of all arrests, sparking xenophobic attacks in the press.)

Some among the few thousand Americans living in Paris had been there from before the war, and many more were ex-soldiers or support staff among the two million Americans who'd served and chose to stay on after the Armistice. Several Black GIs, after getting back home to America, preferred how they'd been treated in Paris and so returned. But the biggest cohort among the city's expats were those who came following the same loose plan as Flanner and Solano, arriving by boat train at Gare Saint-Lazare "richer than most in creative ambition and rather modest in purse." It was easier than ever to reach Europe after the war, as the cost of transatlantic travel fell with the excess of warships being retrofitted for civilian use, and with the dollar strong. But finances were a constant concern for many expats, even as the French assumed they were all "rich because American."

Those American voices that Solano and Flanner heard at the cafés talked often about writing. How and where to do it. How to get properly paid. "We were a literary lot," said Flanner. "Each of us aspired to become a famous writer as soon as possible." To live in a great metropolis, to draw inspiration from the same streets walked by Baudelaire, Verlaine, and Rimbaud, and to do it cheaply: This was the dream they shared.

But Flanner stood apart from her American peers in Paris. Many of them wanted to socialize only with others like themselves. While boasting of their escape from home, they still demanded peanut butter for their bread, and favored the American-run diners that served them the corned beef hash of their childhoods, and made their pancakes from Aunt Jemima's flour. They preferred bars like the Dome where "all the waiters understand Americanese," as Sinclair Lewis wrote. And in the end, many of the American artists and writers in Paris would use the city as a place in which (and through which) to think primarily about America. For Hemingway, something about sitting in the Closerie des Lilas brasserie on cold mornings unlocked his Nick Adams stories, drawn partly from boyhood memories. "Maybe away from Paris I could write about Paris as in Paris I could write about Michigan," he wrote in *A Moveable Feast*.

Flanner enjoyed seeing more and more of her compatriots settling in. At the same time, she went out of her way to connect with the locals and wanted to learn as much as she could about French history and art. She and Solano took twice-weekly conversation classes to supplement what they'd gotten at school, and soon spoke fluently. As she made French friends she discovered that as much as they liked discussing Victor Hugo and Edouard Manet, they preferred talking about Irving Berlin and George Gershwin, Louis Armstrong and Sidney Bechet. Europeans might still believe their Continent lay at the center of the universe, and yet, said Flanner, "we Americans were at first very popular because of what the French wanted from us—our twentieth century."

"I felt I was living both at home and abroad," she said, "living surrounded with the human familiarity of American friends and acquaintances, and the constant, shifting stimulation that came from the native French." And by living between her two worlds, American and French, she'd positioned herself to make her own unique contribution to the "literary lot" whose numbers were steadily growing around her.

When describing her *New Yorker* brief, Flanner liked to say that Ross had only ever given her one directive: "I don't want to know what *you* think about what goes on in Paris. I want to know what the French think." Who knows if he actually said it? He tended to give writers wide berths to pursue whatever interested them. Flanner found it equal parts comical and intimidating that she—who after three years abroad hadn't seen much of France beyond the capital—was now supposed to give an inside account on all things French.

She started reading ten French papers a day. People said France had more dailies per capita at that time than anywhere else on earth and that the typical French person might read as many as five versions of the same news item before lunch. Readers so spoiled for choice had the luxury of wanting their news delivered with style: a cutting description of a politician known for his terrible speeches, written to mimic his jumbled syntax; some broader philosophical question tucked into a review of a humble gallery show; a track report that made you feel each fleck of mud flying from the horses' hooves. Flanner absorbed some of that journalistic flair. She credited the French papers with teaching her how to use minimal language for maximum effect. "I learned more by being in France about writing the English language than I could possibly have learned in America…I was excited by the exactitude of the French language…a taxi driver will say, 'I don't think you mean quite that word, Madame. Now, let's see, the more exact word, if I may say so, Madame, would be…' And then we get into a long talk about linguistic accuracies while he is dangerously talking to me over his shoulder continuing to drive."

She found it easiest to think of Ross as her lone reader and said she "strove, first of all, to please him," learning how to write in part through his editorial comments. She'd geared her first, overly chatty letters toward introducing would-be tourists to various Parisian pleasures; he pushed her for more direct reporting on events. She veered toward the lyrical; he favored tight, balanced sentences. She wanted to develop her own idiosyncratic style; he tried to show her that she could use good grammar and precise prose to do just that. She said that Ross taught her discipline, both as a writer and as a person.

She found him endearingly odd: his clothes hanging poorly, his face "homely, with a pendant lower lip" and gap teeth, "his butternut-colored thick hair in a high, stiff pompadour, like some wild gamecock's crest." Though never true friends, they connected intimately through language. "I had the very good fortune of working for a lunatic," she said. "He kept us completely on our toes, completely aware, completely awake...We chased words around the office together." He demanded excellence and she wanted to make him proud. They did fight. She ignored his requests for what she considered "cheap glamour," giving as example his wanting to know which members of the aristocracy had frequented the Ritz bar on a given night. And she would voice her anger anytime she learned that someone she considered an equal was getting better pay.

Flanner and Ross collaborated to hone the Paris Letter "formula" and the Genêt persona, creating a new kind of correspondent letter, more literary than the usual polemic, diaristic, and dry political reports from Americans abroad found in *Vanity Fair* or *Town & Country*. Flanner's Letters helped to shape what would become the classic *New Yorker* tone of its founding era: wry and irreverent, immune to hypocrisy and attuned to absurdity. On the state's ceremonial honoring of the eighteenth-century "farmwife," Marie Harel, who invented Camembert, Flanner noted that "Harel's monument, a stone shaft, unfortunately resembles a slice of Gruyère. There is no justice."

Thanks to her androgynous pseudonym, she felt free to write like "a gentleman of the press in skirts." Even as Flanner felt she and Solano were still flailing about like "an innocent pair of green horns" in Paris, on the page she came across as fearless, comfortable in any social situation. Genêt could be cutting. She called the dadaist writer Tristan Tzara "a great man of small stature." She judged the hit show *La Revue Nègre*, which had quickly made Josephine Baker the biggest star in the city, "tuneless" and "dull"—though she thought Baker magnetic, with a voice like a "magic flute."

While her style and humor made it impossible to imagine her Letters being written by anyone else, she almost never inserted herself into a piece. She said she avoided using "I" because "'I' is like fortissimo. It's too loud." Ross discouraged writers from weighing in directly on any issues of social impact. "Let's let other magazines be important," he liked to say. Following his lead Flanner strove for detachment in her choice of subject and was careful to avoid telegraphing any strong sympathies through her choice of words.

She was happy to keep her views to herself. At that point she believed that culture existed somehow beyond the grubby reach of politics, and that all she had to do was confine her writing to the world of arts and society to avoid showing where she stood politically. Once—only once—an editor tried to add an "I think" to one of her Letters. Flanner said that it made her feel nauseous.

The Letters were in some ways group efforts. With so many like-minded people living nearby, friendship was on offer all around, and Flanner leaned on people in her circle. Intense relationships, working and romantic, formed quickly among this group whose members usually had no family close at hand, who in many cases had come there precisely not to have family close at hand. There were only so many cafés, so many salons, and it seemed as if all the same people were going to all the same ballets and concerts and costume balls and gallery openings, which felt endless.

While Ross and other editors made suggestions which, as Ross told her, she could "disregard or not," her friends in Paris often pitched stories as well, and then helped her to gather information. Doda Conrad, a Polish-American bass singer who'd lived in France for years, provided many contacts; he seemed connected to everyone from cabinet ministers to chimney sweeps. For an inside track on crime stories Flanner had help from a neighbor, a ballerina dating a loose-lipped detective. She made connections with journalists at the big papers and sought lines into as many facets of French society as she could. She tried to see and hear as much as she could fit into a day. "I always attend more than I can use." She would clip whatever caught her attention in the papers to see if it could be worked into her Letters, often going herself to reinterview the subjects or sources quoted, hoping to tease out some new angle.

Her job, as she saw it, was to soak up whatever was taking place around her "like a sponge" and then "squeeze it out in ink every two weeks." Research done, she'd sequester herself for long bouts of writing, sometimes going forty-eight hours without sleep, her brain blinking like a light bulb needing the tap of a fingernail to come right. Hunched over an old Olivetti, she would peck at its steel keys with the pointer fingers of her small, elegant hands between long pulls from her constant cigarettes.

Solano provided a calming presence, sometimes stepping in to type as Flanner dictated, and giving editorial guidance on the fly. Solano was an experienced and skilled editor, with significant literary connections from her newspaper days, and offered her services freely to friends in need, including Hemingway. A woman living three floors below remembered the "faint clackings" of their twinned typewriters reverberating down the stairwell.

When she finished a piece Flanner would rush it to the Gare Saint-Lazare, where a desk clerk collected the weekly mailbag bound for New York via boat train and ocean liner. "I trust only that mailbag at the station and...only my own hand and foot to take the Letter there." She timed her deadlines to coincide with the scheduled sailings of ships such as the *Aquitania*, *Majestic*, and *Europa* out of Cherbourg and Le Havre.

Her Letters usually ran in two columns toward the back of an issue. French-themed ads surrounded the writing: Madame Cusson, the Fifth Avenue boutique, boasted of its exclusive right to show the latest fashions from the house of Aine Montaillé on Place Vendôme; a Parisian couturier calling herself "MyRBoR, the great creator" announced her impending visit to New York and that she was taking appointments for fittings.

One early and key connection in Paris—socially, professionally, and politically—was the writer and shipping heir Nancy Cunard. Raised by servants, an only child haunting her family's sprawling, spooky countryside estate, she, like Flanner, had needed to put a body of water between herself and her mother, the American-born Lady Cunard. After the dissolution of a brief marriage (entered into only so she could have a home of her own), and hungry for a poet's life, she'd left London "without looking back at all, as is my habit," she wrote. She, too, considered Paris the place where she could truly "begin." She'd been there two years when a mutual friend introduced her to Flanner and Solano.

Four years younger than Flanner, she had a fast mind, spoke it freely, dressed well, and had been published, all attributes Flanner prized. They had in common that people found them intimidating. Cunard stood tall, with high cheekbones and impenetrable, sea-colored eyes. A friend noted that the "crystalline quality" of her beauty "made some people think she was cold to the core." That she had a celebrated name and a great fortune was obvious and of less interest to Flanner, drawn more by Cunard's perpetual dissatisfaction and seeming inability to experience regret, her poetic skill. When Cunard arrived somewhere, often with an unfamiliar companion on her ivory-bangled arm, she always brought with her the promise of elevating a mere good time to a major event. "To be in the presence of Nancy was more like coming to grips with a force of nature than being out for an evening of gossip and dancing after a hard day's work," said Solano.

They soon spoke of themselves as "three happily married women," a joke on their tripled histories of marital strife. They would sign off letters to one another as "1/3," their correspondence decorated with doodles of trios: three owls in a row, three legs of a stool. They traveled together, edited and critiqued one another, wrote long letters about what they wanted and what they hated. The writer William Murray, son of the woman who shared much of Flanner's later life, Natalia Murray, suggested that Cunard "became a fixture in both Janet's and Solita's lives, almost certainly sexually as well as spiritually," though offering no evidence to back the claim. Solano wrote in an unpublished memoir about a wild night when Cunard convinced Flanner and herself to go "brotheling" with her, but left what that entailed obscure.

Cunard paid for dinners and drinks and trips for her friends and protégés. She had the money and enjoyed helping people she liked. Flanner and Solano borrowed her dinner dresses, hand-me-downs from her mother, from the Parisian ateliers of Vionnet and Poiret, and worn once. Flanner sometimes sported the top hat that Cunard kept as a keepsake of her father. While Cunard played the patron, Flanner took on the caretaker role in their relationship. She felt she had to guard Cunard from her own intensity. The trio often started evenings at Cunard's inexpensive, unheated apartment on the Île Saint-Louis, the red walls decorated with tableaux by Picabia and de Chirico. All sorts of people joined them there: Constantin Brancusi, Marcel Duchamp, Man Ray, Berenice Abbott, Peggy Guggenheim. "We were lively and hip," the screenwriter Anita Loos reminisced with Solano more than fifty years later. "Most of all, we took amazing good luck for granted."

Hemingway, too, would provide encouragement and understanding. Flanner met him not long after she arrived in Paris, likely in 1922 when he'd returned to the city, suffering from malaria, after reporting from Constantinople on the Greco-Turkish war. But then he was off again. Only two years later, after he and wife Hadley returned to Paris, would they and Flanner and Solano start to see each other regularly, usually at the Hemingways' bare rooms above a sawmill. "There was something magnificent about [their] hospitality," recalled Flanner. "There was always a glass of wine, usually some boiled potatoes. Ernest cared far less than I about aesthetics. What he cared about was the action and the emotional body of the traveler. He was a born traveler and a born novelist. I was not." He took her to a fight at an outdated ring near Place de la République. She was struck by how quickly he'd picked up the local boxing slang, hurling insults at the boxers with ease, the sign of a fellow excellent listener.

When they hosted Hemingway he would flop down in their chair, a flea market find, slung low as it had originally been meant for nursing mothers, which they'd had upholstered in a fabric print of tall ships. Flanner thought him drawn to it because the sailing pattern resonated with his yearning to travel; or maybe it was just "the only one big enough to hold him." They took to calling it "Ernest's chair." Flanner remembered him leaning back among the yellow wallpaper and leopard print throws, forever "laughing, talking, his long legs crossed and cocked up in front of him." Hemingway was then pulling away from journalism to focus on his short fiction and was full of advice and enthusiasm. They shared their love for detective novels and talked shop about everyone from contemporary mystery writers to Stendhal. Hemingway told Flanner that all that mattered was to write "so it feels good."

Raised in neighboring states, they bonded further over having lost their fathers to suicide while in their twenties. They discovered that "piece of personal duplicate history" by chance, and later discussed it at a back table at the Deux Magots, "which he always favored for serious talk…I had taken a more rationalist view than he of suicide as an act of freedom—in my mind and conscience a possible permissible act of liberation from whatever humiliating bondage on earth could no longer be borne with self-respect—and our talk ended with the mutual declaration that if either of us ever killed ourself, the other was not to grieve but to remember that liberty could be as important in the act of dying as in the acts of living."

In the fall of 1926, Flanner and her friends celebrated the publication of *The Cubical City*. "Grand news—your book in print," Cunard wrote when planning the fete. "And let us go to that neggro (sic) bar together, get drunk, and weep, palm-clasped or hand-clapping if need be on the way back—yes, but back where?" Years later Flanner would write to Solano to thank her for pushing her to finish a book that in her view had "so little life of its own to begin with. Had you not driven me by your energy and indeed your ambition for me I would never have started it, let alone completed it."

A Los Angeles reviewer compared Flanner to John Dos Passos and Sherwood Anderson, saying either one would have been "proud" to have written the book, while also suggesting that "Miss Flanner's story seems too masculine in thought and construction to invite comparison with any women novelists." That one tickled her. A Boston reviewer judged her "too brilliantly attuned," explaining that her "virtuosity" obscured "the meaning of her thought." In Chicago she was "incandescent," in Tulsa "peculiarly vivid," in New York "nothing very original" and "too electrical," in London "overburdened [by] irrelevant physical detail." Flanner recalled the most brutally honest critique came from her friend in Paris, Virgil Thomson, who told her, "I did not have as much talent for fiction as I did for wishing to write." [More recent critics have had their own interpretations. Flanner left her protagonist Delia Poole's desires ambiguous and her gender expression fluid enough for some readers to interpret the novel as a ground-breaking work of queer literature, a modernist lesbian roman à clef published two years before the landmark books of Virginia Woolf (*Orlando*), Djuna Barnes (*Ladies Almanack*), and Radclyffe Hall (*The Well of Loneliness*).]

Flanner must have felt some sadness at not being in New York for the publication, to meet Putnam in person and to be available for the American press. In the end, *The Cubical City* did not propel her to the great literary heights she'd hoped to reach. Reviews were widespread but uneven, sales modest.

6

TRUE NORTH STRONG AND FREE

It felt good to end the day with a body that had been pushed too far, still feeling the sting of sweat in his eyes. Each day demanded certain tests of strength and each day those tests would be passed. On Saturday you played pool. On Sunday you begged forgiveness. He ate well, slept well. They called him Gene and left him to his labor.

He would recall these years in Canada as "the happy period of my life." His greatest ambitions were to see Saskatoon and maybe Vancouver, though in the end he saw neither.

Eugen couldn't fault his family for sending him to this cold country across the ocean. He'd gotten into trouble again. He could last only so long at the fishmonger's before snapping. His parents had arranged for him to work for a Canadian wheat wholesaler through a Catholic youth exchange. After docking and passing quarantine in Saint John, New Brunswick, it had taken him a month just to cross the country and reach his new home.

But anywhere was better than his grandparents' house in Cologne, the other place to which he'd been exiled, back during the war while his father went off to the trenches and his mother put their savings into opening a restaurant. He'd felt marooned there with his elderly guardians. They'd seemed frightened by him.

Now here he was across the world and still surrounded by German voices, even if these Germans had accents different from his own. These Germans had come from the Volga before the war, settling the village as part of Saskatchewan's St. Joseph's Colony. They'd arrived already suited to life on the Prairies. They'd learned to draw out all that was needed from an unforgiving land.

Even among these kinfolk he tried to speak English as much as possible. The language came easily to him.

Here were the familiar smells of fried dough, the vinegar tickle of boiling beets. Here, too, was constant toil, which now, away from everything and everyone, calmed him in a way his previous jobs hadn't. He'd found a place to put aside the visions of himself as the lone, enlightened superman striding the mountaintops. Here, where the tallest structure was the grain elevator, followed by the Church of the Sacred Heart, his mind went as flat as the land. He could spend hours staring at the white sky.

Slowly, through steady work and quiet devotion, he gained the trust and eventually friendship of his employer. He was put in charge of going into town to sell the weekly collection of wheat and to bring back the proceeds.

7

BECOMING GENÊT

Flanner and Solano relocated to the Loire Valley for the summer of 1927 to work on their fiction. Flanner was calling her second novel *A State of Bliss*.

It would be about a mother and daughter in California, she proudly told Mary. "I know I must try to conquer my periods of gross despair," she wrote her. "When I can't work, I want to die and weep that's all. I've been so terribly ambitious and have done nothing. It's a constant grief to see myself at thirty-five of no consequence to public or art... The worst is over since I have decided what kind of book to do and I feel my *New Yorker* Letters have afforded me a facility in writing that will aid me infinitely. You've given us all [Janet and her two sisters] every chance to be artists—Result?—We are 'talented women,' which is something."

She set a goal of four thousand words a day and a deadline of a few months. But the book got the better of her and she put it on hold, disgusted with herself. She escaped into her role at *The New Yorker*. "I need and long for work," she told a new colleague, Katharine Sergeant

Angell. Flanner in those first years often filed her Letters in the casual, loose style of the café conversations she shared with her friends, leaving it to her editors to refine her prose. Angell, a sharp and stylish Bryn Mawr graduate, hired by Ross in *The New Yorker*'s first year to do a bit of everything, soon emerged as both his favorite editor and the person who drew out Flanner's best work.

Their bond grew quickly, with Angell progressing over a few months from opening her editorial letters with "Dear Miss Flanner" to signing off with "Love, Katharine." Flanner came to know about her young children, about her divorce and remarriage (in 1929 to E. B. White, after which she became Katharine White, which she'll be called from here on), about her difficult pregnancy, about family illnesses (real and imagined), professional setbacks, and many joys. Flanner moved more slowly in revealing the facts of her own life, sometimes mentioning "my friend here with whom I live, Miss Solano."

Each woman felt charged by the other's encouragement. White would lobby and protest on Flanner's behalf to Ross and other staffers many times over the decades. And at the same time she never avoided speaking frankly when Flanner had missed the mark. She rejected one piece by saying Flanner's subject ("the elderly American lady stepping out in Paris") was "fairly old over here," and her prose "too complicated and not quite new enough." She made no secret that she thought Flanner wrote cryptically, leaving it to her and her colleagues to "edit her obscurities out."

Flanner came to trust in, even depend on, White's interventions. About one piece, which she thought too heavy on society news, she told White, "If there's any doubt in your polite, considerate, wise, *bien-elevé* head, darling, chuck the whole letter. Whatever you do will be the right thing to have done." Filing another Letter, she wrote, "I hope you like. If you don't then I can't." She admitted to White that while her edits often left her sentences looking "warped and spread," she understood that "the only way...you can do anything with a sentence of mine is to blow it apart with dynamite." She enjoyed how White challenged her. Replying to one tough-talking letter she wrote, "I couldn't help it, I roared when I read your indignation...you looked even on paper like a small very righteous very angry wren." (White stood just over five feet tall.)

The limits of the transatlantic mail system made back-and-forth revisions difficult. Flanner only got to see the final version of her Letter along with everyone else when it appeared in print. Copyeditors sometimes made late additions or altered her work without her knowledge, and she often disagreed with their choices. They "shingled my vocabulary, and castrated my japes," and even substituted their own arguments for hers, she griped to White.

She moved on quickly from such offenses. She could tell herself they were editing Genêt, not Janet Flanner. She also knew that her editors were only following what one among them, St. Clair McKelway, reminded her was Ross's "absolute, relentless policy...as continually expressed...when he picks up a sentence in the magazine and tosses it, indignantly, at the assembled editors in the news meeting: that if the thought isn't clear enough to a lay and nervous metropolitan reader it shouldn't be in the magazine." Ross "asks, simply and with a sort of bland rather than blind faith, for perfection and doesn't know why it can't always be had."

In her first years Flanner half feared each new letter from the office would be the one where she finally got "sacked," as she told White. But it soon became clear how well suited she was to writing about her chosen milieu—"the city on the Seine...the most capital capital of the world."

She did as much as anyone to shape popular conceptions of Paris in the 1920s as a frenetic wonderland, as intellectually curious as it was culturally innovative, while still retaining its Old World charms, big and intimate at once. She played to the idea that expat living was simply more fun than American living, not despite but because of things like bad plumbing and worn-down buildings, the absence of customer service, the absence of puritanism, the absence of commercial ambition. Genêt's Paris was the kind of a place where, after a threatened rise in the cost of tobacco caused a run on cigarettes, people just shrugged and happily drank more brandy to make up for it; the kind of place where you could head west on a whim and discover, just a few miles out of the city, a country inn serving "blue trout, boiled alive and served with mysterious, perfected sauce" and, "for a few coins," bottles of excellent wine.

As good as she was at capturing the era's madcap spirit, she also wrote elegiac pieces against its frenzied roar, trying to document as many disappearing people, places, and ideas as she could before they were gone from memory. She became the unofficial historian of the fading *vieux Paris*, lamenting the closings of once-iconic cafés and the shuttering of specialized shops. Not for nothing was she a fan of the funereal urban photography of Eugène Atget, "the first to utilize the beauty of the empty street."

She saw that an epoch in French history was passing and devoted much space to memorializing figures well known in France but less so in America, especially keen to rescue those beloved but more obscure members of the recently deceased. On the death of one of the "great servers of the French palate," Françoise Fillioux of Lyons, known for her "*volaille truffée demi-deuil*" (truffled chicken in half mourning), she wrote: "She died with a knife in her hand in her kitchen, where she had cooked for fifty years, and her death was solemnly listed in [the French arts and culture paper] *Comoedia* as that of an artist." And like an especially gleeful anthropologist she explained colorful local rituals, such as "the Lenten trade balls," the annual spring charity galas hosted by "furriers, dressmakers, barbers," and other trade associations. "These balls are not fashionable: they are merely altruistic outbursts on the part of workers who make everyone else fashionable. The proceeds are given to those innumerable vocational *maisons de retraite* [retirement homes] which are the backbone of high French craftsmanship and low French wages."

She was drawn to the ecstasies of high culture and the thrills of criminal lowlife. She said it was the middle that bored her. She straddled both sides of the Seine: the Right Bank of the Champs Élysées, the Opéra and its wide Haussmann boulevards, the fashion houses and the American banks; the Left Bank of small galleries and experimental art schools, warehouses converted into studios, and the cafés and jazz clubs of Montparnasse. She made connections between these different worlds with ease. On the consumerist fantasia of the 1925 Exposition internationale des arts décoratifs et industriels modernes (International Exhibition of Modern Decorative and Industrial Arts), she remarked on seeing the influence of the sleek high modernist innovations on display there at flashy new nightclubs like the Florida, with its "big gobs of color, star rays, and whatnot." Genêt was seemingly everywhere that mattered in Paris at once.

Her eye was always on the search for novelty. She spotted right away in the fall of 1925 the new fad for pearls being draped backward over spine-exposing dresses, originating with the sprezzatura style of the American expat Sara Murphy. Dresses that season "must come from the mint: cloth of gold, cloth of silver, or cloth of copper, at least, or lead, and pewter, maybe, and highly colored. Except when they are black, which is confusing."

She would write in the 1920s about masked balls, gallery openings, horse races in the suburb of Saint-Cloud, and gambling in Deauville; the witticisms of French waiters (one of whom wondered if the word "Prohibition" referred to some American religion because otherwise he couldn't understand the concept); celebrity divorces; sightings of handsome heavyweights and reclusive designers; the heroic landing of Charles Lindbergh (when high-end nightclubs in Montmartre "stood champagne to the Americans, as did excited patrons in humble bars, to their Yankee clients"); screenings of experimental films; the exploits of diamond thieves on the Riviera; and profiles of controversial artists such as Isadora Duncan: "The clergy, hearing of (though supposedly without ever seeing) her bare calf, denounced it as violently as if it had been golden." On rare occasion she strayed from France, as when reporting on Nancy Cunard's opulent summer fetes in her Venetian palazzo.

Her Letters helped to develop the *New Yorker* hallmark of making people feel they'd gained access to the shared and special knowledge reserved for the cultural elite simply by reading the magazine. She would make an offhanded remark about Colette's favorite restaurant without first introducing Colette, assuming it to be a familiar name among her readers, or implying that it had better be. She covered the wedding of an actor to a minor aristocrat as if she was pitching a bad movie, giving the reader the superior sense of one who'd seen all this before, sophisticated enough to know that such unions rarely involved romantic love. "It was Paramount Night the other afternoon in the village of Seraincourt, not far from Paris, when pretty Pola de Chalupec-Domski-Negri became the bride of Prince Serge Mdivani. Our advance to exhibitors is 500 feet of this special, which has some pretty scenic effects in French scenery and fine close-ups of a champagne buffet, might go well in a neighborhood house but would flop for the first big runs...Certainly came the old subtitles with which every cinema sinner is familiar. 'I-am-very-happy-the-prince-was-my-childhood-sweetheart-this-is-the-happiest-moment-of-my-life-kiss-fadeout-cut.' However, if the direction was bad for Pola Negri's wedding, the lighting was excellent, it being a sunny day. Besides, no one should be too critical. This was the first time she had been married in France."

Rarely in her Letters from the twenties did she address the lingering sense of mourning that helped to fuel the era's great artistic innovations alongside its excessive pursuits of pleasure and release. Collective grief was such a constant part of French lives that she found no need to voice it. More than a million French soldiers had died, the highest toll, proportionally, among the major combatants. More than three million had been wounded. Riding the *métro*, one saw the *mutilés de guerre* (war-wounded) taking their reserved seats. If one traveled beyond Paris, especially to the north and east, one passed through a dead landscape: Eight million acres of France had been laid waste. And then came the influenza pandemic that killed as many as a hundred million people globally, taking more lives than the Great War itself. In the wake of so much pointless death, the main directive now was to see the world as it was, in all its beauty and its terror, without any illusions or moral certitudes, while dreaming of another world yet to be. "May all things bear a new name," the poet Guillaume Apollinaire had written from the trenches in 1917.

Parisians felt they were dancing on the volcano's edge. Parties could stretch into multiday affairs. The postwar abandon took place against a backdrop of highly contentious politics. Paris in the twenties was at once the most cosmopolitan place on earth and among the most polarized. Musicians, writers, painters, dancers, and others found themselves questioning tradition and expanding their worldviews amid this furious mixing of cultures and classes: Dadaist draft dodgers from Zurich, White Russians and ardent Bolsheviks, eastern-European Jews fleeing pogroms. The rush of immigrants came bringing their home politics with them.

The terms of peace felt unsettled. Repaying the debt to America, which many of the French thought should be waived altogether, was a hotly debated issue. The franc was unsteady. The state had to draw on its treasury to repay its war debts, and yet the postwar economy showed (ultimately unfounded) signs of strength. Racial hatreds flared, often over labor-related issues. The Russian revolutionary example energized the French workers' movement while doubling the right-wing resolve to crush any chance of something similar happening in France. A large contingent of communists and socialists lived along the periphery of Paris, in the so-called Red Belt, while municipal politics and the police force were dominated by conservative forces. "The storm had died away, and still we are restless, uneasy, as if the storm is about to break," the French poet Paul Valéry said in a lecture a few years after the Armistice.

And yet political engagement was, for many among Flanner's crowd, an afterthought. "Politics interested very few people," said the Russian writer Ilya Ehrenburg of his time on the Left Bank in the twenties. "People thought that whoever did not succumb to chauvinist propaganda must be a firm believer in peace, and this suited everybody: people wanted to enjoy life peacefully." Diplomacy was something done "behind the scenes and had little interest for the spectators." One might read about the Rif War or Great Syrian Revolt, but "the shooting was far away, and life in Paris went on as before...The trenches...soldiers' mutinies, the demonstrations had receded into the distant past...*Dancings*, boxing matches, coachloads of tourists, vacuum cleaners, crosswords, and a number of other innovations made their appearance."

By 1929, as she finished a profile of Edith Wharton, Flanner had given up on writing a second novel. She decided she had no talent for fiction. Perhaps while reporting on the critically and commercially triumphant novelist, Flanner saw some quality in Wharton that she would never manage to possess. The Wharton assignment seems to have bothered her. It was a short piece, and yet Katharine White had to hector her for months to get it done, though in the end she called it one of the finest profiles "we have had in a long while." (After the issue with her Wharton profile appeared, Flanner joked to White that the piece had helped to sell three times the regular amount of copies at her corner kiosk, "in other words, fifteen instead of five! Ah, fame, fame...") Flanner sent most of what she earned for the Wharton work to her mother and spent the rest on a typewriter and some crystal beads for Solano.

A few months after abandoning her novel she tried and failed to write a history of seventeenth-century women, to be titled *Without Men*. She stopped corresponding with her mother for a stretch, embarrassed to report on her lack of progress. When she did resume contact, she explained, "When I can't work I have a guilty conscience, and when I have that, I can't write you. It's something old and secret and subconscious, perhaps."

Late in 1929 she described in *The New Yorker* how "the recent unpleasantness in Wall Street" was barely registering in Paris. France, with its strong gold reserves and low unemployment due to its postwar population shortage, was for the time being shielded from the worst of the effects of the stock market crash—so much so that Flanner felt comfortable joking about it. She suggested that the French people sympathized with "our disaster," which she found "polite and astonishingly sincere, considering that for the past ten years they have seen us through one of the worst phases of our prosperity—which consisted of thousands of our tourists informing them that we were the richest country in the world, that they should pay their debts, that we had made the world safe for democracy." For now the only real change she saw was that "at the Ritz bar the pretty ladies are having to pay for their cocktails themselves."

Recognizing that the market crash limited her potential for other American freelance work, it was beneficial that *The New Yorker* had started attracting a steady flow of advertisers and by the end of the twenties was earning two million dollars in yearly profit with a readership of more than sixty thousand. Flanner had gone from the cautious optimism of her first years to telling Ross that *The New Yorker* was "the best magazine in the world," the great American successor to Britain's *Punch*, for the two publications shared "the same civilized anger, the same impertinent snobbish criticism against snobbery, the same dry nourishing page style." She would later say that she took to her assignment "like a duck takes to water—tentatively at first and then with wild abandon." Without entirely realizing it was happening, she'd channeled all her energy into becoming Genêt.

And yet by putting herself out of sight across the ocean, she'd lost out on developing the chummy rapport with the staff that her American colleagues enjoyed in their overstuffed offices, where flimsy partitions were all that separated one worker from another and the lack of amenities once prompted Dorothy Parker to quip to Ross that she'd had to cancel coming in to write for the day "because somebody was using the pencil." Around the office few considered Flanner among the magazine's top echelon of contributors. Copyeditors joked about what they called "Flannerisms," those times when she reached so far for originality that her sentences became huge, filled with straining metaphors. As Ross's managerial and editorial duties expanded with the magazine's rise he'd stopped editing her directly. He communicated with her largely through "Mrs. White," who "does most of the work around here, especially the letter writing," as he explained to Flanner. "I don't like to inject my personality into things when they're going well…I devote my life, it seems, to the things that are going wrong and it wears me down."

Flanner tried using humor to disarm potential opponents at the office. "Who in God's name is my editor now, if not you?" she once asked White. "Do drop me a note, at least, to tell me your news and promise you have slain whoever cuts my Letters: the castration of the few bright lines they contain is really *idiotic* editing: it's so much simpler and sensibler [*sic*] to cut out one whole paragraph and leave the others intact. (If you did the editing, darling, I'll have to start by cutting my throat!)" At the same time she recognized that whenever she placed pieces in other magazines her writing never quite sang in the way it did once someone at *The New Yorker* had taken a look at it.

Flanner knew she was considered second-tier and wanted to do something about it. In 1930 she wrote her most successful piece up until that point, one that foreshadowed her coming evolution as a journalist. It was another profile, this time of Francois Coty, a pioneering French perfumer whose scents sold widely in America, and who also happened to be one of France's leading fascist agitators. He was "one of the most curious, self-willed, self-satisfied…reformers that ever appeared here, and one of the most powerful men in France," she told White in her pitch. "Also the most enigmatic: one can never tell which way an idealist, with money, will blow." Coty had used the millions from his perfume empire to buy *Le Figaro*, pushing the already conversative French daily farther to the right, while also publishing a populist anti-Communist paper, *L'Ami du peuple*, filled with nasty rhetoric. "A paper written by capitalists to be read by the working classes," Flanner called it.

But she could already hear Ross telling her not to judge Coty as a political being. And so, her profile, titled "Perfume and Politics," couched her critiques of Coty's publishing pursuits and funding of hateful hard right political groups within a broader story of his rags-to-riches climb as a man of business, while providing a tour of the art and science of making perfume. She was astute in noting how easily someone might slip from their role as a business figure into something more nefarious in the political sphere. Coty established "personal contact with the masses, so necessary to a man so determined to stamp out Communism…via his comforting curly-haired profile and his evangelist's message pasted on the boulevard billboards." Coty, "powerful, hot-tempered," was "a man with views," who "takes his new Fascism…seriously," while spewing out wild ideas for fixing any pressing issue. She understood how far a wealthy and influential public figure could go with such buffoonery. "In a government crisis he can always be relied upon to offer, not a solution, but a gesture which is magnificent, usually unacceptable, and which makes delicious reading…Harassed by falling cabinets and fallen francs, postwar politicians in France are a solemn lot. Against them Coty… seems like a red-wigged character from the old Italian comedy—one of those sympathetic and declamatory *saltimbanques* who from the top of a tight-rope offer marvellous cure-alls which have the high merit of relieving nothing but public tedium. Such humorists (even when they take their jokes seriously) are peculiarly useful to an impatient, critical people."

Reporting on Coty meant learning as much as she could about his ideas and their context, which included getting tutored by a friend, the journalist Germaine Beaumont, on French politics. Flanner grew increasingly aware of fascist ideology and of the inroads it was making in France. She was meanwhile reading and hearing of more and more people across the country losing jobs or taking pay cuts and of their growing sense of resentment, much of it directed toward foreigners and Jews.

She asked Ross to let her do some more reporting on events in Europe beyond Paris, broadening both her own gaze and that of the magazine. She would start with Berlin.

8

DEPORTED

One day in 1929, two years into his time in Canada, something broke. Eugen stole the cash from the week's wheat sales (163 Canadian dollars) and spent it on a drunken weekend with a woman he met at a pool hall. He was arrested by the mounted police, jailed for three months, and although forgiven by his employer, deported on his release according to Canadian law.

What he saw back in Frankfurt shocked him. The squalor. The beggars. Young men and women selling themselves openly. People standing around doing nothing, preferring the pointless streets to homes they could no longer afford to heat. He heard of otherwise respectable citizens breaking into shops to steal bread. Newspapers had gotten so expensive that libraries posted them in their windows as a public service. People gathered to gawk at the headlines.

It hurt him to see his mother with her hair so white and her face so drawn. He asked if she was ill but she told him no, she'd just gotten old.

Some friends dragged him to a dance marathon, the new craze. It was depressing, watching people dance for days and nights on end, dancing themselves into delirium. Germans like him, debasing themselves for the entertainment of other Germans, for the chance to win some lousy pittance. It made him sick.

9

SMOKED PORK, SWEET CABBAGE, AND MOSELLE WINE

In the summer of 1931, a friend, Esther Strachey, invited Flanner to join her on a car trip to Berlin led by her sister-in-law Noël Murphy, famed for her daredevil driving as she guided visiting American friends around Europe in her small Ford sedan. In the Black Forest, Flanner, Strachey, and Murphy shared picnics of smoked pork, sweet cabbage, and Moselle wine. In Berlin they listened to jazz over cold martinis. By the end of the trip Flanner and Murphy had fallen in love.

Two years Flanner's junior at thirty-seven, Noël Murphy was the expat scion of a well-known New York family, the Havermeyers. She'd married Frederic Murphy, star son of a clan that had grown rich with its Mark Cross leather goods company, and brother of the artist and expat luminary Gerald Murphy. When Frederic died of lingering war wounds in 1924, Noël wanted to stay close to his plot in a suburban cemetery west of Paris, so she bought a two-story stone farmhouse nearby in the village of Orgeval.

She was a classically trained soprano and had been an actress. Flanner praised her intelligence and her rarified "Pahk avenue mahner," as she put it, mimicking Murphy's patrician accent. She was taller than most men, with a sharp chin, aquiline nose, blonde hair cut short to accent her long neck. Friends said she looked like Marlene Dietrich. They called her the Viking. Hemingway told Flanner that Murphy made him "nervous the way cats do some people." Murphy, in return, said she had no time for Hemingway's "false manliness."

While Flanner was taken by Murphy's "maddening" beauty, relishing how everyone turned to watch her as she entered a restaurant, a deeper attraction grew out of her admiration for Murphy's sense of loyalty to the causes and people she cared for. Flanner was always flitting from one assignment, place, or person to the next, with no grand plan, but Murphy had put down roots in France, held strong political convictions, owned property. For her part, Murphy liked how Flanner made her laugh.

The farmhouse in Orgeval on Rue des Bouillons, with its cheerily painted rooms and lush grounds, would become Flanner's emotional lodestar for the rest of her life. Murphy stocked a vast wine cellar and cooled champagne in her well. She kept four cows, a few horses, pigs, ducks (strangely subdued, they almost never quacked), chickens, and rabbits. Flanner admired Murphy working in slacks, shirt sleeves, and espadrilles, planting neat rows of beets, cabbages, tarragon, thyme, sage, chives, chervil, and oregano—her "garden kitchen," as they called it—interspersed with messy clumps of poppies. Flanner recalled the grounds filled with "zinnias, marigolds, asters, fading carnations, calendula, purple haze and orange sunshine. And CHIGGERS." She liked to wander through the pruned orchards below the property, escaping the high winds that sometimes blew. Djuna Barnes came to suntan nude in the yard. Gertrude Stein and Alice B. Toklas came often for Murphy's Sunday luncheons, arriving in their own Ford sedan, which Stein piloted while Toklas rode in the back, fighting her wide-brimmed hat from flying away the whole time. Stein asked all sorts of questions about the animals—Flanner chalked that up to her "American grass roots...though as a San Franciscan she was not rural"—while Toklas ignored them to pore over the herbs which, as Flanner noted, she would have known how to use in "making delicious food" in which Stein "was not interested."

Though Murphy enjoyed preparing bountiful meals, she was cash poor and guarded her money closely. She refused to pay for heating. She'd received none of the Murphy fortune from her husband; before he died, he had transferred his shares in Mark Cross to his father, who'd been considering selling the company. The shares never went back to Noël, who'd kept afloat thanks to a small trust she'd secured after her mother's death, although its value abroad was dropping quickly in tandem with the dollar's weakness against the franc.

Flanner bought a Citroën roadster to travel the thirty kilometers from Paris to Orgeval more quickly. She continued living with Solano, who remained devoted as Flanner's passion turned elsewhere, still editing and typing Flanner's pieces as always, even packing Flanner's clothes for her trips to Orgeval. Murphy knew about Solano, and the two women were mutually impressed by each other. Solano, who'd started writing her own Parisian correspondence in a column for the *Detroit Athletic Club News*, described Murphy to her readers as a "careless, flamboyant Amazone in bright shorts and skirts—something the peasants had never seen before, either for costumes or formidable motoring energy." High praise from Solano, whom friends similarly described as flamboyant. Sometimes Solano and Flanner traveled to Orgeval together and the three women got on well; Murphy would relieve Solano to take a turn typing out a Letter while Flanner dictated.

The arrangement confused some in their circle. One of Flanner's college friends now living in Paris wrote to a mutual acquaintance, "Janet Flanner is now in love with Noël Murphy but she still keeps house with Solita Solano. Solita has a house in the country where she is in love with another girl and where Janet visits. Noël doesn't visit in that house but has another friend, some French woman, where she visits until Janet returns from Solita's. X plus Y equals???" Friends marveled at how Solano, outwardly the bigger personality, even bordering on a bully, had over the years become subservient in her relation to the seemingly milder Flanner. Solano balanced her days between helping Flanner and writing her own dispatches from Paris while also pursuing her fiction. (She'd published two more novels with Putnam's since her debut, neither one a success.) As Flanner spent more and more time in Orgeval, Solano joked to her readers that "Genêt…lives with me when she remembers it."

Their relationship had been built from the start on the sense of "complete freedom" that Solano gave Flanner, as their friend Margaret Anderson described it, a freedom meant to flow both ways. More than fifty years after meeting Solano, Flanner would tell her "rarely does a day go by that I don't think of you…yes, we have known each other very, very long." And Solano in her own old age, arranging to have Flanner's papers donated to the Library of Congress, would proudly describe herself to the Head of Manuscripts as "Genêt's friend, amateur sec'try [*sic*], and guardian of the thesaurus: birth to retirement."

Shortly after meeting Murphy, Flanner wrote to her mother that, usual financial worries and health complaints aside, "I love my life and am succeeding at it, late, it's true, but I like [my] work increasingly."

She continued to write as one inoculated against all financial illness. She remained unaffected, although "the tales one hears and the absence of one's friends on incoming boats" had convinced her that Americans were indeed suffering, and she worried that if the franc kept up its "altering mystical quality much more, we'll be using buttons or barter."

She was earning well, especially after she'd casually mentioned to White that she'd been approached by *Arts and Decoration* magazine to write a Paris column for them as well. White got her a raise, which came with the understanding that Flanner would do no such thing.

Despite having a few letters cut that summer of 1931 (Flanner wanted the editors to note her "extreme disapproval" of that decision) she and Solano were making enough money to take over the room next door to their own and to install their own bathtub and a gas burner.

Financial crash or no, she counted on the public's insatiable appetite for enviable Parisian lifestyles, such as was offered in her 1931 profile of that "peculiar genius," Coco Chanel. And since harsh economic realities infringed on her ideas about the art of living she continued to assure her readers that, despite higher prices for champagne and some fluctuations in the art market, Paris was "still happy."

10

THE CHAUFFEUR

Eugen convinced his parents to buy him a car, a red eight-cylinder Horch limousine designed for attention. He'd promised to use it to start a chauffeuring business. He told his mother that he'd met friends in Canada who'd shown him how to make a fortune in chauffeuring. They might even help to invest.

In truth he wanted the car for other reasons. He'd read a lot of crime novels in Canada. Bank robberies, kidnappings, smash-and-grabs: They always started with a car.

He would later tell investigators that after he'd come back from Canada he started seeing a young Frankfurt woman, whom he'd met at a swimming pool. He referred to her as Myriam. She was older than he was, he said, and a cocaine addict. She introduced him to the drug and he developed a habit as well. High, they listened to records together for hours: Beethoven, Mozart, and always Wagner.

Had he taken an excessive amount of cocaine on that August day in 1931 when attempting the kidnapping that would land him in a Frankfurt prison? It would help to explain how the caper was carried out. The arresting officers might have wondered if they were doing him a favor. It looked to them as if he'd engineered his crime to get caught.

First, he and his two accomplices, friends from the neighborhood, hadn't bothered to check if their target, the son of a Frankfurt financier named Riefstahl, was even home before breaking in. And then finding no boy to take for ransom Weidmann had settled for some inexpensive jewels, though not before a nearly hour-long chat with the lady of the house, her maid, and her masseuse as his accomplices searched for anything else of value. He'd tried explaining his actions to the three terrified women, citing that the financial crash had made things difficult for everyone. He took the time to cover Frau Riefstahl's bare shoulders with a shawl and he went to turn down the gas on the oven so that a dish that was cooking wouldn't burn.

He'd parked his bright red car so badly when they'd pulled up to the house, and then had driven so erratically through the quiet neighborhood when leaving, that he'd drawn the attention of several witnesses and was arrested the next day while in line to buy tickets to the movies.

He looked bored by the trial and indifferent to the verdict. He was sentenced to five years and eight months in Preungesheim Prison. To his parents' shame, the *Frankfurter Zeitung* described him as "the son of a good family, who'd gone down a bad path."

11

CRACKING UP

Sparked by her attraction for the Germanophile Noël Murphy, Flanner returned to Germany in 1932 and would continue to do so at least once a year.

She felt both drawn to and terrified by France's eastern neighbor. She'd first seen the country at seventeen, straight from boarding school, traveling to Berlin with her family to join her sister, who'd gone there to study piano. She would remember that winter of 1909, passed in a pension full of musicians, as the beginning of her "passionate yearning, a kind emotional necessity, for aesthetics, for beauty. It was the selfishness of the joy of the eye. My eyes—I wanted to see with both of them." On that trip she'd first realized how badly she longed for "the beauties of Europe...the beautiful gardens, the beautiful palaces, the towns made with what they call promenades so people can promenade about. I was consumed by this necessity, a kind of magnificent malady, a fever to take part, if only as an onlooker."

There had been so much for young Janet to see, a lot of it unsettling: the mad pomposity of a zeppelin crowding the sky for the

Kaiser's annual military review, the multitudes roaring below in a collective delirium, the strutting of the young officers with tortoiseshell glasses—"quite fantastically effeminate," as she remembered them—who "with their elbows pushed women off into the gutter." She was unsettled, too, by encountering a young woman named Carlotta Nehring, just a few years older than she was and already married to an officer. Flanner accompanied her a few times to the theater and would keep a photograph of Nehring in her scrapbook until she died.

In Berlin feminists argued for the rights of women to love one another openly, while the vanguard sexual theories of Richard von Krafft-Ebing and Havelock Ellis were discussed without shame. Flanner had fluent German from school; how much she absorbed of what she overheard in the cafés and theaters is unclear. Undoubtedly the city offered new clues through which to decipher the codes of adult life: She learned to look for the ways in which one's social standing was woven into the fabric of one's outfit, one's choice of words, one's posture; to follow the nuances of light conversation to divine its deeper, unspoken meanings. Above all, she'd discovered in Berlin that one "could fall in love with life."

Austria had provoked ambivalent feelings. She'd first seen Vienna in 1922 on a spring visit with Solano on assignment for *National Geographic*. She would be dazzled by the palaces and stables and greenery of the Ringstrasse one day; and the next, following Solano on her investigation of the city's outer reaches, she'd be horrified by the sight of women and children rifling through the garbage for food. Inflation had so decimated the middle classes that while visiting the university Flanner saw a professor gathering crumbs from the table to bring home for his family following one of the simple communal meals the faculty took at the mess hall. Hatreds arose easily in such an environment. She passed bookstalls "full of shabby little anti-Semitic pamphlets, which sold for a few groschen." She watched a Schnitzler play that sparked an anti-Jewish riot, "the first beastly public anti-racial melodrama I had ever witnessed." (Somewhere in that same city, perhaps passing them on the street or at a beer hall, was an angry and disillusioned thirty-three-year-old "house painter" named Adolf Hitler, Flanner recalled decades later.) Still, she'd returned the following year, taking in *Der Rosenkavalier* at the gorgeous Opera House, and then again the next summer, happily waiting out the heat one day by playing ninepin bowling in a café basement.

Years later, after she'd affiliated herself with all things French, and after two World Wars, she would claim to have always harbored a deep dislike of German culture, so obscene and militant and lacking in taste. "I should think that, innately, I was a wine drinker rather than a beer-drinker," was how she would explain it. But as a young woman she seems to have found many of her German experiences thrilling. And apparently her repulsion toward much of German culture only heightened those thrills.

Sometimes Solano tagged along on the trips with Murphy. Most often, Flanner accompanied Murphy alone to hear Wagner at the summer Bayreuth festivals (Hitler, too, loved the Judeophobic Wagner, and Bayreuth) or to Munich where Murphy took singing lessons. Though ostensibly visiting for the sights and music and to please Murphy, she kept watch for potential material. "It's always been swell having Murphy to travel with," she told one of her editors. "She'd go any place once to look at nothing."

Berlin, especially, lit her up with its decadence in the face of economic crisis, in the wild, waning years of Germany's first flirtation with democracy, the Weimar Republic. Berliners, as one writer described, made up "a giddy society that was weirdly out of kilter, sparkling, brilliant, yet constantly on the verge of a nervous breakdown."

Knowing the bottom might drop out at any moment, they lived as if anything was possible. And if anything was possible, then *everything* was worth doing, if only for the adventure of it. Good or evil, moral or amoral, productive or wasteful: pointless distinctions. It was the era's contagious, invigorating idea: "Do anything, but let it produce joy. Do anything, but let it yield ecstasy," as Henry Miller voiced it in *Tropic of Cancer*. "So much crowds into my head when I say this to myself: images, gay ones, terrible ones, maddening ones...Lust, crime, holiness...the evil, the sorrow, the discord, the rancor, the strife...but above all, *the ecstasy!*"

In Berlin the "old forms of everything current to the surface of European life seem to be cracking up," Flanner told White after her 1931 trip, adding: "Must get to work now." Though more than a decade had passed since the Kaiser's humiliating abdication and the loss of the Great War, Berlin's atmosphere still felt charged with the same unruly energy Flanner imagined must have accompanied those first days of experimentation and disorder in the wake of defeat. And she found that energy intoxicating. In a *New Yorker* Letter from Berlin filed that year, she acknowledged Germany's financial failure, which had produced "workers without work and capitalists without capital" as well as "terrible want in certain quarters." But she moved quickly from that gloomy material to how there was still no other place on the Continent "where overeating, fine restaurants, mocha, tobacco, music, flowers, and courtesy so warm the tourist's heart... And if banks close down for weeks, cabarets rarely do before dawn." She saw this as evidence of the Teutonic determination to continue to host Europe's most raucous party even while everyone was certain "that their country is going to the dogs."

Flanner hadn't been ignorant of Nazi ideology. She, Solano, and Murphy had seen terrible things on their summer trip of 1933, coinciding with the first days of Hitler's taking absolute power. After he'd been sworn in as chancellor in January of that year, Berliners celebrated with a five-hour torchlit procession, twenty-five thousand strong, through the Brandenburg Gate and along Unter den Linden, the city's majestic main boulevard. "Today, Germany, tomorrow, the world," they sang. "It's like a dream," the Nazis' chief propagandist Joseph Goebbels had written in his diary. "The great decision has been taken...The nation erupts! Germany is awake!...The German revolution begins!"

Now Flanner was experiencing the "revolution" up close. She saw signs announcing "Jews Not Welcome" at the entrances to towns. In Murnau soldiers made Solano change out of her trousers because women had to wear skirts. On reaching Nuremberg in Murphy's conspicuous black-and-white Ford with French plates they were harassed by officers and civilians: German women had been banned from using lipstick and powder, and the three Americans were wearing makeup. They were barred from smoking in public. Soldiers demanded their papers, threatened to send them home. "Hitler flags everywhere," wrote Solano. "Hitler emblems on every male arm and on every handlebar. Hitler photographs in every window. The Hitler salute from every passerby. A 'Heil, Hitler' from every child." They saw a Jewish boy being marched down a street with a placard around his neck, confessing to the sin of kissing a non-Jewish girl.

A few weeks after that trip, Flanner, writing from Lucerne, brought attention to the forced resettling of German Jewish refugees in Switzerland, though this came in a single paragraph tucked into a longer, breezy "Swiss Letter" reporting on the opening of a new Wagner museum and the auction of a royal library. She came the closest she'd been to writing an explicitly contentious political piece that same year when in one of her Letters she briefly shone a light on the plight of German Jewish refugees in Belgium who'd been forbidden to work. The only other words she wrote that could be connected to what she'd seen in Germany were in the closing paragraph of the year's final Paris Letter, noting, in the passive voice as if on behalf of the collective zeitgeist, that "all over Europe, 1933 has been a worrying kind of year."

She wasn't alone among *New Yorker* contributors in failing to comment meaningfully on troubling social or political issues. E. B. White once joked that even as late as the mid-1930s *The New Yorker* had only once ever taken a political stance: strongly opposed to the proposal to relocate Penn Station's information booth. Not entirely true, as a handful of writers, most notably White himself, did manage to talk about the Depression and other issues, but chiefly as they affected Americans. Party politics and elections were covered, but often jokily, as in a 1928 piece with the mock-serious title "The Political Outlook, By Our Own Political Correspondent" and bearing the news that "it looks as if the nominee for the Democratic party...would be a member of the democratic party in good standing" and that "Abraham Lincoln is definitely out of the race for the presidency."

Finally, Flanner was starting to feel the effects of the economic crisis. Ross in a rare letter directly to Flanner (White was on vacation) told her that "the depression has finally hit us and the issues are away down in size." He asked to furlough her for a month to cut costs, wanly trying to comfort her by saying that her work ranked "among our very best departmental stuff and, believe me, we hate to drop even one department." She answered that *The New Yorker* might as well start paying her in bananas because at least she could eat the bananas. Ross had already reduced her pay by 10 percent a few months earlier. ("Your letter about the cut was so sweet and so personal that I nearly enjoyed the loss of money!" she'd told him.) At the same time, she wanted him to know she understood the forces they were facing. "When the necks start being shaved, remember I have one; the magazine has always been charming to me, Ross, I know and realize it and if pennies are scarce, though I'm no department head to be important enough to come up for immediate guillotining, I should be sorry if you didn't consider me as at least second in line for amputation."

Her insecurity about her job came just as some investments her ex-husband had helped her to make failed to give their usual returns. When her Liberty Bonds came due, she sold them all and with the proceeds bought gold coins, which she tucked into a small bag inside a chamber pot nestled in a corner of Murphy's attic. She still sent as much of her pay as she could spare to her mother and Hildegarde, who were also struggling. With her American income not only reduced but holding less buying power in France, she knew that two or three dry months would be all it took to kill her fantasy and send her back to America, to her mother, back to a conventional life.

She took on any assignment she could get, at the risk of her health, which had always been delicate. She wrote about French banks for *Fortune* despite having no experience as a financial journalist. She took on rewriting work for French *Vogue* (the "vague *Vogue* job," she called it). With Ross's permission she now did start writing a monthly Paris column for *Arts and Decoration*, the tone fluffier than anything she'd written for *The New Yorker.* Again she was capitalizing on her ability to give glimpses of Parisian refinement, still to be found if you looked hard enough. But she predicted that this would be a dead-end project; either Parisians would no longer be able to enjoy such high living, or the *Arts and Decoration* readers would tire of hearing about it. Meanwhile she prodded her *New Yorker* editors to assign her as much extra work as they could. At one point she fell so short of funds after taking yet another pay cut that in a single month, along with her regular Paris Letters, she contributed two short stories, a cartoon, a long profile of Elsa Maxwell that she'd been made to rewrite five times, and an extended standalone piece on House of Worth, the French atelier. She said that she would have written about the Fall of Rome if anyone had asked her to. Ross eventually took pity on her and bumped her pay back up slightly to make up for the exchange rate.

She was starting to realize how drastically she and the place in which she lived had changed since she'd first sailed from New York with a head full of poetry and romantic ideas. By spending so much time reporting on and writing about France, and thanks to her already wide and growing network of sources, she'd developed sensitive antennae to developments across the Continent. People around her were reading newspapers from the time they woke until the time they went to bed, so desperate were they to keep up with events, feeling themselves being sucked into a vortex, helpless to stop whatever change was coming. They wanted to talk about international flows of money, the gold standard, conspiracies, corruption. They'd lost interest in discussing the latest craze at the cabarets or debating the best cocktail at the Ritz. They wanted to make sense of this new France being torn apart by competing visions of what the nation and its empire stood for, and where it was headed.

12

THE STAVISKY AFFAIR

Along with her beer the garçon brought a tip, an unprecedented note of urgency in his voice. This time he wasn't delighting in some minor deputy's bedroom misdeeds or whispering of a wildcat strike soon to come. This time the story was still unfolding. And this story still unfolding, not far from where she sat, was sure to be a bloody one.

Whether at the Brasserie Lipp or elsewhere, the garçons tended to save their highest gossip for Flanner, always the hungriest to hear it. They knew that she understood that their real work had nothing to do with keeping spots off the knives or wiping up crumbs. They were story-makers as she was. She knew that in their mouths the *garçons de café* held the whole secret history of Paris.

This one's tip confirmed her hunch: Tonight's would be the largest of the street protests that had been growing in strength and violence since the first reports of the swindler Stavisky's crimes had set everything alight a few weeks earlier.

She got up and walked west along the Boulevard Saint-Germain, already a tangle of bodies, heading for what she was sure would be the protest's main target, the Palais Bourbon, headquarters of the Chamber of Deputies, France's legislative assembly. Its deputies were meeting that night in an emergency session to decide what sacrifices should be offered to a public outraged by what the press dubbed the Stavisky Affair, the fantastical scandal in which, as the disgraced prime minister had recently shouted in that same Chamber, the crimes of one obscure confidence man in a provincial port town had grown into a monster that threatened "the very existence of the Republic!"

Three years earlier Serge Alexandre "Sasha" Stavisky had finagled his way to overseeing the municipal pawnshops of Bayonne in the Basque country of the southwest. These shops served as public institutions, giving out loans in exchange for holding valuables. They were meant to keep the insolvent from going to loan sharks while boosting local treasuries, as they borrowed from the state at favorable rates. Stavisky had the idea to float public bonds for the Bayonne operation, offering as security some jewels he was holding for an unnamed Spaniard worried about his own unstable government seizing his riches. Small-time investors struggling to find places to park money during those first years of the Depression liked the sound of a bond venture offering steady profits backed by municipal credit. Lost in Stavisky's pitch was the fact of his being a convicted fraudster who'd dabbled in everything from forgery to illegal gambling to gunrunning.

There were no Spanish jewels. By the time the Ministry of Finance caught up with Stavisky in late 1933, he'd pocketed between two and three hundred million francs. Across France, political fixers, bankers, newspaper editors, insurance men, members of the aristocracy, and top-ranking ministers were implicated in his Ponzi scheme. Before the story got out few people had ever heard the name Stavisky—so undeniably foreign, so sharp on the tongue—which only made his apparently tremendous influence more confounding. The police closed in on the now-fugitive financier's secluded chalet in the alpine resort of Chamonix in January 1934. He died from a bullet to the head.

While most papers repeated the official report of death by self-inflicted gunshot, some right-leaning outlets claimed Stavisky was killed as part of a police cover-up tied to a government plot to defraud common French people of their pay. Some insinuated the governing Radical-Socialist party had hired his assassin, pointing to the discrepancy between Stavisky's left-handedness and the bullet's entering his right temple. (The Radical party was not at that time radical but centrist-left, an "anachronistically misnamed party of laissez-faire middle class Frenchmen," in the historian Robert Paxton's words.) Some papers suggested that the plot extended internationally, Stavisky pulling levers for a cabal of global financiers. Such fantasies found wide appeal. No one failed to mention that the culprit was a Jew; few shied away from emphasizing his prominent nose in their illustrated portraits. The Stavisky family had fled the pogroms of Czarist Russia for France during Sasha's childhood, numbering among the wave of eastern immigrants reviled not only by French non-Jews but by their already assimilated brethren.

Flanner shared the affair's many twists with her readers. One day they would learn of Stavisky's operating with government immunity for years, no doubt because he was a police informant; the next they would read that the prosecutor who'd handled his case was the brother-in-law of the prime minister, Camille Chautemps. To the French it all stank of the excesses of the mythic Two Hundred Families, a frequent target for populist vitriol, the supposed secret masters of the French state and economy, the people who drank in a night what you earned in a month. They all had crooked hearts and operated with impunity, protecting one another to further the common interests of their impenetrable circle of graft—or so went the popular thinking. The "Radicals are covered with mud," Flanner summarized, surveying the mess, "with side splashes for every other party and parliamentarianism in general."

And now in the first days of February the new prime minister, Édouard Daladier, badly miscalculated how to consolidate power while forming his government. He tried to shuffle off the head of the Paris police—a fascist sympathizer—to a post in Morocco, to be replaced by a more liberal-minded official. This misstep brought out the night's mob.

And yet, as Flanner understood, the present raging in the streets was only satiating a larger, long-simmering need. With France trudging through an economic crisis, a public outpouring of emotion had come due. Some definitive action needed to take place, there at the center of this once great city at the center of a failing nation at the center of a decrepit empire. (A joke went round in these years: "Why is France ruled by seventy-year-olds? Because the eighty-year-olds are dead.") People dared to wonder if the very functions of France's liberal democracy should be destroyed.

On that February night they spilled out from their offices and factories and homes by the thousands, arriving on foot, by bus, by *métro*. Some came by taxi or chauffeured sedan, because the rich get angry, too. Some rode motorcycles in wide lines, filling the boulevards with the blues and grays of their homemade uniforms, dressed as if for war. They'd been called by their radios—the Eiffel Tower served as the city's main transmitter and nearly half of Parisian homes had radio sets—by wheat-pasted posters, overheated journalists, and would-be demagogues telling them to rid themselves of this "gang of thieves and assassins," to form a "populist wave," to "clean out" the parliamentary filth and regain the nation's lost "soul." One could read the protestors' achievements and grievances in the slogans they sang, the badges they wore, the banners they waved. They traded in the language of skulls and swords and eagles and fiery crosses, the codes of colors and slants of hat and tucking of shirt and rolling of pants and lacing of boots, all the signals to show what you'd done in the Great War and how you felt about it two decades later. Most of the people out that night shared the experience of having served; half the country's male population at that time were veterans. But now men who'd once huddled together in the trenches fighting for France's survival could come to blows over differing visions for its future.

Kids lit fireworks. Men blew trumpets. They were going to storm the Chamber of Deputies and overthrow the government, or so went the rumor. They would breach the inner sanctum of this impenetrable shadowy *maison sans fenêtres* (house without windows), as it was dubbed. There was no rain but only the bracing cold and a light mist. All noncommercial aircraft had been banned. Café owners started shuttering early.

Most of the demonstrators adhered to the hateful blood-and-soil rhetoric of the country's hard-right *ligues* (leagues) and ultranationalistic political associations: the largely Catholic and Royalist Action Française; the thuggish Solidarité Française; the fiercely anti-Communist Jeunesses Patriotes youth group; the Croix-de-Feu, initially a veterans league, which had expanded into a mass movement encompassing civilians, including many women, drawn to its antiestablishment ideology. The leaders of these groups had seen extremist politics take hold in Italy and Germany, where street violence had proved an effective tool for political gain. The less extreme but still right-leaning Union Nationale des Combattants (UNC), another veterans' association, also constituted a significant presence, as did a forceful minority of counterprotestors from the left, including a few thousand Communists. Mixed among these were a handful of misfits, the ones feeling no great allegiance to any cause but who came to watch things burn.

Demonstrators buzzed around the Arc de Triomphe and out front of the Opéra Garnier and at the Grand Palais. The bulk of them were drawn to the Place de la Concorde, spanning a patch of the Right Bank of the Seine about eight soccer pitches wide from the eastern mouth of the Champs-Élysées to the western edge of the Tuileries Gardens. A logical rallying point, across the water from the Palais Bourbon and the Chamber of Deputies, and symbolically weighty as it had served as the nexus of revolutionary fervor nearly a century and a half earlier. There the high executioner Sanson (or his assistant, depending on the teller) had brandished the severed head of Louis XVI from the scaffold.

Army and police trucks lined the width of the Pont de la Concorde. A few dozen cavalry waited behind the trucks. The forces of order had set up early, anticipating a night of unrest that would easily surpass the past scattered protests. In this mix of police, gendarmes, and cavalry one saw sabers, pistols, and white batons. Their orders were to hold the bridge by any means. As the first Deputies arrived at the Palais Bourbon to do their night's work, armed guards escorted them inside.

A man in a leather overcoat lingered too closely to the barricade. He was tackled and searched. He had a dagger. He'd come to kill a politician, he told his captors. Anyone would do.

As the sun set there were perhaps two thousand people in the Place de la Concorde. More kept coming. No one had thought to stop the flow of *métros* into the city center. The police presence swelled as the sky darkened. More of the *hirondelles* (swallows)—the bicycle police, named for their capes that fluttered as they rode—arrived. So did more cars, wedging their way between humans and horses and vehicles to add another layer of protection. Firefighters came armed with high-powered hoses.

People tore benches from the ground and practiced the French sport of making weapons from the streets, dislodging paving stones to be hurled toward the bridge barricade. They smashed the windows of trams and buses. Close to the bridgehead they threw fireworks at the cordon of mounted police. Someone had brought ball bearings from his factory job and tossed them at the horses' hooves like seeds, panicking the animals; a few of them threw their riders as they staggered. One rioter mounted a riderless horse and, after a comrade handed him a UNC flag, charged at the cavalry and got knocked to the ground. Someone set fire to a kiosk. Someone else lit up one of the deracinated benches. A group in the Tuileries set up a bonfire ringed by a makeshift wall of debris and invited people into the circle to heat slabs of iron procured from the smashed protective grates for the trees. These would be thrown at the police. A woman hid under a parked car and stayed there for hours.

A bus driver insisted on continuing his normal route through the plaza even if he no longer had any riders. A circle of rioters blocked his passage near the square's central obelisk. People mounted the bus to rip the driver from his seat and then doused the machine in gasoline. Later a firefighter died in the efforts to maneuver the burning bus away from the melee. The smell of motor oil and charred rubber choked the air.

Three more military units arrived to reinforce the building's southern flank, taking their positions as quietly as possible. The masses across the river remained blind to this escalation of force. Meanwhile other units were converging on central Paris by *métro* from points around the city. At pay phones informants relayed bulletins to the leaders of their respective factions. Radio transmissions led people to believe they were hearing everything important just as it was happening, but there weren't yet enough people on the other ends of those transmissions to gather meaningful facts to relay. A rumor, unfounded, held that the police had set up hidden machine guns along the Boulevard Sebastopol. The police, too, were hampered by misinformation. Officers rushed off to man the entrances to sewers, reacting to the lie that the Jeunesses Patriotes planned to breach the Palais Bourbon from underground.

Around seven thirty the first gunshots rang out, the source or sources unknown—perhaps protestors in the Place de la Concorde shooting into the air, perhaps panicked police officers doing the same. Something shifted then. Witnesses would recall it felt as if the whole plaza was listing like a ship about to capsize. The men holding the bridge felt the surge coming, the menacing crackle of a crowd seeking its breaking point. It was a riot. They were going to lose their position. The forces of order struck first, pushing their way out into the square as the firefighters turned hoses on the first rows of bodies. Hundreds charged back, wresting the hoses and turning them back on the firefighters and police. More gunshots went into the sky. Frightened horses turned away and crushed the policemen occupying the first layer of the barricade behind them, men's and beasts' footing unsure on the slick ground. The throng burst toward the bridge and broke the barricade. Rioters jumped onto the parked vehicles intent on lighting them up. Some brandished razor blades and with them slashed horses' haunches.

The police now fired directly on their adversaries. Some among the phalanx rushing the barricade later claimed to have been met by more than a hundred gunshots, with evidence pointing to many of these volleys coming at close range. Batons flew down. So did handcuffs and nonregulation billy clubs. The Palais Bourbon was not breached. Some of the injured begged to be let into the building for medical attention but were turned away.

Well away from the bridge, in the plaza's northwest corner, a thirty-four-year-old housekeeper to a couple staying at the grand Hôtel Crillon stepped onto the balcony to watch the events. She died of a stray bullet to the chest. Elsewhere a sixteen-year-old butcher's boy took a bullet to the spine. He would die months later from the wound. At the Plaza's northeast corner, someone threw a gasoline-soaked newspaper into the window of the Naval Ministry. Five firefighters were injured handling the blaze.

Around eight o'clock roughly twenty thousand people aligned with the UNC marched along the Champs-Élysées toward the Place de la Concorde. A few police officers saluted the uniformed veterans as they passed. They created a crush mixing among the existing congregation in the plaza. They sang the traditional soldier's song "Le Madelon," as well as the "Marseillaise." Changing the lyrics of a popular revolutionary anthem about killing aristocrats, they sang about hanging deputies from lampposts. A few hundred meters northwest of the Place de la Concorde, a separate group of UNC vets pushed up against the gate of the Élysée Palace, the president's residence, and were met by gunshots from mounted police. Hospitals started to feel the strain by nine. Trains had stopped running to and from Concorde by then.

Some of the wounded stumbled into the Brasserie Weber on Rue Royale, which offered a northern exit from the plaza; it was the lone café in the area not to have closed at the first signs of trouble. The

Weber stayed open because a doctor happened to have sought shelter there after interrupting his usual walk home to see about the fuss in the plaza. He tended to two young men struck in the thigh and neck, respectively. He pressed the Weber's coat-check woman into service as a nurse. They laid out other injured men on a bench and some tables. Eventually, lacking flat surfaces, they hoisted another of the wounded onto the brasserie's roof. They used table linens for bandages. Three other doctors, some medical students, a nurse, and two Red Cross workers soon came to the Weber to work through the night, handing lists to the brasserie's manager, who found supplies from local pharmacists. A police officer discovered what was going on inside and made it his duty to make sure no one, civilian, police, or military, could come in to interrupt the work. Wait staff served rum. Roughly 250 wounded passed through, most of them for treatment of blows to the head from police. Three Republican Guards, flayed by rioters, were treated after being hidden in the cellar for their safety.

Back out on the streets policemen lost their guns, guards lost sabres. Some rioters reportedly used seized arms to shoot police, while others drew weapons they were already carrying to fire from statues, from trees, from balconies. A second bus went up in flames a block west of the plaza. A man who'd heard about the commotion on the radio came late in the proceedings just to watch. He couldn't reach the center of the plaza, but from its edge he bent to help a wounded man. He was killed by a police bullet while leading the wounded man back toward the action.

Close to midnight came a second charge from rioters trying to take the bridge, which the forces of order again repelled. This prompted a final decisive move to clear the plaza once and for all, led by cavalry. Projectiles flew. There were several gunshots. People were pushed or jumped from the bridge into the freezing Seine. By three in the morning the mob had been dispersed and the police and military barricade came down. Fire crews kept working well past sunrise.

The night's official death counts ranged from fifteen to twenty, the real number likely higher. More than fourteen hundred people were wounded, more than two hundred arrested.

Daladier resigned as prime minister by morning, after serving only a few days. The country's greatest outburst of populist violence in decades had brought down a legally elected government.

There would be more street fighting in the coming days, in Paris and elsewhere. The Stavisky Affair was far from resolved. There were more revelations and recriminations to come, more of Stavisky's mistresses to meet, more public figures to pillory, more unsteady steps down dark trails in search of guilty parties. A judge said to possess information on the cover-up was murdered by being tied to some railroad tracks.

"You would not know Paris!" the American bookseller Sylvia Beach had written her sister just after the riot. She could have extended the statement to the whole of France, whose people were highly polarized while also united by a collective distrust of their elected officials and of their fellow citizens. "People observed each other covertly," recalled one union leader. "I tried to categorise the people I passed on the pavement. In which camp did this one fit?...Others looked at me and asked themselves if I was friend or foe."

For right-wing extremists who might have thought themselves a fringe minority, seeing so many like-minded souls had shown them how many people shared their antidemocratic views, and how far they might go to make themselves heard. Moderates could meanwhile console themselves with the bitter vindication that they hadn't been paranoid in fearing that Italian- and German-style extremism had come to a vulnerable France. The Republic had seemingly come close to falling to a rightist coup. The forces of the left would need to organize themselves to protect democratic institutions perhaps too fragile to survive another such threat. Rarely since the Revolution had the future of the nation and the safety of its people felt so precarious.

"What a time to be living in Paris and yet I am sure you would not miss it," Katharine White wrote to Flanner.

But Flanner had missed the Stavisky saga's single most dramatic moment. As she'd tried making her way toward the Palais Bourbon that night she'd struggled to penetrate through the masses and gave up, returning to the Brasserie Lipp where she drank more beer with friends.

Only in the pale light of the following morning did she cross the eerily calm Seine and descend into the Place de la Concorde. She found it stained by grease and blanketed by a thin layer of ash. The square was "empty of people and strewn with glass, bricks, trees, coat sleeves, embers, brass helmets, and one pair of ladies embroidered drawers," she would write in *The New Yorker* a few days later. "By beautiful accident, all the lights were extinguished except for the illumination on the horse statues." She saw spent cartridges, ripped-up benches, and a few medals that had either fallen or been ripped from veterans' uniforms. Even in such a wide-open space the acrid stench was overpowering. Two city buses were still burning.

Flanner understood how harshly the Stavisky protests had been exposing the country's internal divisions, and that someone aiming to write authentically about France should be there to document each one as it happened. And yet on that night she'd been unwilling to push her way through to see it for herself. "The odd thing here is that five minutes walk from a murderous riot, you don't know it's going on, the rest of the city being calm," she told White.

Why did she turn away? Maybe it was just fear. Maybe she'd intuited that this was a crowd bent on destruction.

Or maybe she just didn't see herself as that kind of journalist. *The New Yorker* hadn't hired her to be a political correspondent, after all. Tracking violent extremists through the streets wasn't meant to be her job. In fact she'd received a Western Union telegram not long after Americans learned of the riot: "AVOID DANGER TAKE NO CHANCES—THE NEW YORKER."

In her next five Letters from Paris, Flanner reported on the scandal and the sometimes deadly confrontations it continued to spark, fighting to gain clarity on the situation while awash in "rumors so thick that one can almost see them." She diagnosed the cause of much of the discontent: "The public is angry in the streets because it is overtaxed in the shop and ashamed in its heart." But she struggled to gauge the broader stakes of the Stavisky-related street violence. While contemporary coverage in American venues such as *The Atlantic* freely used the term "French fascists," Flanner tried to convince her readers—perhaps herself, above all—that France did not have true fascism, that in France fascism was still "only a term, usually a reproach, against the veterans and youthful patriotic societies." She maintained that "while Rome is capital of Italy, Vienna capital of Austria, and Berlin capital of Hitler, Paris is still capital of Europe for a kind of obstinate civilization, cerebral style, ideology, and suave, formulated, independent, liberty-loving living."

The fighting in the streets continued. "Am worried about you," White wrote to Flanner. "Don't take any chances and get out if you ought to."

The Stavisky scandal and its aftermath solidified Flanner's belief that her *New Yorker* writing might meet the needs she thought would be fulfilled by writing novels—especially now that "European and

French politics had started developing their appalling capacity for sounding like fiction, for sounding like horrifying thrillers," as she later said. The aspiring novelist with a magazine job penning witty letters about life in Paris had now unwittingly positioned herself to become one of America's key foreign correspondents, in the early stages of an era when a single day's events in Europe could remake the world.

Flanner confided to friends that she felt she could no longer make sense of her era. But she knew where to look to start trying to figure things out. There was a man she needed to see, up close.

13

THE LIBRARIAN

Weidmann dropped off books for the two Frenchmen sharing a cell near his own. They'd been caught in Frankfurt a few weeks earlier running a phony currency exchange. Weidmann had targeted them from the start. He was teaching himself French and wanted practice.

He'd found his opening through the Preungesheim Prison library's collection of foreign editions, which was unexpectedly extensive, even after he'd been ordered to destroy hundreds of "un-German" titles two years earlier alongside the book burnings then taking place in so many public squares across the country. He could still find plenty of French pulp with which to ply the two new inmates. He'd cemented their connection by smuggling in contraband between his bookstacks. Chocolate, tobacco, sardines, sausages. A receiver he'd made out of spare parts lifted from the prison workshop, which just managed to catch the signal of a nearby radio tower.

The guards let him linger in the Frenchmen's cell long after he'd finished his deliveries. They liked Weidmann. People were easily drawn in by his soft-spoken, somewhat wounded manner. Any alarms that might have been rung by the remoteness in his blue-and-gold-flecked eyes or by the whiff of ill health in his sallow complexion were dampened by the softness of his long eyelashes, the gloss of his thick pompadour, his easy, full-lipped smile.

He was on year four of his sentence. He'd served quietly, an example to his six hundred fellow inmates, which was how he'd earned this soft job among the ten thousand titles of the prison library.

The Frenchmen were both serving eighteen months. The smarter of the two was Roger Million, twenty-two, short, skinny, and twitchy, with angular, feminine features and a hyena's grin. He wanted people to call him Scarface though he had no scars. Born just outside Paris, he'd made his way as a petty smuggler and confidence man working mostly along the Riviera and in Tunisia. There was a prior conviction in Paris for waving a gun at one of his father's former business partners. When the family furniture company had failed and his father had been forced to take a job as a waiter in a friend's restaurant, the shame had driven his mother to suicide.

Million's cellmate, Jean Blanc, shared his age but little else. He'd grown up rich in Paris, shy, doted on by his widowed mother. He had a small, squeaky voice and a doll-like face framed by thick, owlish glasses; he read constantly but lacked any practical intelligence. Prosecutors would later describe Blanc as "dim and listless, spoiled by a constant and abundant flow of money, someone who sleepwalks through life, weak in character though not inherently amoral." He sought the thrill of mixing with criminals and was always getting dragged into one scheme or another. Knowing he had little to offer as brains or muscle, he'd tried to make himself useful by learning to print counterfeit bills.

The two men had met only a few months prior to their arrest.

Million had promised to teach Blanc how to orchestrate complicated international cons, so long as Blanc promised to keep him funded by passing along the hefty allowance he received from his mother. They'd started their partnership with the amateurish currency exchange that had been their undoing.

Now Weidmann rigged up the makeshift radio, and the three of them followed the scratchy updates on Italy's invasion of Ethiopia, as if listening to someone reading them a boy's adventure story. Weidmann uncreased the small map he'd made from scraps of paper to be adjusted in tandem with the news: the Italian forces in yellow, the Ethiopians in red, British and French naval ships in green and blue.

14

HELL ON WHEELS

In the fall of 1934 Ross wanted Flanner to profile Gertrude Stein, a sudden celebrity at sixty with *The Autobiography of Alice B. Toklas* and her return to America for a lecture tour that took her to nearly forty cities. "Gertrude Stein Has Arrived" flashed electric letters in Times Square on her first night in New York. (Amid the frenzy over *The Autobiography* Hemingway had written to Flanner, "By jeesus [*sic*] will write my own memoirs sometimes when I can't write anything else. And they will be funny and accurate and not out to prove a bloody thing.")

Flanner's friendship with Stein had grown slowly. At first, she'd assumed the role of awestruck acolyte, addressing her senior as Miss Stein. Flanner didn't take to Stein's writing—"charming nonsense," she called it—but respected the intellect and ambition that had produced it, while marveling at Stein's devotion "to the process of living her own life" on her own terms. Stein basked in the admiration. She always dominated their talks, just as "Gertrude led everything," said Flanner. Alice B. Toklas ("a praying mantis among strawberry leaves,"

Flanner called her) doubted that Flanner had actually read Stein's work properly.

Flanner pushed back against the idea of profiling Stein. "The press is instinctively irritated by [Stein] anyhow," she explained to Katharine White in refusing the assignment. She meanwhile told Stein that she was protecting her from overexposure: Were she to pile a profile onto "everything else they've written and pictured about and around you, thc name of the magazine would have to be changed from *The New Yorker* to *The Gertruder*." Easing the sting with flattery she said that while on tour Stein and Toklas ought to jointly "run for President...you could get the job easy."

In truth Flanner expected American readers to eventually "sour" against Stein's cryptic writing and wanted to avoid associating herself with that turn in opinion. And more important, she had another profile subject in mind, one that would be "hell on wheels," as she told White. Already exhausted from overwork and having been warned that she needed to cut back on expenses, she asked to be sent on a reporting trip to Nuremberg. She was going to profile Adolf Hitler.

Ross would be hard to convince. Though he'd started *The New Yorker* "with a declaration of serious purpose," as stated in the first issue, this had come paired with a "declaration that it will not be too serious in executing it." A decade later he still thought he was running a humor magazine, which he insisted on calling "a New York paper" even as its profile grew. He didn't want his writers profiling major political leaders, let alone non-American ones. Better they should cover people "more or less in the New York public eye," as he told his editorial team. When he was pitched an interview with Mussolini in 1930, Ross answered that "a thing like this is away [*sic*] out of bounds for us, since we never go in for straightforward treatment of such things as serious articles about famous men." He thought he was playing to the tastes of his audience. If Americans wanted to trouble themselves with serious and sober analyses of current crises they had plenty to choose from within their own borders. As William Shawn explained, "In our inattention we were being completely true to ourselves at that time—in those days the people who worked for the magazine were actually proud of being apolitical and socially detached."

The New Yorker hadn't completely ignored Hitler's rise. The journalist Mary Heaton Vorse had documented some of the effects of his "revolution" in a brief piece in July 1933, mentioning "the Jews and their plight," concentration camps, and Communists being "hunted like rats." But that was a four-column sardine compared to the multi-issue, multi-page whale of a profile that Flanner was now proposing.

Flanner meanwhile had to convince herself of her own fitness for the task. She could see that the Nazi party's seizure of power had become the most vital story in Europe. She could see, too, that she couldn't write that story until she understood its central protagonist. And she knew that she'd hook more readers with the chance to know the enigmatic Führer than with a history lesson on the Nazi party. But she was a novice at political reportage and had written only a few profiles so far, all of them centered on fashion and culture. A few times she had cautiously touched on social or diplomatic issues and afterward second-guessed her work. To one of her editors, about a piece she deemed a failure, she promised, "I shan't use politicana [*sic*] as first paragraph in the future (only did it this once for variety's sake)." She'd mocked one attempt to stray beyond her usual Paris Letter format as "Political Addenda, Mostly Not Funny." She still believed that the journalist's job was to collect and recount facts without judgment. She claimed at that time that she wrote for the reader who was "neither

Left nor Right." She needed to "stand close" to events to understand them, which was why she preferred reporting on things observed to espousing grand theories.

But when, charged by the Stavisky Affair, she'd started writing more and more about the warring ideologies in France, which meant writing about European diplomacy more broadly, she'd been surprised that Ross had never commented on this new direction (he "seemed not to notice it," she later recalled) and interpreted his silence as encouragement.

As the people around her grew more willing to entertain the possibility of some kind of war, be it civil or between nations, she knew she had to continue exploring that track of political writing while looking beyond Paris, to keep her readers informed, but also for her own professional survival. "GIVE ME ANY HINTS as to what you hear, believe or want to about Europe," she begged a *New Yorker* editor. "Friends returning from New York say the only thing that interests in a Paris Letter is Europe, not Paris. Yes? Advise, please. Kind of worried." To write about European politics meant trying to understand the German threat to peace. Just before proposing the Hitler profile she'd told White she'd become convinced "Germany will come and gobble France as sure as we sit here, you and I…the Germans are a medieval people, still intent on saving and subjugating the world."

She had a newfound confidence on her side, after completing work that Ross had called "superb" and White "perfectly beautiful," a two-part profile on Queen Mary. It had been "odd, exciting and hemmed in" work, she'd told White; "I keep trying to make her human and I fancy after twenty-five years queening maybe she isn't." Despite being stonewalled by the royal press secretary and barred access to her subject, Flanner produced a thorough look at the monarch and by extension the role of the monarchy in British life.

By talking with local journalists, titled friends, and a few "unwitting sources," including palace employees and suppliers, she got at minutiae ranging from the angle of the Queen's cursive to how she selected her gowns. The profile, for which she was paid a bonus for "outstanding merit" and which got reprinted in other publications, also fetched her the biggest paycheck of her career so far. She said she couldn't eat for a day after the $1,100 arrived, she was so "astounded." She opened a savings account for the first time in her life.

Capitalizing on the goodwill Flanner had gained through the Queen Mary piece, White championed her Hitler idea to Ross, even while passing along that Flanner herself had said she feared it would be an "almost impossible job." Ross submitted. Though it would push the magazine into new and risky territory, the prospect of a Hitler profile was ultimately "just too fascinating for us to resist," as White told Flanner. "If anyone can get it we feel you can."

Ross knew Flanner was close to burning out after having taken on so many assignments and travel in recent months, but once he'd approved "the Hitler stuff," as he and White called it, he pushed Flanner to complete the reporting quickly. Perhaps, concerned for her health, he hoped she could finish early enough to give herself some time to relax before returning to her Letters. More likely he'd gotten so excited by the idea he worried a competitor would beat them to it. Hitler remained somewhat of an unknown quantity in America, and what had been written about him in English was full of psychological speculation and falsehood. A deeply researched profile, if done well, would draw much attention to *The New Yorker*. "For God's sake, see Hitler through before leaving [Nuremberg], if you can," Ross told her. "If you do half the piece on him that you did on Queen Mary, your fame will be nation-wide, or at least will stretch from here to the Mississippi."

As she started preparing to write the profile, Flanner's anxieties about the potential for German aggression began creeping more and more into her work. Much of the American Hitler coverage remained superficial, and President Roosevelt refused to publicly denounce him as a dictator, but the foreign press was already reporting on party-sanctioned murders and on the persecution of Communists and of Jews. The American Jewish Congress knew enough to put Hitler on mock trial in front of a crowd of twenty thousand at Madison Square Garden in the spring of 1934, drawing sympathetic luminaries including newly elected Mayor Fiorello La Guardia, and garnering *The New York Times* headline "Hitlerism Denounced as Crime Against Civilization." The Nazis had by that point established their first concentration camp, at Dachau, for political prisoners. And in Paris Flanner had encountered some of the German intellectuals who'd fled and were either settling in France—with difficulty, as refugees could neither take any job that could go to a French citizen nor draw state assistance—or heading further afield. A German-Jewish refugee family moved in below Flanner and Solano at the Bonaparte.

By the summer of 1934 Flanner swerved between discussions of political, economic, artistic, and military matters, her tone sometimes frightened and antagonistic, and other times reassuring and diplomatic. In an August Letter she joked that tourists traveling to Vienna no longer asked what plays were on but rather if they should be concerned about being shot, and that people heading for Munich had less interest in what their favorite restaurant was serving than in verifying the rumors that its owner had been murdered. And then she swiftly turned to warning that if "European business doesn't get livelier,

European politics will. It's the empty old cashbox that is filling people's heads here with new ideas."

That September, with the twentieth anniversary of the outbreak of the Great War dominating the conversation in France, she wrote that another Franco-German conflict felt "inevitable." She predicted that this next war would be fought on all sides, not with the same initial sense of sacrifice and hope for glory that had gripped people like a mass fever in the summer of 1914, but with a kind of suicidal resignation. She jumped from that remark to covering the latest developments in Parisian theater, although even there her anxieties rang out clearly: "Paris is in a bad way theatrically as well as financially, artistically, politically—like everyone else on the Continent and on earth."

Two weeks later she was fretting over Hitler's "plebiscite radio speeches in which his excited voice sounded like the screams of static," and cataloguing facts of the previous year's Nazi purge still coming to light, while also passing along the rumor from the German-expat "grapevine" that most Germans were against him but had been terrorized into submission. It struck Flanner that people had become resigned to their own annihilation. In that especially temperate summer "everyone has loved the sun and stopped thinking. There is a general impression in Europe that thinking won't get you anywhere, anyway. All over the world, events seem to be taking place without a thought having been given to them first." And again she wrote that war looked certain, this time in April 1935 in response to news of German rearmament. "Things here [in France] look alarming...the worst fright since the fearful fighting in 1914." She described how, instead of panicking or hoarding food, French peasants living near the German border had figured that they'd be bombed to oblivion before getting the chance to enjoy anything they might stockpile. With the introduction of German labor service for nonmilitary units she noted how, according to her sources, "Berlin volunteers could be seen exercising at night in the Tiergarten, crawling on the ground on their stomachs as if hunting imaginary violets in imaginary shell-holes." The prevailing feeling was that "if war comes this year, it might come at the beginning of July, if it's hot, heat and history having an undeniable affiliation in European affairs. Otherwise, war should open in about three years, of its own momentum."

Even while making these predictions Flanner remained in thrall to German culture, with all of its abject fascination and dark eroticism. In that same Letter from April 1935 she beamed about the release of *Triumph of the Will*, Leni Riefenstahl's Nazi propaganda film that masqueraded as a documentary of the previous year's Nuremberg rallies. Riefenstahl's Hitler appeared to Flanner as "a surprised messiah, astonished at his holy success." Riefenstahl had turned him into a screen god from the opening sequence of his arriving at Nuremberg by plane, coming from high above the clouds as if a deity descended from the heavens. Flanner judged the film "the great Berlin event...it gives you two hours of Hitler, fabulous flags, acres of marching men, shovelers, trumpeters, etc.—undoubtedly the best recent European pageant."

Now, in September 1935, after months of research that included reading her French version of *Mein Kampf* purchased from a pornographic bookdealer, tackling the prescient anti-Nazi critiques of the exiled journalist Konrad Heiden in German, and wading through a sea of official and unofficial misinformation about Nazism, Flanner was headed for Nuremberg to witness the annual Nazi party rallies.

For the first time Flanner would visit the country alone. She had to move carefully. No one would be close at hand to help if her hosts turned nasty. The Nazis had banned her fellow American correspondent Dorothy Thompson from Berlin a year earlier for mocking the Führer in her book *I Saw Hitler!* ("I bet he crooks his little finger when he drinks his tea," she'd written), a shocking expulsion that had *The New York Times* predicting on its front page that Thompson wouldn't be the last journalist to suffer such a fate. Another American correspondent advised Flanner that if she told anyone what she was really doing in Germany she shouldn't expect to ever return there under the Third Reich. "OK by me but sounds a little neurotic" was Flanner's reply. In the end she crossed on a tourist visa to avoid attention.

When her family had worried about her travel she'd tried to calm them by saying she would keep her distance from Jews. Despite the crudeness of that statement and others like it, Flanner had also shown herself to be sympathetic to Jewish causes. She'd taken to *The New York Times* in 1922 to denounce the anti-Jewish riots she'd seen in Vienna, and she was deeply affected by the struggles of Jewish refugees. Her mother, who did actively dislike Jews, reprimanded her for what she saw as Janet's liberal views. And yet Flanner certainly traded in cruel and careless stereotypes. She rendered a Jewish theatrical agent as a grubby caricature in *The Cubical City* and shared in the family lore that her large nose gave evidence of hidden Jewish ancestry. Her attitudes toward Jews seem marked more by arrogance and ignorance than by outright maliciousness, not uncommon among her social set in that era.

Once she'd reached Nuremberg, Flanner realized that too much caution would cost her the story. She needed to get close to the center of things. She risked connecting with an old acquaintance, Ernst "Putzi" Hanfstaengl. Half-American and half-German, he'd been one of Hitler's earliest financial supporters and had gone from being a kind of court jester as Hitler's personal piano player to serving as his foreign press chief. Flanner had first met Putzi in New York. He was a Harvard graduate (Class of 1909, as he liked to remind American journalists) and had been briefly engaged to Djuna Barnes. Flanner's fellow correspondent William Shirer described Putzi as "an immense, high-strung, incoherent clown," who'd asked the foreign press to, as Shirer quoted him, "report on affairs in Germany without attempting to interpret them [since] history alone...can evaluate the events now taking place under Hitler." Shirer admitted that his colleagues among the English-speaking press actually "rather liked him." Flanner's main complaint about going to see Putzi was that she would have to spend time with his wife, who was "pretty stupid (stupid not pretty)," as she told White, unless Putzi was "off with a blond." She also visited Putzi's mother, a Bostonian with whom Flanner shared mutual friends and who knew Hitler well. She "loves to talk and be kowtowed to," Flanner told White. "I'll do it." Flanner figured that Putzi shared even the most closely guarded state secrets with his mother: She was American and intelligent, meaning he was unable to "treat her like a parlor maid in wits, as he can his German wife."

She decided to attend the Nuremberg rallies as a journalist after all, to get the best seats possible. She had to see and hear him closely, to understand how he managed to seduce so many, she told White. No sooner did she ask Putzi to officially invite her to the Party Congress than all doors opened. Now she would be watched more closely, and, her hosts hoped, used to advance their aims. Hitler "took special satisfaction in the foreign visitors and delegations who came each year [to the rallies] in growing numbers," wrote the Nazi architect and Hitler confidant Albert Speer, "especially when these were from the democratic West." Flanner was treated as an "Honor Guest [*sic*]" and given "room, food, drinks free, tickets to all the shindigs, an autobus or a private car to get about in," as she crowed in a letter to Ross.

"Instead of hiding the fact I was a writer; I should have vaunted it." She told Ross of how the other correspondents all failed to mention these perks in their reports—just as she would fail to do when her own time came to file.

Flanner sent false postcards to *The New Yorker* as she went about her reporting; she said only good things about Germany, assuming they would be read by Nazi officials. "I think your flattering postcards from Germany to all of us (flattering to Germany, that is) were a great stroke of genius," White told her. "You are a very canny newspaper lady."

She avoided interviewing or meeting Hitler, anticipating that all she would hear would be bluster and that the only way to really "squeeze any truth" from the profile would be to chronicle how he worked, how he achieved his "messianic effects" on large crowds. She trailed him for a week, observing carefully how others responded to their Führer. She connected with a few German friends collected on previous trips. They helped her gather conflicting thoughts on Hitler from a variety of sources, from members of his entourage to anonymous citizens who risked speaking to her. A young Reuters correspondent also offered tips and made introductions. As with her profile on Queen Mary, she was searching for all possible side-door entrances into her story. "She looked beyond what the ordinary eye could see, and she heard vibrations too delicate for the ordinary ear," William Shawn would say of her years later. "She picked up signals, intimations, atmospheres, dim forms, ambiguous voices, and out of all this she constructed as accurate a representation as we have had of what was going on in Europe."

She was surprised by how easy it was to get people talking. "The great drawback of my German trip of nearly a month was that I believed what American correspondents, still there or just out of it, told me and so went without journalist's visa; not only would I not have been jailed (of all the damned tosh) but would have received even more attentions and help than I did incognito," she told White. "The amiability, politeness and friendliness of all the Germans now—from peasants who...had no idea whether I was a writer or a lunatic, up to men high in secret diplomacy, was astonishing, especially to me who lived in Germany before the war and have visited often since and have always found them inclined to severity and stiffness, plus rudeness. It's childish to fancy such a change is occult propaganda; I can only deduce that Hitler's treating them all like one class, peasant and aristo alike, pleases and frees their better natures; it is certain that being now amply fed and sure of their future (good God, how) makes them better tempered than three years ago when I was last there. Whereas the French, out of European fear, are getting crosser and crosser." While she talked to plenty of "liberal educated anti-Nazis," she said that among the true believers she never met one who struck her as particularly bright. "The intelligent Nazi didn't exist, don't exist. Intelligence is wiped out on faith."

On Friday, September 13, 5 p.m., at the Zeppelinfeld, there on the outskirts of the fairy-tale town of Nuremberg, she witnessed the spectacle of the Nazi party rallies firsthand. The gathering had started at the beginning of the week, doubling Nuremberg's population and turning the whole place into "a city of jubilation, a city gone mad," as one observer remarked. Hundreds of trains converged on the station recently built to accommodate the masses. A lucky few among the pilgrims slept in the gothic gabled inns; many more in tents. Day and night uniformed men pushed through the cramped streets like rivers of black, brown, and red in search of an ocean.

Under the deep blue banner of a late summer evening Flanner watched the pulsing lines of service corps men goose-stepping in sync to the unquestioning hails from the grandstands. (Six months earlier

Hitler had reintroduced compulsory military service in a shocking defiance of the Treaty of Versailles.) The crowd echoed the perfect cohesion of those marching checkerboard squares by chanting in unison with one giant voice. As night fell Flanner watched the beams of 130 antiaircraft searchlights placed at forty-foot intervals gathering to make an incandescent dome in the sky, connecting hundreds of thousands of men and women below under the white light, ringed by the red of twenty-one thousand Nazi flags. (This "Cathedral of Light," as its designer, Albert Speer, called it, "had the advantage of dramatizing the spectacle while effectively drawing a veil over the not-so-attractive marching figures of paunchy party bureaucrats.") Later came the eerie pageantry of a torchlight procession through the medieval streets, ancient and avant-garde at once.

Speed. Power. Noise. Color. Weapons. Smoke. People, in every direction, dead-eyed, ecstatic. Blaring horns. Metal tonnage. Shouted promises and secret oaths. Flags drenched in blood. Crisp, snapping heels. All of it meant to mask the private internal divisions of a party in chaos. All of it meant to quiet the individual doubts of a citizenry still far from united around the self-proclaimed messiah. It was opera. It was melodrama. It was cinema.

Flanner, the great lover and critic of the arts, could not help but be aroused by the sheer magnitude and precision and planning of the performance. ("It's not our place to decide whether M. Hitler is greater than Napoleon or Bismarck—as he himself claims," a French film critic had commented after seeing newsreels from the rallies, "but he is certainly just as strong as Cecil B. de Mille.") Flanner couldn't have been completely immune to the thrill of realizing that she was witnessing something historic in all this bedlam, nor that new journalistic opportunities might be opened to her alone as a result.

Whether going on to preach the gospel or sound the alarm, anyone who experienced a Nuremberg rally left permanently stamped. For the French writer and Nazi sympathizer Robert Brasillach it was the sight of "German children playing like wolves around the memorials of civil war and sacrifice," the way the "nocturnal ceremonies" left one with the sense of "an easier life, but most of all the surprising mythology of a new religion." For William Shirer it was the terror of "the little men of Germany who have made Nazism possible...[shedding] their individual souls and minds—with the personal responsibilities and doubts and problems—until under the mystic lights and at the sound of the magic words of the Austrian they were merged completely in the Germanic herd."

And for Janet Flanner it was the "parading of military strength and of equipment of a blitzkrieg type then unknown in England or western Europe—the public premiere of Panzer divisions, of a brand new Luftwaffe roaring overhead, of demonstrations by the ace [Ernst] Udet of dive-bombing, of flame-throwers in rows, of motorcycle corps in formation, of solid city blocks of whippet and giant tanks, of miles of marching, goose-stepping, uniformed men, and, above all, of hundreds of thousands of civilian German faces lifted to bay to the blue Bavarian skies, Today Germany, tomorrow the world."

But she would only write those words much later, after the war.

In the immediate Flanner wrote nothing, at least not for public consumption. She would keep her experience at the rally totally out of her profile, aside from a single sentence: "Hitler's use of flags, banners, scarlet, gold, of music, of singing, and of marching, massed men, made last summer's Nürnberg Nazi Congress a week of unusual sights—especially to the two hundred foreigners he allowed, by special written invitation, to attend." She didn't specify for the reader that she had numbered among those two hundred guests.

She did leave one other written trace from the event. At some point—maybe that Friday night at the Zeppelinfeld, needing a moment away from the barrage; maybe on the train home, trying to keep other, darker thoughts at bay—she made a list in pencil on the back of her official pass to the rally.

> Japonese [*sic*] anemones
> Aster frikati [*sic*]
> Dwarf aster
> Lilium rubrum speciosa

She may have been considering planting options for the Orgeval gardens.

Flanner would guard that pass to the 1935 Nuremberg rally, with its eagle and swastikas on the front and its catalog of flowering plants in gently sloping cursive on the back, for the rest of her long life.

Back in Paris after nearly a month in Germany, typing through her notes, the full scale of the horror hit. She'd seen Hitler and she'd seen people reacting to Hitler, and the second sight scared her far more than the first. "He is the strangest most unattractive inexplicable male in high position I ever saw," she told White. "[But] the view point which pretends he is nothing because he looks like it, that he is a mannekin and the others the men, that he isn't the whole works in that vortex of ambition and personal fanatical belief where Nazism is still functioning—that minimizing attitude is certainly wrong… He has the most completely catalytic effect on the mind of mankind I ever heard of…He sums up the kind of godhead and mythology of silly bloody maleness and flatulent pride that suits [the Germans] to a T. Those who hate Fascism better start knowing he is not a mere hysterical heliotrope. He's the fanatic and dangerous *exalté* he says he is, and his sobbing occasionally doesn't interfere, alas." In another note to White just after her return she wrote: "I can't tell you how discouraged I feel. People are crazy. Germans craziest."

She was still fighting through the headwinds of the Nazi media machine, struggling to sift reported facts from official lies. She worried about how to capture "the most nebulous personality, the most cypherlike individual in history," she told Ross. It would be a "hard job to make this entertaining," while telling the "truth about him physically and psychologically." While she anticipated that whatever she wrote would "please neither the Nazis or the antis," she would focus on doing "a good job for you."

By the late autumn of 1935 she realized that she'd been working for nearly fifty days straight at ten hours a day trying to finish. She had too much material. She felt like she was drowning in it. She took three days off (which went "like a breeze") and got back to it.

She feared Hitler and understood that others should fear him, too. But she also feared devoting the whole profile to denouncing him, lest her work stray from factual reportage and into the realm of propaganda. That the propaganda served American purposes offered no consolation. She hated how her peers wanted to "jack up the facts to suit the American anti-Nazi attitude." She told White that while "more than ever" she shared that anti-Nazi attitude, she couldn't abide her colleagues slipping into editorializing while showing their "ignorance of the simple physical Hitler truths." Just "because one hates autocracy is no reason to lie about it." The more she turned her personal observations into public prose, the more she saw how easily her words could be turned to advancing a particular group's interests. Complicity was not a feeling she liked. She was a writer, not a publicist. She was certainly no diplomat.

She decided she had to cover Hitler the same way she might cover a Coco Chanel or an Elsa Maxwell—the way she would profile "anybody," as she put it to White, giving "the life story, inner and outer, of a human being, without adding whether or not you or I or anybody agrees with his sectarian views." She would chronicle his political rise just as she would follow a captain of industry's journey from mail room to head office. While it had been "awfully hard to get any truth" out of his inner circle, she thought the profile would succeed chiefly by taking seriously those surface details about Hitler the man that so many others had glossed over or avoided. "You have to catch hold of interesting personal stuff about H the way you'd catch hold of a flea—crack it between your nails," she told Ross.

After months of intense fact-checking and revisions, the first installment of Flanner's three-piece profile, "Führer-I," ran in the February 29, 1936, issue. It was among the earliest, and first, truly in-depth studies of Hitler that many Americans would have encountered. (When Dorothy Thompson interviewed Hitler five years earlier she could only ask three questions, submitted a day in advance, and had afterward decided that he had no political future.)

Flanner opened with a joke. It was odd, she wrote, that a man who didn't drink, smoke, eat meat, or, apparently, sleep with women, should be "dictator of a nation devoted to splendid sausages, cigars, beer, and babies." She highlighted his physical weakness, from the time he was a "small-boned baby," to an underfed, unpopular, tubercular teen, to a war-wounded adult. "Like many partial invalids, he has compensated for his debilities by developing a violent will and exercising strong opinions." Hitler, then, was just another bitter, loudmouthed veteran. She judged his mind "limited" and his "face inappropriate to fame," while allowing that his eyes were his one good feature. She mocked him for his lack of friends and rumpled dress. She explained the real reason he avoided alcohol and nicotine stemmed from his already being a malformed eccentric, since such substances would only "heighten the exciting intoxication his faulty assimilation already assures."

She described how he decorated his homes and offices; the cars in which he was driven; how he was fed and coddled and clothed and entertained by his lackeys; his preferred Bavarian recipe for porridge (butter, browned flour, a touch of vinegar, carraway seeds, lightly salted); his insomnia; his mania for films; his unexplained "fits of weeping"; his hatred of invitations to dinner; his ability, when needed, to charm women by talking them into submission, as do "many small, dominant men"; his laughable interpretations of art history, proceeding from the assumption that Chinese and Egyptian art had never happened; his lifelong outsider's susceptibility to being easily impressed by a title or diploma; his tortured genealogy ("born of a lusty father past his prime"); his embrace of the bits of Nietzsche that fed his views of a world where the strong decimated the weak; his love of police dogs; how he could no longer take his solitary walks, "his one sport," for fear of assassins; his wartime failure to connect with his trench-mates who "thought him courageous but queer"; how mountain speedways were built to shorten his drives from Munich to his favored alpine chalet; how, "like many mistaken middle-aged men," he'd brought his receding hair forward "in a wiglike wad."

She had praise as well, commending his skills as a "mob orator," capable of shutting down any challengers—"a born spellbinder of the emotional type...who, when heckled, could find an explanation as quick as lightning and make it sound like thunder"; his knack for advertising and organizing; his craftiness; his pragmatism and patience; his singlemindedness; his "furious energy"; his fearlessness. All praise that could also be read as a warning.

Her harshest criticism was that Hitler "has mystical tendencies, no common sense, and a Wagnerian taste for heroics and death. He was born loaded with vanities and has developed megalomania as his final decoration." But she also wrote lightly about his love of South German sweets and other details meant to present a well-rounded figure of the man.

With deft sleight of hand Flanner, through this great accumulation of anecdote and trivia, achieved her goal: to present Hitler, a man with foibles like any other, as the embodiment of the new and terrifying realities imposed by the Nazi party, her true quarry. By chronicling Hitler's career, she was able to give readers context on what Nazism represented and explain how this formerly fringe party came to dominate all aspects of German life. She was narrow in approaching Hitler chiefly as a national rather than an international problem, one that would have to be left to German citizens to solve by themselves. And yet without saying so directly—by recounting the killing of SA chief Ernst Röhm on Hitler's order—she was also able to imply that he was someone capable of murdering any number of people he saw as threatening: "In over sixteen years' struggle for power and its maintenance, the Führer has been loyal only to one man—Adolf Hitler." While focusing tightly on the idiosyncrasies of their leader, she did more to expose the broader Nazi threat to the global order than had anyone yet in the pages of *The New Yorker.*

Flanner laid bare Nazi dogma using Hitler's own words, translating the German herself. "Its 'principles are based on a racial conception of the world' and it is a militant, hierarchical form of responsible, patriotic society with 'the good of the State before the good of the individual,' 'with obedience going upward, authority going downward.'"

She highlighted that dogma's anti-Semitism, quoting from the original twenty-five-point Nazi party platform of 1920: "Only those who are of German blood can be considered as our countrymen, regardless of creed. Hence no Jew can be regarded as a fellow countryman." She gave examples of German persecution of Jews, from the forced removals of Jewish business owners to the posting of signs reading, "Jews are like moths in the coat closet, like mice in cupboard. They are not wanted here." She empathized with the German Jewish plight of having to flee and so "embark on a journey as momentous as crossing the Red Sea must once have seemed." She questioned the logic of accusing a tiny segment of the population of somehow secretly dominating a nation of millions, and of Hitler's assertions that Jews completely controlled America's media and banking industries.

She revealed the coterie of German elites and industrialists who propped up Hitler's reign, while also naming his supporters abroad, including the aristocratic Diana and Unity Mitford, adherents of Diana's soon-to-be husband Sir Oswald Mosley's British fascism. She pointed out sections in *Mein Kampf* that had been deleted in French translations, detailing Hitler's plans to wipe out "the French hydra." At the same time, she tried to understand Hitler's appeal to those Germans who felt safe that they would not one day be victims of persecution, the ones free to imagine themselves taking part in some great, modern experiment, offering all sorts of new opportunities and advantages, the ones who would be welcomed into a new kind of "national community" that would amplify their voices after so many years of being too embarrassed by their country's ignoble past to proclaim its true grandeur.

By the last sentence of Flanner's final installment, many readers would be convinced that Hitler, however bizarre a character, could not be laughed away, and that those who ignored him did so at their peril. Remarking on his speechmaking, which he performed as constantly as if he were a man seeking power rather than one who had attained its heights, she closed: "Hitler still talks more than any other man in Europe."

She'd always wanted her profile work to stand apart from her Letters and so planned to sign the Hitler pieces not as Genêt but with her name, just as she had for all her other profiles. White worried that she might never be allowed back into Germany, which would put her "in a fix" as a foreign correspondent, perhaps even get her "locked up" if she tried returning. "I suggest that (if it worries you) that you not sign the profile," she advised.

Flanner shared White's qualms but felt compelled to write "as herself." She signed all three pieces Janet Flanner.

15

SHE DOESN'T DO VERY WELL ON THE SLIGHTER SUBJECTS

Flanner was back in America by the time her Hitler profiles ran. She'd sailed in January 1936 to catch up with friends and to relearn New York after "being ignorant of it for too many years," as she told White. She wanted to see what was new at the Metropolitan Museum and to "see even Radio City, which I'm unacquainted with." Most importantly she needed to cross the country to see her mother, who was ill in Altadena, California. It "curdled her blood" to take the time away from her Paris Letters to make the trip, but it "curdled it more" to realize it was "a necessity if I'm to see mother alive again." Still, that was no reason to stop working. "Maybe in California I could do one Hollywood Letter," she suggested to White.

By the beginning of that spring, "Führer-I–III" was making Flanner famous, just as Ross had predicted. A gossip columnist spotted her in New York, "a great gal—one of the smartest...taking merited bows for the series of pieces [on] Hitler. She's no longer girlish-looking, but she still storms up and down Gotham with the same mannish stride that used to wind me in Paris a dozen years ago, when we all used to frequent the same little café on the Île Saint-Louis, for onion soup and cheese soufflé." She was seen in San Francisco, dining with the drama critic Alexander Woollcott and her old friend Neysa McMein. In a "Snapshots of Hollywood" column, sharing space with Tallulah Bankhead, she was "Janet Flanner, now considered a vital European political reporter." Her former employer, *The Indianapolis Star*, described her as "chic and radiant, with a grand sense of humor and an oh-so-wise intelligence." Having read the Hitler pieces, the *Star*'s reporter assumed Flanner "must have known the dictator well."

She'd come a long way from writing about the latest cocktails at the Ritz. She'd shown her readers, her colleagues, and Ross that she could reach to the very center of European political action. She'd brought *The New Yorker* new acclaim. Freelance offers came from *Collier's*, *Time*, *Harper's*, and *McCall's*, the last especially lucrative, all wanting more of the same. So did a more permanent job offer from the Hearst Corporation.

While she received some fan mail for the Hitler pieces she gained many critics as well. By failing to directly and personally condemn his moral character in the strongest terms, she'd been, for some readers, too flippant a reporter for the story at hand. Malcolm Cowley, her close colleague and friend among the Paris expats, called her a fascist because of the profile's soft touch. Although Raoul Fleischmann told her he found the piece enlightening, other Jewish readers accused her of being a Nazi sympathizer. While she'd made a keen diagnosis of the Nazi pathology she'd offered no ideas for a cure. And the need to understand Hitler had never been more pressing. On March 7—the same day the magazine ran "Führer"'s second installment—Germany occupied the demilitarized Rhineland, violating the Treaty of Versailles and blindsiding the international community.

The criticism seemed not to bother Flanner. She told her mother she could understand why Jewish readers might dislike what she'd written. To a *New Yorker* staffer she recounted that when she was in Hollywood "the Jewish film gentlemen candidly said they thought my Hitler article was not unfriendly enough! No pleasing everybody." Defending her approach to Gertrude Stein, she said she hesitated to use harsh labels in print because people labeled others far too quickly and for superficial reasons. She would often complain during the thirties that if you didn't declare yourself a communist people automatically labeled you a fascist, and vice versa. She was, however, unprepared for how the profile was apparently received by its subject. "Latest is that [the profile] is all over Germany," she told White, and "is considered a fine pro-Hitler article which I refuse to believe. It is said to have been translated (and cut) and given to his nibs who liked it; don't believe that either."

If unruffled by the negative reactions to the profile, Flanner was evasive when talking about how she'd produced it. She lied to *The Indianapolis Star*, saying that she hadn't even seen Hitler, claiming that she purposely avoided him since "she never would have been allowed to have printed what she wished if she had entered the country as a journalist," and failing to mention her attendance at the rally. She might simply have been trying to keep herself out of the story. But maybe, stirred by the overwhelming beauty of that massive festival as much as by the collective insanity that fueled it and unable to reconcile those two feelings, she thought it wise to keep quiet about her own role in that drama.

She'd told Stein she hated superficiality. Perhaps she feared that even after all her months of research and reporting, her work on Hitler hadn't led her to any deep insight or true catharsis. Her real feelings about Germany—a place so horrible, so beguiling—were still too disjointed and disturbing to exhume. At least not in print, not yet.

As her stature in America grew, Flanner enjoyed time with her mother, who seemed "much better" but would "certainly slump when I leave; you know how mothers are, the darlings." She luxuriated in California's sensual delights. "The orange trees and freesia are in full bloom in the garden and the air smells like a perfume shop," she told White. She then returned to the east coast, visiting old friends, seeing how comfortable they were in their coastal vacation homes with their grown-up children. She felt the pull of home. The Hearst offer tempted her with its promise of a steady salary and a New York office. But there was only one magazine she really cared about.

To Ross and White she proposed continuing to write for *The New Yorker* but now based in New York, where she would focus on doing profiles, and on a regular salary. She said that she felt too old and set in her journalistic rhythms to go out and chase stories at the speed needed to keep up with the demands of being a European correspondent, now that the Continent felt so unsettled.

She knew she was good, but far from the best, at staying on top of new developments. She understood that her real skill lay in her ability to pull down those select shining stories from among the many floating by and then to plumb for the deepest truths, digesting and distilling each one in a few choice words. Her way was to read everything she could on a subject, to think things out slowly, to approach her contacts with care and precision, one at a time, for proper meals of conversation, not morsels, and then to write in long, uninterrupted, meditative stretches. "The trouble with me," she told McKelway, "is that I really adore to write and I go into a kind of séance with every page."

Eventually, she threatened to quit the magazine business altogether. She would go out to Hollywood, where, she said, she could easily pull in five hundred dollars a week.

White told Ross that they needed to "consider very carefully" her desire to "make more money and save for her old age," and to take her Hollywood threat seriously, despite how misguided she was about how much she could make out there, given that she had "no particular qualifications in the fiction line, nor...the lurid touch" that Hollywood craved. White also predicted "financial loss for us, and in the end for her" if she was to set up writing for them in New York as she'd proposed. "She doesn't do very well on the slighter subjects, and she is an extremely slow worker. One reason she is so good a reporter in Europe is that she knows the European ropes. She doesn't know the American ropes and might not turn the trick so well here. Moreover, if we brought her over here we should lose our one intelligent representative in Europe."

White suggested giving Flanner a raise, and to have her always working on "one important profile." They had to "make it increasingly pleasant for her to stay in Europe and hold the franchise there for us." She advised Ross to offer Flanner something enticing enough for her to want to stay on at least two more years, after which "if she then feels she must come back I think we could put it upon her to select her successor, and train him or her before she leaves Europe." She added "P.S. I'm trying to think in all of this of both Flanner's and *The New Yorker*'s ultimate good."

Flanner would have to figure out some way to adapt to the needs of the moment. Ross gave her a slight raise and encouraged her to seek out more assignments that took her beyond France, with a bump in expenses. She could write London Letters regularly, too, if she wanted. But because this would mean more work and travel, all parties knew this wasn't much of a reward.

Flanner sailed from New York in April, disappointed. But she knew Ross and White were right. Paris was her home, Europe her subject. And her time with her family, though pleasant, had reminded her of how stifling a loving home could be. "Hildegarde is so intellectual," she'd joked to White. She'd dragged Janet out to Death Valley, boring her with her passion for "early American Indian archeological evidences." Her mother, meanwhile, was "so fond of her children (me because of [the] *New Yorker* letter, poor dear) it's pathetic."

She decided she hadn't really been serious about returning, that her grasping for an American job had been only a momentary failure of nerve, that things were getting scary on the Continent and she'd been looking for a way to hide. Instead she would get back to work with doubled enthusiasm. From her ship she wrote White: "Thank you for all you did, even more for all you tried to do." Later she cabled Ross: "My re-decision based on thinking your ideas probably better for us both and don't [think] that I will go to London reluctantly. Having decided now to go will go and do good as I can."

But before she could think about her expanded role as a London correspondent, she would have to prepare for her next big non-French assignment. Ross had asked her to cover the 1936 Summer Olympics in Berlin in a series of reports, to which she'd mildly protested that she knew nothing about sports and "didn't know one end of a runner from another, unless I look close."

And this time Ross requested something new: to "get something of the [German] political and economic situation" into her Letters.

16

THE BUSINESS

Weidmann was back in Blanc and Million's cell. Speaking freely in French, confident they wouldn't be understood, the three men returned to their most recent preferred topic of conversation: "*le* business"—here using the English word, a bit of French gangster slang—they would pull off in Paris once they were free.

Weidmann had designed their future scheme to play to their respective strengths: Blanc's access to money, Million's ability to gain the trust of strangers, and his own intelligence and skill with languages. They would open a beauty parlor and teaching school in Paris. They would make shoddy beauty supplies to sell at inflated prices to students and clients. Blanc would fund it. Million would seduce a young woman and bring her in as the face of the operation to ease the minds of the women on whom they'd prey, since a beauty school run entirely by men would seem odd. And Weidmann, who told the Frenchmen he'd trained as a chemical engineer, would figure out how to make the products while also scouring the city for marks, hunting especially for American women, who were the perfect combination of rich and gullible.

He'd always wanted to see Paris.

17

NOT WHO WON, NATURALLY

Flanner got back to Paris in April 1936 having missed a brutal winter that spilled into early spring. To welcome her back the deaf woman who sold flowers on her block sent a bouquet, the wife of the local barber made her chicken soup, and Monsieur Louis painted her rooms at the Bonaparte. Katharine White arranged for fresh orchids to greet her as she walked in. "Thanks exquisite orchids. Don't worry feel fine. Working hard. How about Eden," she cabled White, charging ahead by pitching a profile on the British Foreign Secretary Anthony Eden (which never came off).

There were new openings to go see, new books to read, new people to meet. She reported on Britain's *Queen Mary* ocean liner completing its maiden voyage to Manhattan, robbing France's own *Normandie* of the Blue Riband given to the passenger ship crossing the Atlantic at the highest average speed, a slight the French were determined to avenge. She critiqued Louis-Ferdinand Céline's *Death on the Installment Plan*, his much-anticipated follow-up to *Journey to the End of the Night*, which she dismissed as a hollow work, joking that it was because she didn't know enough French slang to catch all of its obscenities.

Most of her attention she devoted to the election of France's first Socialist and first Jewish prime minister, Léon Blum, who'd wrangled an unsteady coalition of left-wing parties collectively dubbed the Popular Front, promoting workers' rights and antifascism. She wrote with approval of Blum's appointing for the first time in French history three female ministers: the chemist Irène Joliot-Curie (a Nobel Prize winner like her famed mother and father) as undersecretary of scientific research; Suzanne Lacore, a village schoolteacher, as undersecretary of child welfare; and the feminist Cécile Brunschvicg as undersecretary of national education.

Flanner admired Blum as much as she did any politician. An "odd man," but she liked his style, seeing him as a fellow person of refined taste in an age of populist buffoons, one who had no fear of alienating his audience, fussing over an argument from so many angles that he made people dizzy. She introduced him to her readers by playing up his paradoxes: as the country's leading Socialist who had also been legal advisor to one of its biggest motorcar companies and occupied a finely appointed manse on the Quai Bourbon; a "myopic and absent-minded" literary critic with degrees in philosophy and law, author of books about Stendhal and Goethe, and at the same time an earthy, twice-married bon vivant able to recite "good kitchen recipes" as fluently as he could Victor Hugo's poetry. She praised him for being bold enough to foresee "a millennium in which man will work only one-third of his day."

The Popular Front's victory showed the world that at least one European electorate (or at least its majority) could envision an alternative to the ultranationalism and authoritarianism dominating so much of the Continent. Still, the electoral process had been marred by ideologically motivated street violence. The ultraright league Action

Française had been waging an anti-Semitic attack on Blum in its eponymous newspaper. The movement's leader Charles Maurras, who claimed that Jews brought "lice, plague, and typhus while awaiting the revolution," told his followers to "sharpen their kitchen knives" for Blum's throat, or better yet shoot him "in the back." A few months before the election thugs from the Action Française's goon squad, the so-called Camelots du Roi, had been walking along the Boulevard Saint-Germain following the funeral of a monarchist writer when they happened to see Blum in his Citroën being driven by one of his Socialist deputies. They took his closeness to their mourning as an insult, dragged him from the car while shouting "It's the Jew Blum!" and beat him close to death. He might have been lynched had he not been shuffled away by some nearby construction workers. The next day members from various parties among the ever-fractious left joined together for a march through Paris in protest. Blum's beating added an urgency to mobilize against those who wanted thuggery over democracy. A heightened awareness of the need for unity carried over to the ballot box. (Once in power Blum would outlaw paramilitary leagues such as Action Française, though some simply morphed into new organizations with different names.)

The French workers' movement, emboldened by the Popular Front's victory, launched thousands of sit-down strikes and factory occupations; in some cases they held executives captive. Businesses shuttered spontaneously and the streets transformed into arenas for impromptu concerts and dancing as hundreds of thousands took part in a mix of carnival and protest. Striking department-store workers cleared merchandise for a makeshift soccer pitch on the showroom floor. Foreign capitalists pulled their money out of France.

Flanner laid out the strikers' grievances in an unusually sober Paris Letter that June. She commiserated with the underpaid workers as much as she did with their employers. Blum's government eventually made significant concessions. Progressive French citizens celebrated the adoption of a forty-hour workweek and increased wages, fifteen days of paid vacations, immunity from punishment for striking, and nationalization of certain industries. Newspapers ran photos of smiling factory workers on bicycles heading out from smoky towns for the countryside to enjoy their vacations. And yet funding those social advances fueled further inflation and higher interest rates, ultimately negating some of the gains achieved.

Flanner noted that the French hoped their new "forty-hour schedule" would apply to everyone, except of course "creatures such as housewives and farmers, whom nature and economics always ignore." For all its idealism the Popular Front failed to provide French women with the right to vote. When the forty-hour week finally did get implemented, Flanner said that it "struck Paris in a way to change all our lives; this ordering food on Saturday for next Tuesday's breakfast (unless you don't mind pickled pork for breakfast) is confusing; the bank being closed on Saturday is a shock for us week-enders too; prices are mounting like the wind."

That year's Bastille Day festival doubled as celebration for the new government, with red flags flying alongside the usual *tricolores*. Blum, the French communist leader Maurice Thorez, and others were hailed by hundreds of thousands at their rally. People also noticed a newfound vigor for France's armed forces, the cheers for the parading military spanning the political spectrum. The historian Eric Hobsbawm, then a nineteen-year-old visiting Paris before taking up his studies at Cambridge, would recall how "the whole of popular Paris was on the street to march…or to watch and cheer the march, as families might cheer departing newlyweds…for a brief moment France became not only the refuge of civilization, but the place of hope."

Flanner had missed the Bastille Day party. She was in Berlin. She'd crossed the border as a journalist, feeling that any fears about fallout from the Hitler profile were unwarranted. "I hate to go to Germany feeling uncomfortable and secretive," she told Ross, adding that as a journalist she'd have "the privilege of carrying papers, clippings, etc; these are frequently taken away from foreigners going over the frontier...If the Germans don't want me to come, they'll say so... if they didn't know I was a journalist and discovered it, they might make trouble on that account even without the Hitler thing, because I'd failed to make out proper papers which are damnably sacred in bureaucratic Europe."

Not much interested in sports, she wasn't sure how to write about the Games. She'd asked one of her editors, R. A. Hague, "what sort of sport news does Ross want, have you any idea? Not who won, naturally." She thought maybe she would highlight the "extremely strange and pretty awful contents" of the official Nazi Athletes Guide and Curriculum, which "states that there has never been a good Jew athlete, among other oddities." (Katharine White would yield much of the responsibility for editing Flanner to Hague, St. Clair McKelway, and William Shawn in the late thirties as her duties to the magazine shifted.)

Flanner and Noël Murphy found Berlin "handsome and hustling," everything freshly painted or planted. On the first of August she listened as Hitler opened the games with a few simple words, and watched in wonder at the final torchbearer, carrying a flame that had traveled from Greece, sprinting through the wide Unter Den Linden, which she judged more pleasant than she'd ever seen it, airier now that its famed linden trees had been cut back to make way for a new subway addition. Twenty thousand doves were released into the skies where Luftwaffe gliders put on aerial displays. As with the Nuremberg rallies, she was taken by the visual drama of it all. At that evening's festival inside the stadium there was "pageant, dance, and melody, the whole being given, by novel application of cinema principles, a brilliant nocturnal beauty. Under faraway lamps, the arena's green grass and red-clay lanes looked like long shots in a colored movie."

The spectacular displays and exceptionally well-mannered crowds and "perfect organization" were all part of an act for the foreign press, a projection of surface civility under which lay the powder keg of German military might, ready to blow. "As the newspapers carried Goebbels' statement that foreigners are to be treated elegantly well, even policemen smile and cheer when a French Ford goes by, with me smiling and cheering in it," she told Hague. She decided that the act was the story. She wrote, in an issue featuring Jesse Owens on the cover, of how members of the SA and SS had been ordered "to wear uniforms as little as possible, not to discuss racial problems in public, and to give a foreign lady, no matter what her profile, their seat in a tramcar."

At the same time she revealed how well the act had worked on her, as it had on many other foreign journalists. "The past year has been closer to physical prosperity and farther from political nervousness than any Germany has known since the war, and its capital city shows it," she told her readers. "Probably the only blot on Berlin's beauty will be the still unoccupied new American Embassy, discolored, drab, three windows broken and boarded, a solid, homy reminder of American depression amid Germany's prosperous facades." Noting that Hermann Goering had recently offered official favor and protection to an actor-director who'd feared he would have to flee, she wrote, "Goering is apparently the most liberal official patron of the arts in Germany today." Maybe she was trying to be glib, but it's not clear.

She went so far as to use France's lackluster performance at the Games to air the popular concern that the country lagged behind Germany in birth rates, illustrating the "increasing difficulty in finding fine physiques in a population which was already making a poor showing at the Paris Olympics in 1924."

The one bright spot in her Letters from Berlin was the obvious pleasure she took in the dominance of Jesse Owens and other Black American athletes, and in the sour German reactions to those victories. And yet her writing gave no evidence that she'd talked to any Black or Jewish American athletes, nor did she mention the hateful contents of the Nazi athlete curriculum, as she'd originally suggested to her editors.

Where was the woman who fretted about Hitler's rise? A few months earlier in the same magazine she'd written that while "it is all very well for theoreticians to point out that for France and Germany to fight again is insanity...everything Herr Hitler has done in the past few weeks—the soldiers he moved into the Rhineland, the speeches he made in the Krupp works," had given people good cause to think it all might "lead to future trenches." She had apparently put those fears aside.

Friends wondered if the Nazi spectacle had now actually won a true convert in Flanner. In trying to justify the contents of her Berlin Letters she told Hague, "I arrive at a conclusion [about how well Germany seemed to be doing under the Nazis] which everyone except an editor of the *New Republic* here would have to arrive at. I suppose stray ex-Jewesses will now again write in to Mrs. White, complaining of my Fascism and my loving governments without liberty; I also wish they would explain why they think the government of Moscow is full of liberty."

She stopped in Salzburg on the way home, continuing her nearly annual pilgrimage to the music festival, which she'd anticipated would be "THE big music-fest of summer Europe since Bayreuth this year will permit no Jews to attend."

In a jolly postcard she told White of her purchase of an accordion there, which she couldn't play but could "make a fine racket on."

18

THE CROSSING

Weidmann gained his release just before Christmas 1936. He returned to his parents' home and to a neighborhood he no longer knew. He saw a mess of cranes strung high with lights, heard nonstop rumbling and hammering. There were new businesses, new cars, new signs, a new Nazi *Oberbürgermeister* to replace the once popular Jewish mayor, Landmann, who'd been driven from his office and home. (Frankfurt had one of the largest Jewish populations in Germany, though this was still a fraction of the city's overall population.) The streets were clean and devoid of loiterers and beggars.

His parents told him how everything had been "revitalized" by the new regime. Hitler's color portrait hung in the living room. Although the family had once followed the Catholic line of voting for the Centre party, they'd happily joined the Nazi party in 1931, terrified, like so many of their class, of socialism and of the Social Democrats, above all, and hateful toward the French and the heavy war reparations they'd demanded. Their paper of choice was the Nazi-approved *Frankfurter*

Zeitung, which had been purged of its Jewish contributors. They now owned the building in which they lived, were admired at church and at work. They were proud to take part in Germany's great awakening.

A few days after his release Gestapo agents knocked on the Weidmanns' door. They took Eugen away and returned him four days later. He told his parents only that he'd been to Wiesbaden. What happened to him there is unknown. Once back he slunk into idleness. He read his Goethe and Schiller and Nietzsche. (He couldn't abidc books by contemporaries like Thomas Mann or Erich Maria Remarque—their heroes were too weak.) He wandered the streets without purpose.

In the first days of the new year he ran into another recently released inmate. They'd worked together in the library. Siegfried Sauerbrey had been a celebrity inside, caught after three years on the run, pinned as the mastermind of a massive insurancc fraud. Now Weidmann tried to sound him out about his plans, looking for a short-term venture to bring some cash. Sauerbrey disappointed. All he wanted now, after once having graced the front pages for his crimes, was to hold on to the mind-numbing clerking job he'd just secured.

In mid-May Weidmann left Frankfurt abruptly. He told his parents he was off to visit relatives in Cologne but headed instead for the border town of Saarbrücken. Despite Nazi policy barring ex-convicts from leaving the country unless expelled for subversion, Weidmann somehow crossed into the French town of Forbach on the afternoon of May 15, 1937. It may be he boarded a train with false papers, or just made a run for it. Weidmann himself would claim that he'd climbed into a ditch and shimmied under barbed wire, dodging a spray of bullets from the border guards. Some would later suggest that the Gestapo agents who'd taken him to Wiesbaden after his release had arranged for him to cross unmolested, perhaps forced him to, for reasons unknown.

On the other side of the border Jean Blanc waited on his motorcycle. They reached Paris by nightfall. They stayed at the Hotel Idéal on Rue Saint-Sebastien in the city's gritty eleventh arrondissement, where Roger Million was waiting. Weidmann spent the next night on a foldout cot in the back of the Café Guichonnet in the same neighborhood. There he met Million's destitute father, who waited tables for the owner, Marie Guichonnet, the family friend he'd turned to after his bankruptcy.

Weidmann loved Paris. He loved the big noise of its cars, the fur-draped women who smiled and held his gaze without shame, the intermingled smells from the rows of restaurants showcasing all the ways the French had for cooking flesh in its own juices. Here was a city where you could be seen, striding the wide boulevard in the glittering night; a city, too, where you could disappear, losing yourself in narrow streets that dead-ended without reason. Here was a city to possess.

He'd arrived at the start of what would be an especially pleasant spring, marked by an unbroken string of sunny days. He later said he'd never encountered a people so free of concern as he had in Paris that first season he saw it.

19

ALL I AM TRYING TO DO IS WEATHER EVENTS

While Flanner had been covering the Olympics in Germany and listening to Verdi in Austria, General Francisco Franco and his allies launched a coup in Spain, ousting the democratically elected left-wing government, also called the Popular Front as in France, from control of much of the country. As with many intellectuals of her era, Flanner would come to see the battle between Franco's Nationalist forces and the Republicans as both a physical conflict and a war of ideologies, a litmus test for the health of European democracy. As the Spanish Republic's delegate to the League of Nations worded it, "Today it is Spain. Tomorrow it will be some other country."

As soon as Flanner got back to Paris she wrote a Letter that opened by implying that the world's democracies would be foolish to treat what was happening in Spain as a local skirmish, boldly speaking on behalf of "Paris" to make her own point. "Paris feels that Spain is having a civil war which might well be anybody's civil war, but most especially France's. Paris is therefore following events with attention…it is fatalistically accepted here that whoever wins will automatically quicken the momentum of the Communist-Fascist struggle which increasingly seems to be Europe's future balancing-of-power." French communists were raising money for the Spanish Republicans, and Flanner elicited sympathy for their cause by reporting that sources along the French border said that what was needed most was "morphine [since] the more constant fighting is guerilla warfare in the mountains, from which the wounded are slowly carried down on donkey back, undrugged." But then, trying to appear objective, she went on to say that some of those same sources had told her that foreign reporters were exaggerating the scale of the most recent battles nearby. "Maybe Paris, being so far away from it all, is mistaken and the Spanish civil struggle isn't worth wasting ink on, let alone blood."

Fascist Italy and Nazi Germany would support Franco's Nationalists. France, after a first burst of arms shipments, would give no aid to the Soviet-backed Republicans, despite Blum's having been elected on an antifascist platform. Blum declared a policy of nonintervention, believing that pushing French citizens to adopt an official stance reflecting his and his party's own natural sympathies for the Republican cause would have prompted major civil unrest, while also antagonizing France's main European ally, Great Britain, which, like America, also refused to intervene. Flanner at that time similarly thought it best to leave it to the Spanish to sort out their internecine conflict, reasoning that outside influence from more powerful neighbors could only lead to escalation and therefore more bloodshed in Spain, and perhaps even beyond its borders.

She knew there were many things she still could not see clearly, and many things she and her fellow journalists weren't being allowed to see at all. She spent the rest of the year in a relentless rush between Paris, Berlin, and London, striving to grasp the evolving political situation from multiple perspectives. She struggled to maintain her pace. The Channel ferry crossings were especially grueling due to seasickness. The Paris-to-London trip was "the longest, most costly in cash and discomfort of any on earth that is so short in actual distance."

How was she supposed to understand Europe when she could hardly figure out France? The country had only descended further into ugliness and polarization in the two years since the Stavisky riot. "NOTHING doing in Paris but political dissatisfaction, monster meetings, worry and watching Spanish war like an eagle," she told R. A. Hague. She'd heard that "war is considered family joke in America; no joke here but regarded as writing on wall; France is NOT sitting pretty, workmen insolent on street to rest of us poor modest bourgeoisie." She told him how a flower vendor had jerked Solano's arm and said, "You've got to buy, you're a foreigner, France for the French." She sensed a "lot of anti-foreigner feeling; not pleasant, believe me."

In an October Letter she translated the unease she'd privately voiced into what were perhaps the harshest words she'd yet used against the French in print. "Verbal violence in all political discussions, street arguments, and party-paper headlines have been the audible and visible accompaniment of France's increasing doctrinal intolerance. It is the intolerance of thought and violence of tongue which, even more than the fractious relations between hypersensitive capital and overconfident labor, may bring about the revolution that certain Parisians are prophesying."

Late in 1936 Flanner took on some speechwriting work for Carmel Snow, the glamorous editor-in-chief at *Harper's Bazaar*, as well as some freelance work for the same magazine. She outlined a book of essays, "not politics or personal biography [but] on things that seem fundamental to me, at my time of life, and that I've never argued before," as she told White, adding that she also wanted to write a "novel about crime."

In the middle of all this change and confusion and overwork she teetered on the edge of manic. "My brain can't hop around that fast," she said in reply to Hague's proposed schedule for some upcoming London Letters. She felt as if she was forever getting off a train somewhere in the rain and dark with poorly packed luggage and nagging pain, forever sleeping in some strange new room with her "trunk under foot," forever running "behind the times," forever worrying that she hadn't "really seen" whatever play, ballet, or exposition she was meant to cover because she was always on the move. She missed the "domestic feeling one has for one's home, even if it's only a hotel room, as mine is in Paris," she told White.

In a daze one night at the Bonaparte, she tossed a *New Yorker* check into the fire. She found herself regularly canceling meetings and social engagements, sometimes at the last moment. She grew nervy under so many deadlines. Her body gave out. She suffered shooting pains in her arms and legs, and was diagnosed with sciatica, which kept her bedridden for nearly a month. She worked with her typewriter on a breakfast tray, hot water bottles and painkillers at her side. Most terrible of all were the "night attacks," as she called them. "I walk with a cane and look like a broken down statesman," she told Ross. She suffered through bouts of anxiety and depression, and for a time withdrew from her social circle, seeing almost no one aside from Murphy and Solano. "Doctor says I must be careful not to joggle inflammation into chronic condition, in which case I would cheerfully shoot myself," she told Hague.

But then, as soon as she could manage it, she was back to her fevered clip. In early December, after having just reached Paris from a

London trip, Flanner had to rush back to London so as not to miss the biggest story of the season: Edward VIII had just abdicated so he could marry the American Wallis Simpson. As Virginia Woolf noted in her diary on December 7, "Spain, Germany, Russia—all are elbowed out. The marriage [meaning the couple's plans to marry; the wedding itself would not take place for another few months] stretches from one end of the paper to another."

Flanner had already been planning a long profile of Edward VIII, her next big subject after Hitler. But in the end her trip yielded only a short piece, and not on Edward but on Wallis Simpson, after Ross pushed her to shift focus despite initially thinking it distasteful to cover the affair at all. "What the hell? It's a strange and funny mess," he'd told Flanner. "For years the English publications...razzed Americans every time they could think of anything to say. It's our patriotic duty to slap back, I think." Flanner didn't share his enthusiasm. She told White that she felt sorry for Simpson. "She's getting the works here."

It was "a difficult job." She had to promise all her sources that she wouldn't mention Edward anywhere in the piece and that she would write it tastefully, "in that more elegant evasive manner—as if it made any difference." She managed only a superficial sketch better suited to a fashion magazine, angled on Simpson's fame as a society host who served fine food ("in addition to being a good cook herself, she can make her own cook be a good cook"), danced beautifully, and played bridge passably. Flanner judged Simpson "not pretty in any conventional manner," adding that "her face has the length formerly seen in nineteenth-century portraits, and she can't look her best in photographs, as she easily would have in a velvet-framed daguerreotype." She conceded that Simpson's "figure is flawless and impersonal in the modern manner; her skin is of the smooth vellum variety that takes modern makeup well," and that she had gorgeous feet. Meanwhile she told White: "Gossip is King will have to abdicate if marries so she won't marry, not wanting a harder seat than she now has, poor devil. She gets menacing letters. Sex, my child, makes lots of trouble here on earth."

Flanner accepted she would never know London the way she knew Paris, and that her outsider status muddied her writing. "One will always be a foreigner in England, without the foreigner's impudent privileges granted in France," she told Hague. "All those traditions which it takes a lifetime to learn and which England knows too well to bother to explain and which actually motivate existence, finally alarm." London was a "peculiarly sealed institution to a newcomer." And besides, she joked, she could never feel truly comfortable in a city where they drank expensive gin instead of good cheap wine. "I'll be glad to be back in Paris and have a drink I can afford." For the time being, the London Letters were accounting for too much of her yearly income for her to walk away from them. And at least her usual Paris-to-London route had just added an overnight service "with the pullman [sleeping car] put right on the ferry boat," which would help her "very much as I then don't lose a day being seasick in the sunshine of the Channel."

Solano, who'd joined Flanner in London to help with the Simpson profile, was taking more and more time away from her own work to assist, becoming, as one writer put it, "in effect, a housewife and part-time secretary to Janet." Ross, White, and others at *The New Yorker* knew that Flanner lived with Solano and assumed that they could depend on her to relay any letters or cables by phone to Flanner if they needed to reach her urgently while she was traveling. Flanner spoke openly with her editors about using Solano to do basic reporting on her behalf in Paris, should she be out of the city while a pertinent story developed there or if she needed some Paris-specific information on a deadline.

As Flanner continued dashing around the continent, her health still unsteady, Solano shared her concerns with Flanner's family. "Yes, Janet sounds far too busy," Hildegarde wrote back. "We don't like to think of her under such a strain. And we wish you would both come back to America, away from the threatening hard times of Europe."

Many among the expats in France had indeed had enough of those "threatening hard times." Their dreams had ended. The twenties had been the party, and now came the hangover. Gerald and Sara Murphy had abandoned their gilded lives in Antibes to return to America in 1934. F. Scott Fitzgerald left, too, the decade of postwar abandon he'd called "the greatest, gaudiest spree in history" now well behind him. After publishing the exquisite, nostalgic *Tender Is the Night*, he'd gone out to Hollywood because he needed the money, drinking furiously, his books selling more modestly than they once had, while Zelda was in and out of institutions for her schizophrenia. And as the expats were leaving, few people were arriving. Paris had welcomed just under two million in 1929. By 1935 that number had dropped to four hundred thousand.

Flanner saw less of Hemingway as he moved base from Paris to Key West. There had been an excruciating dinner in 1932, arranged by Hemingway's second wife, Pauline Pfeiffer, at Michaud's, a favorite of James Joyce, who was the guest of honor. Hemingway sat in near-silent awe and Joyce hardly spoke. Both men drank steadily. Flanner and Pfeiffer got bored and snuck away while Hemingway was off in the bathroom. Solano stayed, saying later that Joyce begged her not to leave him alone with Hemingway. When Hemingway returned, he wound up the restaurant's bar-top phonograph, after which Joyce, seizing a chance to avoid the awkwardness of the table, leapt up, grabbed the restaurant's tiny *patronne*, and began waltzing madly with her. In Solano's memory Hemingway said, "Gawd, he'll kill himself," before Joyce stumbled back into a table. Hemingway told her to fetch a cab while he hoisted Joyce over his shoulder, carried him out, and deposited him at home, later telling Solano he had to kick in the door as Joyce had no keys.

In his wandering Hemingway sent Flanner poetic letters, as in 1933 when he suggested she join him at a harborside hotel in Havana, "in a good clean room where you can work for $2.00 a day" while "the marlin swordfish go by, swimming up the stream like cars on a highway...They have beaches miles and miles long, hard white sand and no houses for twenty miles...Finest life you ever saw." He told her how much he'd appreciated her saying she'd enjoyed his *A Farewell to Arms*, writing, "I don't know anybody that I would rather have had like it (and I don't think very many people did like it very much)." Complaining about an unspecified disagreement with the publisher Jonathan Cape over the British edition, he said that publishers "are our natural enemies."

Flanner wasn't moving to Havana or anywhere else. To letters from her family urging her homeward she'd repeatedly answered that she couldn't justify it professionally, especially since the best she could hope for in America was an editorship. *The New Yorker* still seemed on solid footing, which meant she was still on solid footing, too, while so many of her peers weren't. The magazine had more than seventy thousand subscribers and consistently ranked among the top three American magazines for advertising pages sold throughout the 1930s. Its already healthy profits had gotten a boost with the end of Prohibition, after which it could carry liquor ads. Flanner felt herself becoming more valuable to *The New Yorker* as she devoted more thought and column space to political, military, and economic news, anticipating, before many others on the staff did, that these were the subjects Americans would care to know most about when reading of Europe. Her value as an observer on this sinking continent could only increase as other expats abandoned it.

She'd meanwhile been sharpening the Letters, honing the format that would carry her through the decade. She would write about the most important developments in Europe, no matter how far they took her away from her preferred focus on arts and culture, but she would do so by treating these developments—whether at an embassy, on a stock exchange floor, or a battlefield—as if they *were* artistic or cultural ones. By sticking to her usual tone despite the changing times she struck on a singular formula of delivering hard news as if it was light gossip. She would continue to seek out those seemingly superficial but ultimately illuminating particulars that other reporters ignored when covering the same story, her own version of the Emily Dickinson line that Hemingway liked to quote: "Tell all the truth but tell it slant." And in hanging on to that way of writing, her unconventional approach, mannered style, and absurdist wit, was she not, in her own way, offering a rebuke to tyrants and their followers who insisted that the world should not be beautiful or funny but only hateful and ugly?

And she could stand apart from other American correspondents in her analysis because the biweekly scheduling of the Letters relieved some of the pressure to deliver the perfect take on any still-evolving story. She could let her ideas percolate. She could change her mind, she could keep refining and revising, never with the goal of erasing doubt but rather to embrace as many possible viewpoints on a story as she felt were right, and then to convey them as entertainingly as possible.

Though hampered physically, and ill at ease with where Europe seemed to be headed, she remained committed to the life she'd made in Paris with Solano and more recently Murphy, and to the career that had started off so casually and now engrossed her so fully. "There's no education like discovering who you are, whatever you are," she said later. "Walden Pond was, for Thoreau, a very fine place for him to understand who he was. I am glad I was able to understand who I was, within my limited self-knowledge, and that it came to me in this beautiful foreign city." America remained, for her, the land of retreat. "If you don't go home after ten years, you know you're hooked. You're in the bird's cage, all right. And you won't want to go home...There is a kind of gilt on the cage of life...that is entrancing. Delightful. There's no sense of captivity."

After more than a decade of writing about Paris and Europe for *The New Yorker*, she'd accepted that this was what she loved to do most in the world. She would continue even if Paris and Europe now looked nothing at all like what she'd hoped to find when she first took the job. She would simply change herself to suit the needs of this new era. She saw her assignment from then on in the starkest terms: "All I am trying to do is weather events."

20

THE VILLA

Weidmann's first stop in Paris was Fouquet's, a crowded brasserie on the Champs-Élysées. "High Class Grill Room" read the sign outside in English. There a forger named Maurice furnished him with papers for 120 francs. He was reborn as Eugen Karrer, French citizen, native of Belfort. The choice of that eastern town close to the German and Swiss borders explained his heavily accented French.

He took a train to Saint-Cloud, a leafy outpost about five miles west of the Eiffel Tower, where Jean Blanc had rented him a house in which to launch their beauty institute. Roger Million would stay there, too. The property was a rickety three-room affair without bath, named La Voulzie for a tributary of the Seine. The men just called it the villa. It stood at the edge of some woods, with no neighbor close enough to see inside, as Weidmann had insisted. His choice of location surprised Blanc and Million, who'd thought it more logical to set up the business in Paris as they'd planned. But Weidmann had convinced them of the benefits of keeping a low profile beyond the city. The idle rich who would make up their clientele wouldn't care about the location; they had their cars and drivers.

How they were going to fit a beauty school into a three-room house he left unexplained. Blanc gave Weidmann fifteen thousand francs to get started. Million put in three thousand. Blanc brought him dishes and cutlery and an electric hot plate and linens and furniture. He stuffed the cupboards with food. Finally, at almost thirty years of age, Weidmann had a comfortable bed in a room of his own.

Million had done as promised and secured a female accomplice, Renée "Colette" Tricot, a thirty-year-old from the suburbs, mother to a ten-year-old son, and unhappily married to Henri, an ironworker for Renault. She had a tenuous grip on reality. She told neighbors she hailed from a line of Egyptian "pashas," and that she was the greatest midwife in all of France. These neighbors would describe Tricot as "dirty, lying, pretentious, proud, and unstable." She cut her fine dark hair to her chin. Her features were unremarkable. She attracted men easily with her talk, and sometimes pretended to be unmarried, calling herself Renée Rolls. Her husband figured the best way to keep her was to look away as she channeled her romantic imagination into various short flings. He worried that confronting her about her infidelities would push her toward true madness. She went out a lot, he would tell the police, but always returned in time to make dinner.

She worked at an umbrella store across from the Café Guichonnet, and it was the Million family friend Marie Guichonnet who'd connected her with Roger. She'd first tried to match Tricot with Jean Blanc, knowing that Tricot craved luxury and sensing that Blanc had far more money than Million ever would. Tricot and Blanc were together briefly until she switched her affections to Million, who, though just as ugly as Blanc, offered the more dominant personality. When Blanc discovered them together at the villa he sped off to the coast in anger, though soon returned and accepted the change. The only real difference, as Blanc would later say in court, was that now when he, Million, and Tricot went out for dinner they split the check, "instead of me paying for all three, as usual." Within weeks Tricot had left her husband and child more or less for good, without telling them where she was living. She spent most of her time at the villa sunbathing or puttering in the front garden. She avoided being alone with Weidmann.

And then one spring day Tricot asked Blanc for some spending money, and he got so angry he cut off all communication with her and with Weidmann. Ever loyal to Million, he kept in secret contact with him and sometimes loaned him his car. He'd agreed to prepay the villa's rent for several months, at Weidmann's request, and accepted the futility in asking him to leave. Blanc saw Weidmann only once more at the villa, when he went to collect the dishes and hot plate he'd provided. Blanc brought along a large friend for protection.

Weidmann had been taking the morning trains into Paris, to find their first students, as he told Million and Tricot. They would run the beauty institute without Blanc. By the end of spring, however, his confederates saw that his attention lay elsewhere. He'd never really intended to start the school. Not when back in prison, not now he was free. He'd said what he needed to say to get Blanc to bring him to Paris and pay his way. He'd lied about his training as a chemical engineer. He knew of better ways to use a secluded property than selling shoddy beauty supplies to credulous women. Kidnapping was his true calling. He would employ "American methods," as he later put it, meaning what he'd learned about Chicago gangsters from dime-store novels.

He'd been spending his days in Paris in the lobbies of grand hotels, not looking for students but listening out for the conversation that would reveal his ideal ransom target. He enjoyed his hours, sitting in overstuffed chairs, reading, surrounded by heavy drapes and marble tabletops and oil paintings and the idle talk of fortunate people. Nights he scoured the classifieds, looking for anything to point him to a victim. He placed ads of his own, posing as a German tourist seeking a governess to accompany him and his child to the Riviera.

One June day at the Hotel Continental, an expensive place on Rue Rivoli across from the Tuileries Gardens, Weidmann fell into a conversation with a Baltimore native named Michael Stein, who'd made his fortune in textiles and had come to see the south of France. Weidmann, calling himself Eugen Karrer, offered to drive him down, suggesting they meet the next morning out at his villa from where he could give Stein a quick tour of Versailles before heading south.

That night Weidmann and Million removed the knob from the door of one of the villa's two bedrooms and boarded up its window from the inside. They would lock in Stein and nail the door shut. He would tell them who to contact to pay for his release. The villa's shutters were strong, the roughcast walls thick enough that no neighbor would hear him scream.

But the following morning Weidmann woke to a telegram from Stein to say that he wanted a few more days in Paris. And then the days stretched to weeks. Weidmann was not concerned, but Million lost patience. He borrowed Blanc's car and packed a revolver, a half liter of chloroform, and some rope into the trunk. Then he took Weidmann to find Stein. It was Bastille Day, July 14, 1937, when they called on Stein at the Continental. Weidmann explained that he and his friend were off to buy some fabric just west of the city and hoped Stein might advise them on the purchase. In return they'd give him the promised tour of Versailles.

The three men got in the car, Stein alone in the back. Million drove "like a demon," as Weidmann would recall. They hit traffic along the Seine and then Stein, for whatever reason, jumped out and bolted. Weidmann ran after him, but he was gone.

When Weidmann went to the Continental the following morning, the desk clerk told him Stein had checked out. Something had spooked him badly. He was already on a train for Calais, having booked immediate passage back to America.

Million was furious, Weidmann delirious.

There were plenty of hotels and plenty of Michael Steins. More were coming every day. Paris was in the middle of hosting the biggest event the city had ever seen.

21

EVERYTHING'S JUST FINE!

On May 25, 1937, Flanner surveyed the opening day of the Paris International Exposition of Art and Technology in Modern Life. From the vast terrace of the Palais de Chaillot, completed days earlier, she could see the panorama of Paris and beyond. In front of her three hundred pavilions from forty-seven nations covered the fairgrounds, from the Trocadéro gardens below to the base of the Eiffel Tower and the Champ de Mars across the Seine. At the center of the Palais de Chaillot terrace, between its two colonnaded wings, stood the newly erected Peace Pavilion, which a pacifist group had commissioned to showcase the work of the League of Nations and, with vivid war zone imagery, to remind people of the wreckage that came when international solidarity faltered. One entered under the shadow of the hulking, star-topped Peace Column, fifty meters of sculpted olive branches with the word PEACE inscribed in eight languages at its base. While the pavilion was set to be dismantled at the exposition's close, the Peace Column was meant to stay on as an enduring symbol of the event's spirit of global cooperation.

When floating the idea for an international exposition nearly a decade earlier French officials had harbored the usual hopes of creating jobs and promoting trade. More recently came the added dream that Expo '37, as it came to be known, would help pull the world out of its economic slump and isolationist policies, with the French hosts pointing the way toward a golden era of international exchange and investment. Some on the planning committee felt it was especially vital to celebrate universalist rhetoric and cosmopolitan cultural heritage in the face of Germany's militarist ultranationalism. Others looked to the fair as a Trojan horse for promoting progressive reforms internally, even while pitching it as a way to bolster national pride and quell internal dissent. Many saw the Expo as a chance for reflection during a charged moment of uncertainty about French standing within a shifting world order. In a few square kilometers France's pavilions would reveal all that the empire had achieved or failed to achieve.

Meanwhile a small but influential number of renegade French officials and cultural elites, swayed by the power and confidence of Nazi ideology, wanted to use the event to strengthen connections with France's historical rival. Ultimately their goal of rapprochement with Germany became one of the planning committee's main (if clandestine) guiding visions.

Bowing to German pressure, the organizers quashed a proposal from German-Jewish refugees to build a pavilion to draw attention to their cause, and declared that all anti-Nazi material would be prohibited from the fairgrounds. Anti-Nazi protestors would face the force of French law. Light shows along the Seine would be produced with German projectors and pumps, bought rather than rented. Some of the construction work went to German firms over French ones, and Germany provided the iron infrastructures for many of the pavilions. During the Expo and in the months bookending the event France and Germany would collaborate on hosting youth retreats, meetings of war veterans, Franco-German art shows and academic conferences, and parades. Some of these events, explicitly pro-Nazi in their rhetoric and symbology, were paid for jointly by French and German ministries.

This desire for friendship came at a time when Hitler's loathing for the French was no secret. In *Mein Kampf* he'd called France an "inexorable moral enemy" threatening the "existence of the white race in Europe," its leaders in thrall to the "Jew-controlled stock exchange" and pining for "Jewish world domination." The book outlined Hitler's desire to rearm Germany, suggesting possible alliances with Italy and even Britain to keep France in check. While complete editions were hard to find in France, especially after the state started destroying copies, French papers had published the most damning passages.

Hitler for his part wanted to make a show of German and French alignment to downplay any worries about the two neighbors being in conflict. (Trade between Germany and France had by that point been reduced to a trickle, alongside a wider decimation of international trade due to deflation, failing enterprises, and a string of protective tariffs meant to fight foreign competition.) Not having participated in any fair since 1900, the Germans would return as friendly members of the international community. But Hitler was already preparing his war machine, using the Expo to buy time and goodwill while he massed troops along the French border. By drawing out French investment in German industry for the fair, he'd fooled the enemy into helping to pay for weapons that would one day be turned against it. He did so fearlessly, knowing that the French, still suffering the effects of the

First World War nearly two decades later, would spin themselves in circles to convince themselves there would never be another.

The Expo was meant to be the biggest party of the decade. But touring the grounds a few months before the opening, Flanner had seen that most pavilions hadn't progressed past the foundation stages. The place was "a gopher hole," she told Katharine White. The red flag of the labor movement flew at one of the main entrances. Wildcat strikes had delayed a construction schedule that already seemed impossible under the best conditions. Right-wing observers laughed as the Popular Front's showcase event was threatened by their own beloved working-class constituents. Two months before opening day another terrible clash between left- and right-wing street agitators and police forces killed five civilians and one officer in the Parisian suburb of Clichy. On the eve of making a very public show of national unity to the world, the French remained as divided as ever.

Along with wondering whether "capital or labor would dominate it," Flanner had written in a January Letter that she doubted the fair would open on time. She asked if anyone outside of France could even afford to come to the Expo, regardless of when it opened, since aside from those few rich enough to get to London that May for the coronation of George VI and Elizabeth, "the rest of Europe has no money to throw away on anything so pleasant and peaceful as visiting an Exposition of Arts and Technics on the banks of the Seine." In the end labor issues and some flooding of the Seine did force French officials to push back the opening day by three weeks.

After getting into a squabble with the Expo's planning committee over her pessimistic predictions, she offered an olive branch by devoting a long and enthusiastic Letter to recommending some of the city's restaurants and nightclubs to would-be fairgoers. She stressed to her editors that she was providing the recommendations not because she deemed the Expo worthwhile but because it was her "duty here as French correspondent." Requesting extra column space so that her list could be clipped out and used as a pocketbook guide, she covered everything from the price of a scotch (thirty francs at a club, twelve at a bar) to the typical dress code for dancing (dark suit, black frock). She offered advice: Tip the sommelier 10 percent; don't talk loudly in public ("remember that the American voice carries"), and use *"Doucement, s'il vous plait"* to ask a cab driver to slow down, but prepare to be ignored. Having heard that ten thousand men from the American Legion were coming for the fair,.she'd told R. A. Hague, "God knows I'd like to run a bordello list and one of druggists where the best poisons could be obtained since [the American Legion men] would like the first and I'd like to give them the second."

She advised visitors to Paris to go see Josephine Baker hoof and sing surrounded by "balloons and gaiety" at a club on Rue Balzac, and then walk a few blocks to a pop-up club called Chez Kiki, which would run through the fair, overseen by Kiki de Montparnasse, trading on her 1920s fame as a cabaret star, model, and artist. She summed up Chez Kiki's appeals as "artists; hijinks; don't bring your aunt." Anyone following Flanner's recommendation to go see Ray Ventura at a nightclub on the Champs-Élysées backed by a full orchestra would have heard his hit comic ditty, "Tout va très bien, Madame la Marquise" (Everything's Just Fine, M'Lady), which the French had embraced as an ironic anthem. (Against a jaunty tune Ventura updates an increasingly frantic Marquise about the state of her affairs in a series of phone calls: all is well, he tells her, apart from the death of her favoritc gray horse...due to a fire in the stable...because the chateau burned down...because some candles fell...because her husband knocked them over...while committing suicide—but other than that "Everything's just fine!") For heavier fare, tourists could contemplate an alternate, and yet increasingly plausible, reality in the working-class tenth arrondissement, where the People's Theatre Company launched a stage version of Sinclair Lewis's *It Can't Happen Here*, in which a populist candidate preaching a return to traditional values wins the 1936 presidential election and turns America into a totalitarian state.

Flanner was wrong to expect a low turnout. Parisian nightlife experienced a boom in the runup to the fair and all through the summer. While she considered her guide a "silly idea," it ended up making "the biggest hit officially here of anything I ever did, darn it," after a popular French radio talk show shared it with listeners, and tourist agencies and transportation companies requested reprints.

Now she was finally seeing the fairgrounds up close: this fantasy space promising escape from a grim period even as it put all the era's anxieties and divisions on public display. Flanner paid six francs to enter the Trocadéro gate only to learn that most of the thirty-five entrances still lacked turnstiles and ticket booths. She could have walked in for free, as many others did, resulting in millions of francs lost over that first week. Even with the delayed opening the bulk of the French pavilions still stood behind scaffolding. A few structures had been abandoned altogether midconstruction. Fairgoers had to settle for visiting the foreign pavilions for the first few days.

As she strolled the grounds Flanner passed carnival games, an enchanted river featuring gondola rides through makeshift caves, a parachute tower where people jumped from two hundred feet with a tethered parachute, and the highly anticipated (and German-made) planetarium, which became one of the fair's most popular attractions. It housed a transparent "Glass Man" offering unprecedented insight into the inner workings of the human body, with different organs lighting up in tandem with a recorded description of various bodily functions. Few who enjoyed the "Glass Man" would have realized that German engineers had constructed it long before the fair, for use as a teaching tool to promote "racial hygiene."

In this wonderland of delusion, the era's creeping militarism peeked through at every corner. The gondola rides were supervised by men dressed to look like French naval officers, while actual officers from the French Air Force oversaw the parachute attraction. Children lined up for a carousel featuring not horses but fighter planes modeled on early iterations of France's Bloch 150. The amusement park's shooting gallery featured machine guns rather than the usual rifles. Out front of one of the fair's busiest restaurants and conference spaces, modeled on a timbered Alpine village, daily performances featured little people dressed to look like the leaders of France and its allies: A false Blum, false Roosevelt, and false Churchill pored over a map of the world.

On the main concourse, dubbed the Avenue of Peace, Flanner was exposed to the most blatant symbolism of all. Standing opposite one another on either side of the freshly planted Trocadéro garden with its central fountain, two pavilions dwarfed the other 298. They belonged to the Soviet Union and Germany.

Flanner understood that since all of the pavilions were showcasing the industries of competing nations as much as their "political doctrines," pavilion design had "recently leaped into importance as a special architectural class," and that "the western world, in addition to conducting an armament race, is staging an exposition marathon," as she wrote in *The New Yorker.* She pitied the French who "with their special decorative taste when designing things ephemeral" had squandered their chance to lead the way in this regard, through their squabbling and inefficiency. No one came close to besting the Germans and Soviets.

The Soviet pavilion made full use of the maximum height allotted by the committee's guidelines, its hundred-foot main structure capped by a seventy-five-foot socialist realist sculpture of a peasant couple: he, bare-chested and wielding a hammer; she in a windswept dress and brandishing a sickle. Its architect, Boris Iofan, was a worldly Odessa Jew who'd taken his degree in Rome, corresponded with Frank Lloyd Wright, and cut a dashing figure in foreign-made tweeds and oxfords; he drew inspiration from Rockefeller Center for the pavilion. Inside, under giant photographs of factory and field workers and quotations from Stalin and Lenin (and only a few from Marx), was the fair's most opulent and materialistic display, a map of the industrialized Soviet Union spanning nearly seventy square feet made entirely of gold and jewels, with provincial capitals represented by red ruby stars. "The petrol pipe lines from Baku are like a long bracelet of topazes," wrote Flanner; "aquamarines make a necklace about the northern seas to indicate maritime outposts; lakes are of lapis, mountains and fertile lands are presented in a complexity of all the hues of jasper—red, green, and yellow." A young woman with a big stick stood at its base barking out information. The map was surely "one of the most magnificent, expensive, and beautiful new objects extant anywhere on earth."

When it came to dramatic intensity the Soviet pavilion paled next to the one across the way, representing a regime that loathed everything that the cosmopolitan architect Iofan and his building stood for. Albert Speer, Hitler's favorite architect, had secretly secured the Soviet blueprints from a Nazi sympathizer on the planning committee. This prompted Speer to cap his own building with a ferocious Nazi eagle with a swastika in its talons, the tops of its wings standing several feet higher than the tip of the Soviet sickle, breaking the maximum height rules. Speer once said that his main objective as an architect was to represent an "intimidating display of power," and here he achieved as grandiose and cinematic a vision as he had when designing the grounds for the Nuremberg rallies. Funded in part by France, the pavilion cost nine times more than any other foreign pavilion. French officials saw this splurging as further proof the Germans wanted cooperation and not war.

A mix of Roman temple, Manhattan skyscraper, and Berlin bunker, the pavilion embodied the Third Reich's desire to present itself as highly advanced and yet timeless. While nearly all of the Expo's other structures favored big windows to best show off their nations' wares, Speer opted for a windowless bulk faced with Jura limestone and recessed spaces filled with mosaics of gold and red tile, following a swastika pattern. Hidden light fixtures produced a spooky effect at night when the swastikas glowed as if by magic. Two massive sculptures of bronzed Aryans stood sentinel beside the entrance, muscular and nude.

The fair's general commissioner, Edmond Labbé, unveiled the building with perfunctory remarks crafted to avoid controversy. This was followed by a wild speech from Germany's economic minister, Hjalmar Schacht. After speaking about the Reich's desire for an active role in rebuilding the world economy, Schacht reminded his audience that unlike France, Germany had no colonies to drive its own economy, and suggested that the European peace could only survive if other nations treaded carefully in reaction to any German action to rectify that situation.

Out front of the German pavilion the swastika and the *tricolore* flew side by side. Inside, the millions who toured it experienced Nazi Germany exactly as Hitler wanted them to. The main hall was church-like with its central nave and altar and stained-glass treatments featuring not Jesus or the Madonna but a swirl of swastikas and eagles. Under titanic chandeliers and mosaics of Aryan workers representing "Strength Through Joy," the marvels of German engineering were neatly laid out: a speed-record-breaking Mercedes racer; Bayer's pharmaceutical miracles; Siemens's photographic innovations; mechanical children's toys. The biggest draw was the "TV Phone." In a telephone booth equipped with a monitor, one person could talk to another in a booth at the pavilion's other end, while filmed. The talkers saw each other on screens while the public watched the conversations live on televisions.

In Germany that summer and fall the Nazis purged more than seventeen thousand "Judeo-Bolshevik" artworks from their museums while persecuting artists and intellectuals deemed threatening to the regime. Meanwhile in Paris the German pavilion displayed a pleasant model for the new House of German Art, which had just opened in Munich, as well as many sumptuous works by Arno Breker, Germany's official state sculptor, including a laurel-bearing female nude commissioned for the Berlin Olympics.

The airless pavilion led some visitors' thoughts toward death. One described the experience as what it might feel like to enter a long windowless coffin after passing through a giant tombstone; another said it felt like being held prisoner inside a mausoleum; an art critic among the German émigrés said that the pavilion resembled nothing so much as a giant crematorium, with the tower as its chimney. But while some were put off by the sterility of the interior and the cold efficiency of the objects on display, many, including some noted French intellectuals, left impressed by German advances, especially in the arts.

Riefenstahl's previously banned *Triumph of the Will* debuted in the pavilion's basement cinema space. Already widely admired as an actor and now recognized for her directing, Riefenstahl attended the opening gala. Giving interviews at the rooftop restaurant she looked "more than beautiful, dressed with exquisite taste, and [exuding] intelligence," as one French magazine described. Her film would win the Gold Medal at the Expo's film festival, beating out Jean Renoir's exceptional *La Grande Illusion*, so timely in its exploration of the complicated German-French history of having shared in the senseless suffering of the Great War. Riefenstahl's win marked a coup for the Nazis, who wanted their film industry to rival Hollywood's, with so far limited success, as foreign distributors shunned German films while Germans couldn't get enough of American ones, especially any with "Micky Maus."

Eighty thousand Germans came in all, including ten thousand members of the Hitler Youth. Many more would have attended were it not for the Nazis' limits on travel. Officials carefully selected all attendees from among the "elite of the Nation." They were told not to discuss politics. Meanwhile the top party brass was conspicuous in its absence. Not only did Hitler avoid the event, the only trace of his likeness anywhere in the pavilion was a semi-obscure rendering of him in a painting of the Nuremberg rallies.

Further down the concourse, bordering the Seine, Flanner reached the pavilion of the Spanish Republic, funded without any support from France. To draw attention to their cause, the designers featured Joan Miró's vivid *The Reaper* (or *Catalan peasant in revolt*) alongside Alexander Calder's *Mercury Fountain*, a fountain pumping quicksilver instead of water, built in homage to the lives lost to Franco in the town of Almaden. The American Calder proudly represented the growing support for the Republicans among artists and intellectuals around the world. (He also unknowingly exposed fairgoers to the toxicity of the liquid mercury's vapors.) By opening day Picasso was still working on the mural he'd been commissioned to complete months earlier. Only after reading about the destruction wrought on the civilian population in the Basque village of Guernica by German Condor warplanes that April did he start work in earnest. When it was finally unveiled in July, *Guernica* failed to make much of an impression and the press gave it little coverage. A German book of photographs from the fair described *Guernica* as "the dream of a maniac...a pell-mell of incomprehensible symbols and parts of human beings...drawn by a child of four."

The French pavilions, once they opened, touted the country's innovations in everything from aeronautics to fashion to refrigeration, and displayed treasures gathered from its oppressively governed colonies. At the Pavilion of Modern Times, the architect Le Corbusier and his cousin Pierre Jeanneret dreamed up radical master plans for Paris and its suburbs, including a concrete stadium to serve as "a national center for popular jubilation for 100,000 participants," housing sporting events, political rallies, parades, and other gatherings meant to "awaken the country." Nearby stood a pavilion dedicated to French festivals, similarly conceived in response to seeing how effectively the Nazis used mass spectacles to their advantage. "We don't know how to amuse ourselves anymore," the commissioner Labbé pronounced at the pavilion's opening. "Our daughters and sons ask for Negro-American music...or Apache rhythms to relieve their boredom a bit...A wise government—and the tyrants don't have the monopoly on wisdom—offers festivals to the people."

All the French pavilions in the end bowed to the massive Eiffel Tower, symbol of modernity and cosmopolitanism. People joked, embarrassed, about the Tower being France's biggest contribution to the fairgrounds despite its being built as the centerpiece of a previous fair, nearly a half century earlier. Some enterprising wit published a memoir written in the voice of the Tower as a grand dame remembering her past glories.

Flanner was back at the Palais de Chaillot in time to hear French President Albert Lebrun's speech. Prime Minister Blum was at his side, surrounded by most of his cabinet. Lebrun said that the Expo would "teach mankind yet again that there is no dignity of life but in mutual comprehension of people's needs, aspirations, and genius; no prosperity but in an ever more intense exchange of products and ideas." His was a far less fiery speech than the one Blum had made that past February when, in conscious opposition to those French officials so eager to welcome Germany into the event's fold, he'd promised in his reedy voice that the exposition would be a "battleground in the fight against fascism." Now he left the speeches to others.

Blum had, however, written the introduction to the expo's guidebook. And there he noted that the five previous world's fairs hosted in Paris had "always accompanied or followed serious political crises," citing the 1900 exposition, launched as France was embroiled in the Dreyfus Affair. Just as the nation had survived those earlier emergencies, he argued, so would it continue to survive, so long as French citizens held on to their faith in one another and in the values of their shared republican experiment.

22

AN AMERICAN BALLET TEACHER IN PARIS

People had been telling Jean de Koven she was pretty enough for the pictures since she was thirteen. Never mind that she was a Jewish girl from Brooklyn. Her idol Luise Rainer, Jewish and German, had won the Oscar for Best Actress for the past two years running. And Jean could do more than act; she'd studied ballet with the Metropolitan Opera. Her friends said she already had a star's charisma and could talk to anyone. She was the kind of person who went out of her way to start conversations with strangers. Hollywood fantasies aside, what she wanted more than anything was to travel. Her wanderlust earned her the nickname Gypsy, though what she'd seen so far in her twenty-four years stretched no further than the eastern seaboard. Her greatest trek was the daily commute across the East and Hudson Rivers from the cramped family apartment at the edge of Prospect Park to the dance studio where she taught in New Jersey.

But now, chaperoned by her aunt, Ida Sackheim, she'd finally reached Paris. To her niece, Sackheim, forty-two, seemed to live a life filled with glamour—an apartment in midtown, a job in fashion—and carried herself less like a guardian and more like an older sister, as eager as she was for an adventure abroad. They were sharing a room at a hotel that made up for its lack of comfort with a Latin Quarter location by the Church of Saint-Sulpice. They'd already seen the *Mona Lisa*, strolled the Champs-Élysées, and taken in the sequins and flesh at the Folies Bergère. "All I do is eat, sleep and drink," de Koven wrote home. "I've never felt so well-rested in my life." Above all, she and her aunt had come to see the Expo.

On the afternoon of July 22 they were soaking up some luxury by proxy in the lobby of the Ambassador, a magnificent hotel on the Right Bank's wide and verdant Boulevard Haussmann. After stopping by to leave word for some American friends who were soon to check in, they'd decided to stay for a cool drink after another broiling day at the fairgrounds. They sat discussing a possible trip to Lithuania, from where their ancestors hailed. Sackheim went to ask the hotel's concierge to help her contact a travel agent and to act as interpreter.

Nearby in an overstuffed leather chair a young man sat reading an American magazine. He noticed that the young woman who'd been left alone wore her curly auburn hair long and slicked back from her forehead, different from the usual fringed bobs and spit curls worn by so many Parisian women her age. He waited for her to approach. He'd grown accustomed to women making excuses to talk with him.

De Koven mistook him for a compatriot by his American magazine. She walked over and asked if she could borrow it when he'd finished. He suggested she join him instead. He was no American, speaking English only passably, if in a soothing voice and with impeccable manners. He sounded German, maybe Swiss, yet seemed to know Paris better than the locals. They talked beneath the crystal chandeliers. She learned that his father was an industrialist, owned some kind of chemical plant. They discovered they both loved tennis.

(In truth he'd never held a racket.) She told him she'd just arrived aboard the *Normandie*, an important detail, as he knew it as one of the most luxurious liners then crossing the Atlantic.

He told her the names of which restaurants and nightclubs to visit and which to avoid. Paris was like a giant web, he said, with spiders at each turn, especially during the Expo. He could help her navigate the city. He pointed her to a few of the less popular but still lovely pavilions to go see. He mentioned a car parked at his villa west of the city, close to an estate that had once belonged to Napoleon and Josephine. He could take her on a tour.

When Sackheim got back from her call the young man rose to introduce himself. He gave her what she described as "the most gracious smile" she'd ever seen. She would recall him as broad shouldered and tastefully dressed, with large, full features, brown hair, and a clean-shaven, square-shaped face. Had she looked closely at his suit, hanging so well on his solid frame, she would have seen that its edges were faded and fraying. He said his name was Bobby Hunter, one common enough in Brooklyn but strange for a European. He added that his friends called him Siegfried, like the heroic dragon slayer of Germanic legend. Siegfried Hunter. Killer of dragons, killer of animals.

Sackheim left the young people to their talk and returned to her chair, close enough to watch but not hear. Fifteen minutes later she was bored, and after a conference with her niece she went back alone to their own hotel to change and send some telegrams. After two hours, with her niece still not returned, she took a taxi back to the Ambassador and found Jean still talking with her new friend. She interrupted their conversation. She wanted to go back to the Expo. Siegfried Hunter offered to walk them there. Half an hour later he left them at the gates at the Place de la Concorde entrance, making a date with de Koven to meet up the next day back in the Ambassador lobby. He promised to take her for a drive and show her *la Grande Paris*, the areas beyond the city core most tourists ignored.

Neither de Koven nor her aunt felt any reason to ask at the Ambassador about the man they'd just met. If they had, they would have learned that he wasn't a guest but had recently become a regular presence, haunting the lobby and bar, always reading, always alone.

That night de Koven wrote to her fiancé in New York, a young violinist, describing all the sights she'd soon be seeing and adding that she wouldn't be enjoying them alone. "I have just met a charming German of keen intelligence who calls himself Siegfried. I am going to visit him tomorrow at his villa in a beautiful place near a famous mansion that Napoleon gave Josephine."

Their date would have to be brief. Sackheim had tickets for the Opéra Garnier, and she'd made Jean promise to be back for the eight thirty curtain.

At the Ambassador, at five, de Koven saw Hunter, in a gray suit and matching hat. He explained that he'd had to lend his car to a friend at the last moment for a quick errand. But they could take the train out to his villa and then have the fun of driving back into the city with the summer sun still out. She'd planned for him to drive her to her own hotel first so she could change, and now insisted that they do so by taxi. He waited in the small sitting area, silently cursing the unexpected expense.

She came down in the standard uniform of the American woman abroad: a prim blue and red plaid dress, patent leather shoes, long gloves, and a white handbag, the ensemble topped with what Americans then called a "sport hat," the slouchy feminine version of a fedora.

They took another cab to Saint-Lazare, from where they took a train to the Vaucresson station. The two tickets on top of the cab fares left Weidmann with not enough to buy a pack of cigarettes.

In her handbag de Koven carried ten thousand francs in American Express traveler's checks for emergencies and a Kodak she'd bought in New York for the trip.

They arrived around six and crossed the unpaved roads and muddy fields separating the Vaucresson station from Saint-Cloud. De Koven took some snapshots of the prosperous, rambling suburb, capturing the warm light piercing through the greenery. At the gate of Hunter's property she saw that a newspaper poked out sloppily from the top of the post box. He left it there as he passed, perhaps too caught up with her to bother with clearing the mail.

He complimented her on her beauty as he showed her the garden. She took his picture. He offered her a cigarette and lit one of his own. She seemed just then to be "happy and carefree," he would later recall. He invited her in for a glass of milk.

The next morning Ida Sackheim received a telegram. She'd been up all night and the telegram confirmed her fears that something terrible was happening. It had come addressed to "Secky," a misspelling of de Koven's nickname for her aunt, "Sacky," proving to Sackheim that Jean couldn't be the author. "Jean" reported that she was doing fine, giving no information about where she was nor with whom. She promised to send another update soon. The grammar was off. English wasn't the writer's first language. It had to be Siegfried Hunter. Sackheim berated herself for letting her niece go off with him.

That afternoon came another message, this time not in English but imperfect French. "Jean de Koven is kidnapped and is being held for a five-hundred-dollar ransom," it read. This was a strangely modest amount to demand, barely enough to buy a used car. The kidnapper advised that Jean was safe so long as Sackheim avoided the police. She was to confirm her understanding by placing the message "Jean, please come back, S." in the classifieds of *The International Herald Tribune*. The kidnapper warned that if she said anything to anyone, "you know how Chikago [*sic*] gangsters operate."

Sackheim went straight to police headquarters at 36, Quai des Orfèvres on Île de la Cité, historic heart of Paris. Eventually she made it to the commissioner, André Roches, who explained that she hadn't offered evidence to merit a response. She'd hurt her cause by bringing a press clipping from one of de Koven's performances, showing a young and vivacious woman. There was the mystery solved: A pretty American dancer met a young man in Paris—a man Sackheim herself had just described to them as handsome—and spent a night away from her chaperone. She next tried the American consulate and got the same answer. She went to place the message in *The International Herald Tribune* and then passed three days of excruciating silence.

Finally, she got a phone call. The man on the other end wanted her to confirm that she had the money. She did. Next he asked if she knew where the man who'd left the Hotel Ambassador with Jean lived. She didn't. This satisfied the caller. She was told to wait for further instruction.

Again she went to the police. Again the officers hesitated. Their theory now was that either de Koven had concocted the kidnapping to disguise a liaison with Hunter, or that the pair had teamed up to extort Sackheim and were likely planning to run away together. She failed to convince them that her Jean was a serious young woman incapable of such treachery. Why, they countered, would a real criminal take the risk of kidnapping someone to demand so little ransom? The officers didn't intend to be cruel. They routinely fielded requests from parents thinking their children had been kidnapped or murdered, and invariably these led to a young man or woman trying to escape a repressive family situation, often hiding the fact that they were living with someone out of wedlock.

After much pleading, Sackheim managed to get two undercover detectives assigned to her hotel so they could at least listen in on the next ransom call. It came the following afternoon. The caller instructed that a yellow taxi would arrive there in ten minutes. She was to hand a purse filled with the five hundred to the driver.

Ten minutes later Sackheim met the driver, who said he'd been told to pick up a package from an American woman. Sackheim pretended not to understand and indicated that she would dash back inside to get someone to translate. She came back with one of the detectives who, posing as a hotel valet, tried to get as much as he could out of the driver. All he discovered was that a man had approached the driver by the Brasserie Lipp on Boulevard Saint-Germain. Still posing as a valet, he told the driver that the woman had been expecting something in return for her package and since it hadn't come, she wanted to speak to his client directly. The frustrated driver left empty-handed to go find the man who'd hired him. The second detective tailed him in an unmarked car.

Sackheim got an angry call from the kidnapper saying that he'd seen the taxi being followed. She'd talked to the police and put her niece in terrible danger. She denied the charge and offered more money. "We'll see, tomorrow," said the voice and hung up. The taxi driver returned soon after, now even more annoyed, saying that his client had disappeared.

The police learned that the kidnapper was working with at least one partner, who must have been watching the hotel while the other was engaging the driver by the Brasserie Lipp. Perhaps there was a third confederate, who'd gone to tip off the first man to quit the area while the second followed the police tail. They had both the driver's and Sackheim's descriptions of a suspect, along with the name Sackheim had given them, even if Siegfried Hunter was an obvious alias. (Had there been any linguists on the case they might have explored translations of "Hunter," which while commonly translated into German as *der Jager*, could also be interpreted as *der Weidmann*, the huntsman, though the name Weidmann would not yet have special meaning for the authorities.)

On Friday, July 30, 1937, Sackheim got another letter, delivered by a taxi driver who said that a man had given it to him on Boulevard Saint-Germain. She was told to drop the money in an envelope at a bar on Rue Nollet that night, asking the bartender to hold it for a man named Monsieur Jean. The kidnapper would collect it the next morning and return her niece to Sackheim's hotel a half hour later. Jean was fine, the note said, she'd cried a little but had been given a small dog to play with. The kidnapper warned that Sackheim would receive no further communication. The note ended: "Remind [*sic*], the least sign we have of the police and we don't send nobody to get the money."

The bar's owner allowed the police to survey it for as long as they liked. Sackheim went through the pantomime of dropping off an empty envelope but no one came for it. Weidmann had seen men he'd rightly assumed were undercover detectives at the bar and never came to collect.

On August 3 came yet another message for Sackheim, now as a postcard. Who did she think she was playing with? Why were the police watching the bar? She had a week to think things over, once and for all.

The police showed Sackheim thousands of mug shots without

result. They put the American Express office on alert to look out for de Koven's checks. By the first week of August French papers carried their first reports of the missing American dancer. Some of the headlines put the word "kidnapping" in quotations, still dubious of Sackheim's version of the story.

Jean's older brother Henry, a set designer, reached Paris and announced a ten-thousand-franc reward for information leading to her return. He told the press that "in our modest family my sister is considered a serious-minded girl, incapable of the acts which have been insinuated, either any escapade or publicity stunts." The family was still trying to get the American Consulate on the case, while petitioning New York's governor and the secretary of state to appoint a task force. Henry was convinced that his sister was already dead.

Shortly after helping with the botched first attempt to get money from Sackheim, Roger Million and Colette Tricot had left Paris to stay with Tricot's grandparents in Ligné, a remote village in western France. Though they'd shared in Weidmann's attempt to get the ransom they'd never actually seen Jean de Koven. On the night she'd come to the villa Weidmann had left the newspaper poking out of the mailbox as a prearranged sign for them to stay away. He'd told them the next morning that she was being held at another location by "some friends."

Tricot returned to La Voulzie two weeks after de Koven's disappearance, alone. Weidmann had asked her to come out to do some laundry and grocery shopping. As reward he gave her a handbag he'd bought at Lancel, along with a watch and a belt. She understood without asking that they'd been paid for with de Koven's traveler's checks.

Tricot then abruptly left La Voulzie again with Million, in the second week of August, without telling Weidmann they were planning to quit Paris. They went first to the Café Guichonnet, where Million told his father, in the presence of Mme. Guichonnet, that Weidmann was responsible for killing the young American woman in the papers, and that he himself had arranged the attempted ransom drop.

With the help of his father, Million destroyed the handbag and belt that Weidmann had given Tricot while Mme. Guichonnet, looking on, remarked that it was a shame that such a gorgeous bag should go to waste. Tricot had hidden de Koven's watch before Million could find out about it. (She would later throw it into the Seine.) Million and his father burned the blue suit Million had worn when hiring the taxi driver, which had been described in the papers.

Million fled with Tricot by train to Nantua, a pretty corner of eastern France near Geneva where he'd gone as a boy. They would stay there with Million's aunts for the rest of the month, with Tricot posing as his fiancée.

By mid-August the American Express office had discovered seven traveler's checks cashed in Jean de Koven's name since her disappearance. The spending followed an itinerary that could have logically been attributed to a young American tourist. Small items were bought at the Guerlain perfumery on the Champs-Élysées and the Lancel leather goods shop on the Place de l'Opéra. One check had been used to gain entrance to the Expo; another cashed at the Transatlantic Bank pavilion inside the fairgrounds; another at a tourist bureau a few steps away. There were no major purchases. Weidmann had forged the signatures, ruining a few checks in the process when he'd failed to copy the script accurately enough for his liking. He'd correctly figured that if he switched out her picture for one of himself he could use de Koven's passport as identification when spending the checks, since to the French Jean could also be a man's name.

Sackheim confirmed that the signatures were fakes. Detectives questioned the saleswoman at Guerlain, who remembered a friendly man, who'd asked her, in accented French, about the exchange rate. American Express would eventually track twenty-one of de Koven's checks, all used between July 31 and August 6, always to buy something small so its bearer could get the balance back in cash.

The Paris police were meanwhile looking more carefully at the ransom letters, led by André Roches, the commissioner who'd at first rebuffed Sackheim's concerns. They theorized that the letters had been written by a German, based on certain phrasings and a gothic shape to the *J*s and *T*s, along with the slanted handwriting, deemed "Nordic" in style.

Tips about de Koven sightings poured in after the Paris papers ran her picture. A waiter swore he'd seen her dining with a Frenchman on his restaurant's terrace in Saint-Cloud. A taxi driver said she'd gotten into his cab with two men who overrode her screamed plea to be taken to the American Embassy and instead commanded him to go to the Closerie des Lilas in Montparnasse. A psychic told the police she'd been visited by a vision of the young woman along an ocean's edge. Paris detectives, sometimes calling on international help, followed useless tips in investigations stretching across France and to London, Geneva, and as far away as Tangier and the Aleutian Islands north in the Pacific Ocean.

Weidmann sent another postcard to Sackheim on August 18, telling her he was keeping Jean for good and now threatening the safety of Henry de Koven. This was the last message she received. Out of money, Sackheim and her nephew would have to return to New York by September.

23

OUR MOVING AND TORMENTED ERA

Less than a month after the Expo's opening day Léon Blum resigned as prime minister, after the Senate refused to expand his abilities to direct economic policy while the franc was in a free-fall. Some of Blum's ouster had to do with infighting among members of the Popular Front over his failure to support the Spanish Republicans and confront the fascist foe to France's west. Meanwhile too many investors and entrepreneurs, spooked by his sweeping social reforms, had pulled their capital out of the country.

Added to this was the constant pressure coming from right-wing agitators who'd always hated him. In the city's wealthier neighborhoods, one sometimes heard "Better Hitler than Blum." Another refrain common among well-heeled Parisians went "Communists, get your bags; Jews, off to Jerusalem." "I admire him in many ways," Flanner told White after Blum's resignation. "I think there might have been civil war here had it not been for him, and think that France has been close to it, because of him. *Et voila.*"

The Popular Front government, continuing under new leadership, had no choice but to drastically devalue the franc. Inflation negated many of the past year's labor gains, and the possibility of a total economic collapse loomed. "France is more worried about Wall Street's wabbling than she is of war's breaking," wrote Flanner. "And what she is afraid of most of all is prices, which have suddenly, terrifyingly risen. The new prices of bread and butter are the latest bombs here." People in France were now more actively calling for an authoritarian regime to match those in Germany and Italy, while others still longed for full-scale communist revolution. No one could say for certain that the rules governing civil society would still apply tomorrow. Headlines carried claims of widespread conspiracies, with the identities of the would-be plotters changing with the political orientation of the paper: a cabal of Jewish elites; Catholic conservatives; Bolshevik terrorists; fascist fifth columnists.

Amid the political upheaval, the Expo hit a fevered peak in mid-July, as Paris witnessed a Bastille Day festival unrivaled in size and energy, drawing a record-breaking four million participants. Giant *tricolore* flags dominated every major thoroughfare. In a scene that would have brought to mind the Nuremberg rallies to anyone who'd seen them, fifteen thousand marchers carried torches in a massive procession stretching more than ten kilometers through the city center.

And then on September 11 two homemade time bombs were detonated in Paris, beyond the fairgrounds, killing two policemen. The targeted buildings housed an organization known to be loudly anti-Blum, leading the public to ascribe the violence to Communist agitators. In truth it was a false flag operation. Responsibility lay with a militant hard-right group, the French terrorist organization known as La Cagoule, founded by the naval engineer and future Nazi collaborator Eugène Deloncle. The group had gotten its nickname from the Ku Klux Klan–inspired hoods (*cagoules*) its members reportedly wore to secret meetings, many held at the headquarters of L'Oréal—whose founder, French pharmacist Eugène Schueller, helped bankroll the cell alongside backing from Italian fascists. The *cagoulards*, as members were known, engaged in sabotage and assassinations with the aim of ushering in an ultranationalist regime in France and aiding in Hitler's domination of Europe. They were planning a coup to overthrow the government, a legitimate threat that led to dozens of arrests and the discovery of a horde of munitions meant to be put toward the cause of armed revolution.

As revelations of the group's activities made the papers, hooded *cagoule*-inspired costumes were soon seen at the season's elite costume balls.

The Paris Exposition closed on November 25, 1937. Flanner ultimately judged it a success, having ripened like summer fruit since its difficult spring debut. Privately she admitted that while she didn't think she'd been "unfair to the early condition of the Exposition," which was a "mess of mud, mortar, and recrimination," she'd had her mind changed as the Expo "literally grew better hourly once it started." In *The New Yorker* she praised the event for offering people so much to "rejoice in. Foreigners and money have flowed in, bringing pleasure and relaxation in their wake...it filled Paris with spenders, and took Parisians' minds off political fears."

And yet the fair had revealed and even exacerbated the fierce nationalism and deep rivalries of the major European powers that prompted those "political fears." Rather than promoting an image of French strength and unity, the Expo's botched opening had exposed the fragility of French parliamentarism. Were the French any more firm in their sense of national identity than they had been before the event? Their government continued to sputter while the Soviets and Germans had projected ever more vitality through their propaganda. "I now don't know which I'd hate living under most—the Nazis or the Communists," Flanner told White. "Maybe we democracies and republics are more out of the political future than we know. I'd like to be so far out as to be an epitaph before the change comes."

The presence of so many German citizens in France in tandem with the aesthetic dominance of their massive and modern pavilion had helped in some way to normalize Nazism in many French minds, and in the minds of many others among the roughly thirty-one to thirty-four million people who visited from all over. While some French fairgoers avoided the German pavilion at all costs, many others left their visits feeling comforted by the promise of strong relations with Germany.

A minor politician, Jean Raymond-Laurent, captured the event's significance in a speech at the Palace of the City of Paris (the present-day Palais de Tokyo). "International expositions illustrate a phase of history, express the soul of a generation, reveal its qualities or its weaknesses, and, for the informed observer, reveal the coming destiny of society and races," he said. And this one "in its turn, will appear to our descendants as the symbol of our moving and tormented era."

The massive Peace Column at the center of the Palais de Chaillot terrace did not stay on as originally planned. It was dismantled shortly after the closing of the fair.

Flanner's writing at that moment mirrored much of the confusion and uncertainty she'd felt when first walking the fairgrounds. It was as if she were living in two Parises at once: the one where people were terrified by the rise of ultranationalism, internal terrorism, and the attendant prospect of war; and the one where everyone had agreed to delude themselves with fantasies of peace and cooperation. Even as she wanted to focus increasingly on chronicling events of political importance, she remained tentative in her analysis and arguments. Her Letters from that year were riddled with open-ended questions. She felt pulled in too many directions at once, and that she was failing to see the present with clarity, amid so many rumors and predictions and allegations.

In the summer she'd been full of joy, telling Hague of the easy "dormitory life" she'd enjoyed for a few days in London when her *New Yorker* colleague James Thurber and his wife, Helen, stayed in the room above hers, with nights full of drink and mischievous talk. "Thurber extraordinary. Never knew him before, don't know him now...he fascinates me." But not much later she was confiding dark thoughts to her other main correspondent at that time, St. Clair McKelway, recently promoted to managing nonfiction editor at the magazine. She told him that they were witnessing an especially "morbid year, with plagues, dictators and talk of war; also wars without being talked about."

What she'd seen of Germany in recent times continued to trouble her. She and Murphy had traveled to Munich in late summer and experienced how the Nazis were weaponizing culture through their hateful and heavily attended Degenerate Art exhibition. Joseph Goebbels had conceived of the idea of staging an exhibit of more than six hundred paintings, sculptures, and prints, mostly avant-garde, which had been "confiscated" from German museums and purportedly illustrated the decadence and disorder of the past decades, leading to the terrible decay of civilization for which Nazism was the only cure. Works were hung haphazardly and cruelly captioned. The Degenerate Art exhibition was held alongside and not far from its antithesis, the first annual Great German Art exhibition, a collection of artworks that had been officially approved to demonstrate what "truly German art" looked like. In tandem the two shows were meant to teach citizens the "correct" way to feel about art and aesthetics.

The Munich trip had also shown Flanner glaring signs that the Germans were preparing for the need to defend themselves in some future conflict, "storing enough of what it has to last out a two years' siege," as she reported in her Letter from Munich, and "brilliantly inventing" alternate solutions for whatever raw materials they were currently importing. Despite the "no war promises of their Führer, on whom...the people's devotion and belief still loyally concentrate, Germans see their efforts, hopes, abnegations, and productions all going into the molding of a war machine and mentality." When filing the piece she told Hague that although it reported "information most well-informed Germans know (and some peasants frankly discuss), I have a feeling that the authorities will like it less than anything I've ever done in this land."

Before returning to Paris, Flanner and Murphy stopped at Salzburg for its music festival, in what would prove to be its final year under the directorship of the great Arturo Toscanini alongside Bruno Walter. There they found momentary escape and pleasure, even if the prices were "crazed for a country town where one walks in mud and puddles in evening clothes to enter what used to be a riding hall and looks like a beer hall to hear insanely oversnobbed music," as she told White. Flanner described the restorative powers of the mountain air and said that hearing Toscanini's Verdi *Requiem* was one of the most wonderful hours of her life. She and many others in the audience had wept openly, "it was like a religious experience."

Aside from that Salzburg respite, she'd found the trip horrifying, leaving her more convinced than ever that Nazism was no aberration and soon to crumble, as she'd previously hoped, but rather the true and welcomed expression of the German populace's desires. She returned "in disgust" to Paris. "I'm a pessimist who thinks the Nazi regime suits the Germans; my Communist friends, being optimists, are sure that every German is seething with revolt and starving; as I've twice been in Germany during reported 'food shortages' and ate what they ate—table d'hote with a Wiener Schnitzel big enough for three, plus three vegetables—I always sniff at reports now...Germans don't know, want or appreciate liberty even when they occasionally see it."

While she'd returned to her previous views of Nazism as abhorrent and terrifying, her hatred of Communism still kept her from taking a bolder stand against fascism more broadly by publicly backing the Spanish Republican cause. And yet privately she told R. A. Hague that although she was sick of "the upper-class intellectual sentimentality here for anyone with a pick in his hand and overalls on his limbs," at the same time "if there's anything I dislike more than Bolshies [Bolsheviks] it's Fascists."

She was not unmoved by the suffering in Spain. That June at London's Albert Hall she attended a fundraising benefit for Basque children displaced by the war. Since children were impartial victims, she reasoned that one could help without taking sides. The best explanation she could muster about her relative silence on Spain was to express her abhorrence for all political ideologies that incited violence, using this stance to justify her political neutrality in public life. Flanner thought of her public role as that of a mere witness to the fractures of her time, rather than as one who would use her position to contribute to the deepening of those fractures. Her job was to pay as close attention as she could to what was taking place on the ground. She had to do so without having her perspective altered by the larger political, economic, and cultural forces shaping whatever local action she was covering, or by her own personal preconceptions.

But in that corrosive decade many intellectuals felt a moral obligation to announce their ideological affinities, unabashedly and unwaveringly. They defined themselves as public thinkers chiefly through those affinities. Nancy Cunard publicly declared that the time had come for writers all over the world to "take sides" because "ironic detachment" would "no longer do." Flanner wasn't about to abandon irony, and while her bond with Cunard survived the moment, her failure to take a decisive public stand left some of her friends cold. She told McKelway of a heated dinner with James Thurber, Dorothy Parker, and their spouses. Parker and her husband had just gotten "back from Spain with hair-raising photos. As Jim [Thurber] and I had determined to stick by democracy and refuse to let people call us Fascists because we aren't Communists we got called Fascists." She joked that she and Thurber planned to "straighten out the European tangle at our next dinner, I think by electing Jim president of the ballet in Moscow." Flanner found Communist-sympathizing intellectuals misguided at best, and at worst tourists out slumming, playacting at taking part in the genuinely noble workers' struggle. "Several of my Red New York friends have gone to the Place de la Nation for the [May Day] parade," she'd told White a few months earlier. "As I am not a manual worker, I remain a bourgeois democrat and I hope that if the worst comes to the worst, that I can go down under that name; I therefore didn't go to the parade."

Flanner did, however, write a Letter that touched on the Spanish Civil War. She'd gotten the idea for the piece after Hemingway stopped in Paris on his way to report from Spain for the North American Newspaper Alliance.

Flanner and Solano visited Hemingway daily while he waited for his traveling partner, an accomplished American bullfighter named Sidney Franklin, to get his visa for Spain from the State Department. In Franklin's dirty room at the Hotel Montana on Rue Saint-Benoît, Flanner watched half-amused, half-annoyed, as the men played bullfighter and bull, Hemingway lunging across the room as Franklin did veronicas with his cape, the two of them giving a running report on the action in Spanish slang. Franklin—real name Frumpkin; he was the son of Russian Jewish immigrants and raised in Brooklyn and had taken his bullfighting name in honor of Benjamin Franklin—had been gored in a bullfight not long before coming to Paris. He sat uneasily on the edges of his chairs at the cafés and often chose to stay behind to tend to his cape and swords and finery while the other three went out drinking. When they returned he would spend a good half hour explaining the use of each piece of his ensemble.

Flanner, tapping into Franklin's egotism, saw a way to use him as a conduit to write on the Spanish Civil War. The conflict had forced Spanish bullfighters to relocate to France, where Franklin was set to fight, so by writing about him she would also have to write about Spain. She pitched her idea as a "godsend" and a "gift from heaven" but said she would understand if "the mag is dead against bull fights (like me!)." Ross okayed her proposal but with the caveat, as relayed by Hague: "We'd rather you kept all reference to Spain out of the piece if you can, because of the mixed political feelings over here and elsewhere." Flanner promised "no political stuff except the necessary statement [explaining] why on earth the greatest Spanish bullfighters are fighting in France, nothing more."

After interviewing Franklin about every aspect of the matador's life and rituals, and helping him to dress, she traveled to Nimes to watch the *corridas* herself in the city's exquisitely preserved Roman amphitheater. "I have really swell technical stuff from Franklin," she bragged to Hague, along with "sartorial information I never saw, not even in *Death in the Afternoon*." She admitted to being terrified by his upcoming fight. "He'll be killed as he is ill (old horn wound unhealed) and passé." She was sure she would faint at the fight. (She didn't, and Franklin survived.)

Her "Letter from the Bull Ring" described the routines of Spanish bullfighters who were finding work in France. While Ross had asked her to keep "all reference to Spain out of the piece," by adding seemingly tangential information about the origins of their bulls and the locations of their training grounds, she brought the conflict to the attention of American readers, if indirectly.

> Because men are tragically fighting men in Spain, the best of Spanish bullfighting is being done this summer in southern France. The Fascists hold Andalusia and Salamanca, where blooded fighting bulls grow, the Loyalists have held out in Madrid, to whose ring great bullfighters go. In order to get together, both matadors and animals have passed over the border for special French toros.

The rest of the piece got bogged down with all its consideration of the costs, construction, and care of the toreador's outfit. Hemingway, after reading it, told Flanner, "If a journalistic prize is ever given for the worst sports writer in the western world, I'm going to see you get it, pal, for you deserve it. You're perfectly terrible."

As Flanner clung to her politically reticent position, she feared losing her way as a correspondent in such a polarized Europe. When a reader wrote in to criticize her depiction of English public opinion on the abdication, she exploded on him in a four-page response revealing, to a total stranger, how insecure she felt in her London assignment and how desperately she was still trying to live up to her ideal of the journalist as impartial observer.

> If it's part of one's work honestly to try and report what seems a part of a general opinion…it should also be part of one's work not to report in such a way as to give an impression of personal defection from established former standards of unbiased impersonality…I am not supposed to write such personal opinions and equations; I'm supposed to note those of others who live in the country, and how they react. I had expected not to return to London for the *New Yorker* since I earnestly felt (and your letter may well be an instance in proof) that a commentator more familiar with the English scene would do the job better. It was not easy, the work there…As the magazine has been able to get in line no one who can take over the work, and as I cannot leave them in a gap, I must continue to work there this winter, I hope this time more to my satisfaction, to yours and to that of one or two others.

She had indeed tried quitting the London portion of her assignment. Ross, White, and Raoul Fleischmann (in separate correspondence) talked her out of it, telling her she was being too hard on herself. Seeing no way to escape her London responsibilities without alienating her colleagues, she considered leaving the magazine to take a job with *Time*, whose managing editor, Ralph Ingersoll, was trying to poach her to become *Time*'s own Paris correspondent. Having been so instrumental in *The New Yorker*'s rise, and for so long associated with its level of quality, Flanner knew she could command a higher rate of pay at a rival magazine. She'd already started to attract imitators. "An editor would say to a writer going abroad, 'Send us a Paris Letter from Rome.' Or Cannes or Salzburg," she would recall. "That was a great compliment to Ross."

Flanner passed along *Time*'s offer letter—which promised, "You can have just as much fun and maybe more satisfaction and easily more money coming to work for us"—to White, who shared it with Ross. White's expertly argued reply showed just how well she knew how to play to Flanner's vulnerability as much as to her pride:

> The thought of you leaving us for *Time* chilled us to the marrow of our bones...we realize your financial predicament and don't think it is fair to stand in your way, [but] would you honestly like to do work that would turn you into a reporter and eliminate you as a writer? *Time* doesn't allow their correspondents to sign anything, of course, and anything you wrote for them would be so rewritten that it would not be recognizable by you when it got into the magazine...You would stop being a person whose name was known and become just another anonymous part of a big organization. You would stop being a writer and would be only one of the many news sources that *Time* uses in France...what they would want from you would be trimmings and interpretation of the general news...I think you are a writer and that you ought to make your main job writing something which carries your signature and which also gives you the satisfaction of seeing your own reports reproduced substantially as you wrote them. For them, too, you would probably

> have to be working under pressure, be on cable call all the time, which is an item you ought to consider in relation to your health...You ought to consider...whether your financial security would actually be greater in the future working for *Time* than for us, since here you have a secure berth. So long as you want the job, you pretty well know it is yours indefinitely.

Going to *Time* was like going to Hollywood, White told her. She might get a higher rate of pay but who knew how long it would last. White added that various unnamed colleagues who'd worked for *Time* had been miserable there.

Ross offered to change her pay from $125 per London Letter and $100 per Paris Letter to $5,000 a year for forty letters, plus expenses. White knew they couldn't compete financially with *Time* and wouldn't try, but hoped Flanner found the offer generous. This would make her "one of a half dozen on the entire staff, including editors, paid on a yearly basis. It's a sign that we think of you as an essential and, let us pray, permanent member of the organization."

Flanner turned down *Time*. Quitting *The New Yorker* "leaves one no place except down to go," she later told McKelway. Nowhere else could she find its particular "mixture of lunacy and leniency."

24

THE SPREE

Weidmann spent the summer alone at La Voulzie. His skin had gone dark olive from his daily hours-long regimen of sit-ups and push-ups on the front lawn. Over the past weeks, half out of boredom and half to make money, he'd haunted the Expo's fairgrounds, pitching himself as an interpreter to German- and English-speaking tourists. He spent whatever he earned. Now he had close to nothing.

He took the morning train into Paris. At the grand plaza fronting the Opéra Garnier he retained the services of a chauffeur named Joseph Couffy. Drivers like Couffy knew the plaza as the spot for wealthy Parisians wanting to take short trips out of the city. Weidmann knew it, too. He'd chosen Couffy for his yellow Renault Vivastella limousine, one of the older and less elegant among the cars. A flashier model could attract unwanted attention. Using the name William Dickson, he arranged for a trip down to the coast at the cost of two and a half francs a kilometer. They would leave the following morning, September 7. He didn't have enough to cover the fare but, as he'd expected, Couffy followed the usual chauffeur's code of not asking for payment up front.

Couffy drove his client down the N20 national highway. By the hamlet of Lamotte-Beuvron (Loir-et-Cher), about thirty miles south of Couffy's native Orléans, they passed through a wooded area. Weidmann asked to pull over by the edge of a forest so he could relieve himself. They were making good time, so Couffy took the opportunity to put some oil in the engine, turning his back on his client to lift the car's warm metal hood. Weidmann shot him in the back of the neck with a single bullet. Couffy's large body slumped to the road. With great effort Weidmann propped him up to lean against the car and placed a newspaper over his face, just before a car sped by.

The passing car was followed by a slow motorized wagon manned by a local farmworker, with the prosaic family name of Blé (Wheat). He later testified that shortly after lunchtime he'd driven past a fat man dozing with a newspaper covering his head, his back against a yellow car, while his co-passenger sat next to him on the ground, also with his back against the car, reading his own paper and whistling. Blé said he'd asked the whistling man, "Aren't you afraid you'll wake your friend?" and that the man had answered, "No danger. He's sleeping soundly." He envied them their pleasant moment and drove off.

As soon as the wagon was out of sight Weidmann dragged Couffy's body into the woods, and then removed a wallet holding the small sum of fourteen hundred francs, keys, and papers. He left Couffy his wristwatch. Another car passed just as Weidmann whipped the yellow Renault around in a U-turn, back toward Paris. He drove in no hurry, stopping at Orléans for a coffee.

The next day, September 8, at around six in the evening, a man walked through the thick forest at the edge of Lamotte-Beuvron. In the falling summer light he saw a man propped up against a tree with a newspaper over his face, as though he'd been out earlier to enjoy the stronger sun and had fallen asleep. Worried that the dozing man would get cold if left alone he went to wake him. As he got closer he saw that the newspaper's edge was soaked in red.

Commissioner Jean Belin, head of the first section of the Criminal Police of the National Security, commonly known as the Sûreté, took up the investigation. Retracing Couffy's route meant bringing in police workers from Paris, Orléans, and Blois. Tire tracks revealed where a car would have pulled over to the embankment by the highway heading southwest before leaving again some time later heading northeast. Couffy's wife told the authorities that her husband had picked up a man named Dickson at the Hotel Daniel in Paris. Investigators deduced that Couffy had been shot from behind through the neck by a single bullet at close range from a 7.65 revolver. Commissioner Belin would later note that the style of killing with a single bullet to the neck from behind at close range was the same manner of execution favored by the Gestapo.

Three days later Weidmann bought some dark gray paint in the massive goods hall attached to the Gare Saint-Lazare. He painted the car, and removed the rumble seat and the hardtop. He bought a celluloid plaque at the Place de la République and brought it to a painter on the Rue Amelot, where he paid someone (it's unclear who) to paint a fake number on it. He falsified the existing permit and papers to match the new number, replacing Couffy's name with that of Eugen Karrer.

He finally had a car. But it ate up a lot of gas, so he had to use it sparingly.

On the morning of Monday, October 4, 1937, Weidmann (calling himself Mr. Wender) and Million (calling himself Mr. Brown) drove south in their dark gray Renault limousine. Their passenger was Jeanine Keller, twenty-eight. In the trunk were a borrowed suitcase containing her clothes, toiletries, a few blonde wigs (stress was causing her to lose her hair), and some jewelry. She'd also packed a travel phonograph and her favorite records, including "Under the Moon" and "Oh Miss Hanna." Next to these lay a shovel that Weidmann had just bought at a department store. He'd told Keller that he was going to surprise his daughter with a day of play at the beach.

Keller, a trained nurse, sometime restaurant cook, and mother of two small boys, was then in the middle of trying to divorce her husband, Eugene, a failed businessman. They lived in a cramped apartment at 28, Rue des Juifs in Strasbourg, in the Alsace region of eastern France, with its mixed French and German cultural heritage. She came from Mundelsheim, outside of Stuttgart; Eugene was French. She'd left the children in his care, as she'd finally found a way to free herself from her domestic prison. She'd placed a classified ad offering her services as governess, and a Mr. Brown had responded on behalf of a wealthy German family, the Wenders, who lived near Vichy and had a young daughter with special needs. After collecting the child and Mrs. Wenders they would all travel to South America. She would be paid a decent salary of 750 francs a month plus expenses. Keller's husband hadn't stood in her way, hoping that the job might, in the long term, save their marriage.

About an hour out of Paris Weidmann suggested some sightseeing. They pulled off near the town of Barbizon at the edge of the Fontainebleau forest. Napoleon's castle in the main town of Fontainebleau was the area's main attraction, but Weidmann asked Million about the forest's Caverne des Brigands (Brigands' Cave), which he'd heard so much about and never seen. Million told them of a grotto that had served as a thieves' hideout in the time of Louis XIV, easy to walk to. It was decided: They would go see the cave before heading over to the castle. Million—after rushing back to the car, explaining that he needed a flashlight but in truth grabbing the shovel, which he hid under his shirt—led them into the thicket toward the mouth of the cave, Million in front, Keller in the middle, and Weidmann the rear. They saw a pub near the cave, closed for the season.

They had to crouch to get through the entrance and into the cave's middle section where it was tall enough to stand. Million made as if to read some inscriptions, fishing out a flashlight from his coat, which he then turned quickly to shine on Keller's neck. Weidmann, with his gun a finger's length from Keller, shot her once through the back of the neck. She fell forward into the dirt. Million removed two rings from her fingers and inspected them. Costume jewelry. He and Weidmann removed her shoes and her hat. They dug a shallow hole and buried her. They dumped the shovel, shoes, and hat into a crack between some rocks as high as they could reach.

After rifling through Keller's handbag they found a money order for thirteen hundred francs, which needed Keller's identity card to be cashed. They found one hundred francs cash. Million was disappointed. Weidmann was indifferent. They returned to Saint-Cloud, taking a different route than the one they'd taken down.

That night Weidmann gave Keller's clothing, jewels, and perfume to Million. They could be presents for Tricot. They didn't bother coming up with an explanation because, as Weidmann later testified, Tricot "never asked questions." She did notice, once Million had gotten back to their hotel room in Paris, that his shoes were sandy. She put on her new horseshoe ring. Million said it would bring them luck.

The next morning, at the central post office on the Rue Louvre in Paris, Tricot cashed the money order, pretending to be Keller. Five hundred francs went to paying the rent on La Voulzie. Million and Weidmann split the remaining eight hundred.

A few days later, the owner of the shuttered pub near the cave saw what looked like drops of blood in the dirt by the cave's mouth. He told the park ranger, who dismissed the information. The publican was a heavy drinker, sometimes erratic, and had made a similar report a year earlier after a prankster faked a crime scene by dripping blood around the cave. Later, after he gave rambling answers under examination, a reporter would describe him as "the owner of a tavern in the woods and surely also its best customer."

But not long afterward some tourists saw the same trickle of blood and discovered the freshly made mound in the cave, and the ranger was again called to investigate.

The police were unable to identify the dead woman. The bullet's exit wound went through the middle of her face.

Just over a week after the murder of Jeanine Keller, Million came up with a new scheme. Having gone through life thinking himself the wiliest and worst version of the human animal, Million seems to have been rattled by his encounter with Weidmann, who'd clearly traveled galaxies further than he had toward the darkness. He felt he needed to demonstrate his own capacity for violence. "He wanted to show that he was smart enough to hatch his own plan, taking care of all the details," Weidmann later explained. "I got the sense that when Million saw me kill Keller and learned of how I'd killed de Koven and Couffy, he had the urge to emulate me and wanted to prove that he was equally capable."

Million told Weidman his idea. He would pose as an investor, replying to classified ads from entrepreneurs seeking capital. No doubt one of these dreamers would be so happy to meet with anyone interested in funding his venture he'd abandon common sense. Million, after tricking him into carrying lots of cash, would lure him to the villa and then shoot him, using Weidmann's pistol.

Adopting the alias Pradier, Million answered three ads he found promising, dictating to Weidmann, who despite being a foreigner wrote French better than he did. "Please allow me to tell you a little about myself. I'm twenty-seven years old, from a good family and well educated, and I can provide the capital you seek, as your offer corresponds well with my own goals. I'm eager to hear your response."

An enthusiastic twenty-three-year-old named Roger Leblond answered Pradier's letter the next day. Recently demobilized from the French army, he was working as a publicity agent and wanted to put on music festivals in the underserved suburbs, featuring singers who were popular on the radio.

Million met Leblond at the latter's apartment in Paris's upscale sixteenth arrondissement. Tricot had come along to pose as his wife, meant to put the victim at ease. Weidmann and Million had chosen her outfit beforehand, dressing her in the dead Keller's blonde wig and fake astrakhan coat.

The two men spoke for an hour and a half about their respective business dreams. Million mentioned a brother-in-law, Eugen Karrer, who would come in as a silent partner. They made a deal that they would each put in some funds to launch the enterprise: eight thousand from Leblond and fifty thousand from Pradier, via his brother-in-law.

Leblond drove out to La Voulzie in his olive-green cabriolet to sign the documents that would put him in business with Pradier and Karrer. He'd brought along just over five thousand of his promised eight thousand francs in cash, all that he could get on short notice.

Weidmann had planted his gun in a drawer behind where they would have Leblond sign. Tricot had been told to stay in Paris. Weidmann invited Leblond to sit at the living room table to look over the papers one more time to make sure all was in order. Weidmann sat across from him. As Leblond hunched over, Million went behind him, got the revolver from the drawer and shot him in the back of the neck. He fell to the ground, convulsing. Million, terrified, shouted at Weidmann to shoot him again. Weidmann remained calm, knowing that Leblond would die soon enough. Weidmann then spread ash on the floor to soak up the blood. He went to get Leblond's car from the street and parked it on the property.

Million liked Leblond's wristwatch and removed it. He ripped a ring from Leblond's finger with such force that he fractured bone. They took his wallet, a pen and pencil, cuff links, suspenders, and shoes. They wrapped the body in one of the villa's green curtains.

That night Million drove Leblond's car and Weidmann followed in Couffy's, hugging the bank of the Seine and then crossing toward the suburb of Neuilly-sur-Seine just beyond the western perimeter of Paris. Weidmann didn't know the area and made several twists and turns looking for a quiet street. They made a game of it, pushing the engines of their cars hard, jockeying for position on narrow roads as if navigating the crucial turns at Monaco. Weidmann passed by a cemetery's gates, just north of the Bois de Boulogne, and thought it a fitting place to abandon Leblond's car. He did so reluctantly as it was a beautiful machine, but they already had a car and one was enough.

On the way back to the villa they stopped at a store to grab some ham and wine. Tricot was there by the time they returned. She'd seen Leblond's hat and coat hanging on the rack when she'd come in but asked no questions.

The next day, October 17, a resident of Neuilly-Sur-Seine saw a green cabriolet parked on the Rue Victor Noir by the cemetery, headlights still on though the sun had been up for hours. He went to investigate and in the back seat saw a dead man wrapped in a green curtain, his feet bare. From the license plate, the police identified the victim as Roger Leblond, resident of 1, Square Malesherbes, Paris, divorced from Eugenie Renner.

The investigation led to the letter from "Pradier," followed by the questioning of all the Pradiers that could be found, even while everyone knew that name had surely been an alias. The most promising clue the police had was the smattering of dead leaves in Leblond's car. Since no trees lined the whole of Rue Victor Noir, the leaves (which a botanist identified as belonging to a sweet chestnut) had to have come from somewhere else. Chestnut trees lined Parisian boulevards and grew in its parks, but these were horse chestnuts. The working theory posited that the leaves came from one of the sweet chestnut trees common to roadsides of the western suburbs, or from a private property in the area with grounds large enough for sweet chestnuts. Saint-Cloud had been raised as a possible location because of its prevalence of that species. But with no way to tie any one specific tree to the leaves in question, the investigators soon gave up on that line of inquiry.

As news spread about the Leblond murder, this, combined with the lack of progress in the Jean de Koven case and the discovery of an unidentified body in the woods of Fontainebleau, led to growing worry among the French public, especially in the area of Paris and its suburbs, that a repeat murderer was on the loose. The papers described the man named Pradier and the blonde woman who'd visited Leblond at his home prior to his murder, based on a statement from Leblond's girlfriend.

On the night Leblond's body was found, Million and Tricot returned to Million's father's café in Paris. There they reconnected with their recently elusive former associate, Jean Blanc.

Million alluded to the murder of Leblond and said, falsely, that

Weidmann had pulled the trigger, but that he'd been there and had helped dispose of the body; he added that he regretted his part in the crime. He also said he was scared Weidmann would kill him to keep him from talking. His father told him to go to the police. He tried to craft a confession letter. Blanc didn't like the wording because it implicated Tricot. He argued that she shouldn't have to go to prison, since she hadn't killed anyone. By the end of the night Blanc had convinced the couple to ignore Million's father's advice and instead of confessing go into hiding. He would cover their expenses and lend them his car. Million's father later testified that Blanc had only offered to help them into hiding after Million had agreed to let Blanc "recuperate" Tricot, which Tricot would strongly deny.

Arthur "Fritz" Frommer told his girlfriend that he was going back out to Saint-Cloud again to discuss becoming an agent for his friend Weidmann's real estate firm. He would have to invest a bit of his own money, of course, as an act of good faith. He wasn't asking her for any more money, he quickly added. She'd already given him everything she could. But he'd scrounged up three hundred francs by borrowing from four friends. He was sure this was the opportunity that would set them up for their future, he told her before leaving for the train, and make them financially secure enough to marry.

Frommer, twenty-seven, had been in Paris only a few months. He'd just served three years in Preungesheim Prison for distributing anti-Nazi tracts in Frankfurt. There he'd befriended Weidmann. They'd bonded over their shared love of literature.

Expelled from Germany after his release in March, Frommer had crossed into Switzerland, but as a known Communist and ex-convict labeled "subversive," he was refused a Swiss work visa. He'd headed for Paris, where his father's two sisters lived with their husbands, Arthur Schott and Hugo Weber. He landed with the Glaubert family, fellow German Jews who employed one of his old Frankfurt friends, now also a refugee in Paris. The Glauberts had set up the Maison Mann chocolate manufactory after having themselves been expelled from Germany as non-Aryan business owners. They hired Frommer as a junior account representative.

To celebrate, Frommer's friend had taken him to the large and raucous dining hall on the Place de la République, popular among the city's German-Jewish population, where he'd met a young Polish refugee, Jachweta Kutas. She was a singer in the Jewish theater on Rue de Lancry. Over the following few weeks she'd brought Fritz to a few socialist meetings, but he always left disgusted by the supposed firebrands who attended, who spoke so much while having seen and done so little.

Frommer had dreams of making his own way in the world, freeing himself from the Glauberts' tenuous patronage. He'd told Kutas of his idea: a reversible tie. She'd handed over her meager savings. Soft-spoken, shy, and melancholy, with a round full-moon face and a medium build, Frommer proved a poor salesman. Nobody wanted his ties.

And then, a stroke of luck. One autumn day, walking a Paris street, he'd recognized his old mate Weidmann, who invited him out to Saint-Cloud to see his home. He told Frommer he was selling real estate. Frommer had his suspicions but had returned to Paris impressed by Weidmann's villa with its shiny Renault parked in the back. He'd visited La Voulzie several times that fall, always coming back to tell Jachweta wild tales of Weidmann and his booming business.

But on that night, November 22, Fritz hadn't come back.

Saturday, November 27, found Raymond Lesobre, a real estate agent, waiting at the Saint-Cloud station. He'd left his Renault, a black Celtaquatre decorated with flames, parked nearby. Lesobre had spent the past Thursday touring properties in the area with a prospective client named Arthur Schott, who was seeking a home with many rooms and a big garden. Today Schott wanted to return to one of the villas, Mon Plaisir, owned by a French woman and currently uninhabited. He'd given Lesobre two of his calling cards, listing his address in Nice.

Weidmann (as Arthur Schott) got off the two thirty train from Paris and greeted Lesobre. Saint-Cloud's station agent would later describe him as around thirty years old, with a medium build, brown hair, and a mustache "worn in the American style." He wore a dark gray overcoat and a dark hat of soft material with a rounded cap. The station agent recognized Lesobre and his flashy car. Saint-Cloud wasn't a big place.

The two men toured the villa Mon Plaisir. Weidmann asked to see the cellar. When Lesobre was a few paces ahead, Weidmann shot him in the back of the neck. He took Lesobre's wallet with five thousand francs and a ring from his finger. He drove Lesobre's Renault to La Voulzie, where he installed false plates and doctored the registration. Perhaps this car he would keep. The five thousand francs went immediately to the rental agency overseeing the villa, covering the back rent owed for the last few months.

He'd been sure to recover the Arthur Schott calling card he'd given Lesobre, which was in his wallet. But he'd forgotten that he'd given Lesobre two such cards.

The following day, Lesobre's secretary, Andrée Vogleisen, called on the Seine-et-Oise police department at its headquarters on Versailles's Rue Saint-Louis. Her boss hadn't reported back from his Saturday afternoon showing and had failed to show up to work that morning. He worked regularly on Sundays.

Usually such a call wouldn't get much of an immediate response, but the spate of apparent murders in the area had put the police on high alert, and officers went directly to question Vogleisen. She told them that she'd last seen her boss leaving for the train station to meet a client named Arthur Schott. He'd taken five thousand francs from petty cash. Schott had come by the office on Thursday, but as it had been her day off she had no description to offer. But she'd taken his call to arrange the second Saturday showing and could report that he spoke only passable French and that his accent sounded "Nordic." He'd told her that he'd come up from Nice for the viewing and could be reached at the Hôtel Magenta in Paris. She shared the addresses of the three villas he and Lesobre had visited. And she told officers that Lesobre would have been carrying a lighter with his initials on it, a birthday present she'd given him and which he'd kept with him ever since.

And then she remembered something. Digging through her cabinets, she found the cheaply printed calling card that Lesobre had given her to file, listing Arthur Schott's permanent address in Nice at 10, Boulevard du Parc-Imperial, which turned out be a modest street near the central train station.

Within hours, most of the officers from the Seine-et-Oise department were on the case, led by their commissioner, Marcel Sicot, a veteran with thirty years of experience, aided by his tenacious young deputy, Émile Primborgne. Officers called on the Hôtel Magenta in Paris. No one there had heard of an Arthur Schott. After the Versailles magistrate Jean-Georges Berry approved the warrants, officers searched the properties Lesobre had shown Schott. After the first two villas revealed nothing, they entered Mon Plaisir with the help of a locksmith. Around seven that evening they discovered Lesobre lying face down on the stairs leading to the wine cellar, shot through the back of the neck, once at close range, with a "Baby" Browning pistol. Empty pockets. No decent fingerprints or footprints. The cellar's front door had been closed and locked with a key. Lesobre's car was gone. Whoever killed him could have been in another country by then.

Lesobre's widow, Colette, hadn't reported him missing. She'd learned of his death from his parents. She told the police that she and Raymond had been living apart for the past few months "for health reasons." After a convalescence along the Riviera she was now living with her mother. It was temporary. She didn't know Raymond to have been involved with any other women. She didn't know him to have belonged to any political group, nor to have any enemies.

The Versailles officers, confused by Colette Lesobre's explanation of her marital arrangements, looked to the secretary Vogleisen. She said that her employer rarely spoke about his family life. Perhaps she knew more than she was letting on. Something about that initialed lighter that she swore he kept with him at all times felt overly intimate. Lesobre's parents in their own statement said their son lived a "normal life" and were convinced that he'd been killed in a robbery gone wrong.

To Primborgne a robbery motive made little sense, given the small amount taken and the apparently premeditated methods of the murder. The killer had chosen somewhere secluded, a quiet weekend afternoon. He couldn't have expected his victim would be carrying much on him. Perhaps it was a targeted assassination. But why target Lesobre, with no obvious connection to the criminal world, and whose profile raised no alarms?

Commissioner Sicot and his assistant Primborgne doubted that the killer ever had the means to buy a half-million-franc villa. He'd needed to be picked up from a train station rather than having a car of his own to drive out to tour the properties. The suspect's description, however vague, was distributed to every police department in France, along with the name Arthur Schott.

The next morning, in Strasbourg, the true Arthur Schott saw his name in the paper in connection with a dead body found three hundred miles away in Saint-Cloud. He rushed to the Strasbourg police station. Schott worked as a salesman for a German lingerie company and lived with his German wife in Nice. He'd been in Strasbourg for several days on a sales call. Many people could vouch for his being nowhere near Saint-Cloud at the time of the murder.

After contacting the Versailles station, the Strasbourg police chief told Schott about the calling card from Lesobre's office. Schott provided a list of people who might have his card. Among them was his nephew, Fritz Frommer, whom he singled out for attention. He didn't think Fritz could be a killer, but was concerned he might be an additional victim, for he roughly fit the description of the man who met Lesobre at the station. He owned only one overcoat, gray, the color of the one that man had been wearing. And he rarely removed his round woolen cap, as he was bashful about his prematurely thinning hair. He told the police that Frommer had recently fled Germany. The Strasbourg chief passed all of this along to Sicot.

Schott returned to the station the next day to say that he'd just received a letter from a Parisian friend worried about not having seen young Fritz for more than a week. This friend had shared Frommer's most recent address: Hotel l'Idéal. The Paris police failed to find him there. He'd last been seen there on the morning of November 22. After tracking down a copy of the identity card he'd filled out when registering as a resident of Paris, the authorities found the address of Frommer's other uncle, Hugo Weber, also living in Paris, whom he'd listed as a reference. The young deputy Primborgne, without waiting for any instruction from his superior, went straight to Weber's listed address on Rue Clichy.

Weber, who'd been a wholesaler in Frankfurt and had fled Germany in 1934, had moved a few times in the past months, and it took Primborgne a few days to track him down with the help of local police. He was now living on Rue Véron. Speaking little French, he'd been reduced to doing odd jobs, replying to classified ads. For the moment he was working as an extra at the Billancourt film studio, south of the Bois de Boulogne. He told Deputy Primborgne that he'd already contacted Commissioner Belin of the Sûreté in Paris to try to get them on the case of his missing nephew, after Fritz had failed to show for their usual Sunday dinner.

Primborgne, after learning this, went to Belin to be debriefed before taking Weber's statement. But Belin stonewalled him, refusing to pass along any evidence until he, Belin, consulted his overseeing magistrate. The magistrate explained that the department had too much work to do trying to capture the remaining fugitive members of the Cagoule terrorist organization to spare Belin for another case. Belin begrudgingly passed along all his gathered evidence to Primborgne, including Weber's previously collected statement, which in the end revealed little more than a few of Weber's theories about what had happened to his nephew.

Primborgne rushed back to Rue Véron to interview Weber as best he could given the language barrier. Over many hours Weber managed to impart that his nephew lived a quiet life and couldn't have been mixed up in any kind of murder. He'd sometimes had to help to pay Frommer's bills, but the young man was ambitious and a hard worker. Yes, he was a communist and had been in prison, but his only crime had been in sticking to his beliefs.

Weber also mentioned that Frommer had recently reconnected with someone he'd met in prison and that this friend had been the prison librarian. He'd told his uncle that the man's name was Siegfried Sauerbrey and that he'd gone out to see him a few times at his villa, which he was renting somewhere in the woods of Saint-Cloud. This Sauerbrey was apparently involved in some real estate business and wanted to hire Fritz on as his personal secretary. Fritz admitted to his uncle that his prison friend had "low morals" and that he'd been frightened by something "sinister" about the villa, but that nevertheless he needed the work and wanted to pursue the opportunity. Weber had warned his nephew against getting involved with any schemes, given the precarity of his status in France. He said that his nephew was exceptionally bright and perceptive. Weber hypothesized that maybe Fritz knew something about Sauerbrey, dating back to their prison days, and that this man must have killed Fritz to keep it a secret.

In truth Siegfried Sauerbrey had been a fellow inmate of both Frommer and Weidmann, the prison celebrity who'd been wrapped up in a major financial scandal, whom Weidmann had tried soliciting for work shortly after his release. The French police did not yet know this. It might be that Weidmann borrowed the name as an alias and that Frommer stuck to using that same alias when describing his friend to his uncle, for some reason fearful of revealing his true name, or that Fritz had been the one to give his uncle the false name in the first place.

Weber also gave the police the name of Siegfried Kohn, twenty-eight, another German exile in Paris, whom he knew to be Frommer's good friend. The police learned that he was likely the last person to see Frommer alive. Fritz, said Kohn, was meant to help him sell an electric typewriter to a wholesaler, a Monsieur Bricart, at six on the evening of November 22. They'd met up two hours earlier on the Boulevard Haussmann and ducked into the Café Cardinal to escape the rain. Frommer begged off staying for the meeting, explaining that he had to get out to Saint-Cloud for a business meeting of his own with someone named Eugen Karrer, whom he'd been visiting lately. Kohn doubted there was any way Frommer would be back in time to help him with the typewriter sale, but Frommer insisted he could.

Kohn directed them to Frommer's girlfriend, Kutas, who confirmed that Fritz had been regularly visiting a fellow German exile at his villa in Saint-Cloud.

The Versailles police, working in tandem with the Paris police, deduced the location of Siegfried Sauerbrey/Eugen Karrer's Saint-Cloud villa. From Fritz's description of it as "sinister" and in a wooded area, they narrowed it down to properties that were somewhat secluded. And they knew the villa was being rented.

Commissioner Sicot and Deputy Primborgne suspected that the murderer of the real estate agent Raymond Lesobre also murdered Roger Leblond, the publicist found dead in his car in the same general area, and that both killings were tied to the disappearance of Fritz Frommer.

Sicot thought back to France's most notorious murderer, Henri "Bluebeard" Landru, who two decades earlier had killed at least eleven victims, seemingly for the sport of it. (In French folktales Bluebeard is a nobleman who gleefully murders several wives.) Only capture had stopped Landru's spree.

Sicot feared he was dealing with a second Bluebeard. The longer it took to find him the higher the body count would be.

25

TO BLUEBEARD'S CELL

Enlisting the help of a local real estate agency in early December, Deputy Primborgne learned that a villa on Avenue Pigault-Lebrun had been rented to a German citizen named Eugen Karrer that past June. The absentee owner of the villa, a Mme. Marie Braux, the widow of a jeweler, was descended from the namesake of the avenue on which it sat, the eighteenth-century writer Pigault-Lebrun. The agent who arranged the rental had seen Karrer only once and couldn't recall much about him. He'd always paid his rent on time, she said, until October when he'd fallen into arrears. But he'd just posted the overdue rent with a lump payment on November 29.

Primborgne noted that the date fell just a few days after the murder of Raymond Lesobre. He was now certain that this Eugen Karrer was the same man that Fritz Frommer had called Siegfried Sauerbrey, and that he'd either murdered multiple people or knew intimately the person who did.

He requested a search warrant of Karrer's rented villa from the

Versailles magistrate, Berry. But Berry refused, citing a lack of tangible evidence to suggest that Eugen Karrer was indeed the same man as their suspect. The only definitive evidence they had about the suspect's identity was the Arthur Schott calling card, which had proved to be an alias. However deeply the deputy might have been convinced that Karrer was their man, in the eyes of the court he was following a hunch.

The furious Primborgne went back to the local real estate agent to see if he could learn anything more. In the meantime he sent three officers from the first mobile brigade out to survey the villa on Avenue Pigault-Lebrun, from a distance: inspectors Émile Bourquin and Ange Poignant, and a junior officer named Vedrenne. Their police cruiser got a flat on the way out, and the two inspectors left Vedrenne to deal with it while they proceeded on foot. They arrived within sight of Eugen Karrer's rented villa at around one thirty in the afternoon.

Snow covered the ground. From a short distance Bourquin and Poignant watched the small and tidy property. They saw nothing to arouse suspicion: a gabled roof with a chimney, a cramped front porch, a few tall and nearly bare oaks and birches, a fence of wooden slats cut to different heights so that their tips in line described the bottom half of a circle, or perhaps a smile. They saw a car was parked next to the house. Perhaps it was Raymond Lesobre's missing Renault?

It was impossible to tell from their distance and angle. They approached and saw a second car parked by the first one. Something felt off to the officers. They went on to the property, knowing well they had no warrant. One of them rang the doorbell. No answer. They returned to the road to watch, hoping that they were well hidden by a thicket of trees.

An hour later, Bourquin and Poignant saw a man approach the villa, enter through the front door, and then emerge from it a few minutes later carrying some gardening tools as if to work on the front yard. He roughly fit their suspect's description. He had dark, slicked-back hair and a medium build. He wore a tightly tailored overcoat that looked deep blue or black in the distance. He moved his body quickly against the cold, his breath steaming in the afternoon air. A dog from the neighboring house slunk in and out of view.

Weidmann had seen the policemen in their hiding spot and suspected that they'd come for him. When asked later why he hadn't tried escaping, he would say only that he'd been tired. Instead, he went up to the officers on the other side of the gate and asked them what they were doing there. Again acting on their own initiative, they silently decided between themselves to confront their suspect. Since they were in plain clothes, Bourquin pretended to be a tax official, flashing a notebook and asking to see the man's papers. Neither of the inspectors carried guns that day. French policemen weren't required to carry weapons, though they could choose to do so if they bought a weapon with their own money. Bourquin refused to ever carry one on principle. He said that he'd seen enough of guns and what they could do during the Great War, and found he'd been able to do his job just fine without a sidearm. He abhorred violence. People said he loved nothing more than his pipe, his wife, and his dog.

Weidmann, according to police testimony, paled and tensed up when confronted, before quickly recomposing himself and opening the garden gate to invite the men in. They followed him inside the house, which was even smaller than it looked from the outside. There were two bedrooms, a bathroom, a kitchen, and a lounge. Weidmann led them through the narrow entrance into the lounge, barely furnished with a coffee table, a dresser, a couch in the corner closest to the front window, and a reading chair.

As they entered the room Weidmann reached into his pocket as though to fish out his identity papers. He wheeled on the inspectors and fired two shots. Though standing just a few feet from his targets he missed. Bourquin, a large man, jumped on Weidmann while Poignant grabbed at his legs. The three men tumbled onto the couch. As if possessed with superhuman strength, Weidmann fought off his captors and got off two more shots. Poignant took a ricocheted bullet in the left shoulder. The second bullet grazed Bourquin's face near his eye before passing through the brim of his hat, which had somehow stayed on during the fight. Weidmann fired a fifth time, missing again. The inspectors continued to grapple with their quarry as he tried to free his hand to discharge his revolver.

Bourquin saw that their tangled bodies had landed next to the coffee table on which a hammer rested, along with other tools Weidmann had pretended to use for his garden work and then brought back inside. Bourquin, despite being nearly blinded by the blood dripping into his eyes, grabbed the hammer and bashed Weidmann until he lost consciousness.

They searched him, finding a wallet containing a used train ticket from Paris and tickets for the Metro, as well as a pen and a lighter initialed RL.

By then the third officer, Vedrenne, had reached the property by car. Poignant called out to him through a window and told him to go back to the station to get Primborgne.

When Vedrenne and Primborgne returned, the four men put the semiconscious man into a police cruiser and drove off. It was December 8, 1937.

The Versailles station was crowded with officers and tipped-off reporters jostling to get a glimpse of the arrested man being brought in, bloodied and disheveled. A doctor treated his wounds, wrapping gauze tightly to his forehead and down over his ears to his neck so that his face was framed by the bloodstained white material. One art lover among the officers would recall that when the suspect came in he looked like Picasso's sketch of the poet Apollinaire (*Apollinaire blessé*, 1916), his head similarly mummified. Soon photographs of the bandaged Weidmann were competing for space on the pages of nearly every major paper in France alongside news of Spanish bombs and the Japanese in Nanking.

Versailles officials were still referring to the suspect as Eugen Karrer, also known as Siegfried Sauerbrey. He pretended to speak only German, forcing everyone to wait for the station's German-speaking chief, Sicot, to return from a southern suburb, where a trove of Cagoulard explosives had just been discovered, to take his testimony. Officers hadn't been able to question him in the chaotic aftermath of his arrest, when the shock of the ordeal might have made him more prone to revelation. He'd gotten time to rest and to plan.

Officer Primborgne in the meantime went back out to La Voulzie. Recalling the dead leaves of the sweet chestnut tree found in the car of the murdered Lesobre, he wanted to look at the property's vegetation, which he hadn't thought to do at the time of the arrest. He found a large sweet chestnut tree on the grounds.

Chief Sicot reached the station at eight o'clock that night. He would recall being struck by the suspect's physical beauty, so at odds with the grotesque crimes of which he'd been accused. When Sicot addressed him as Sauerbrey, the man shook his head, and told him, no, his name was neither Sauerbrey nor Karrer, but Eugen Weidmann. His manner remained serene. He spoke gently. He refused to answer any direct questioning about his crimes. He told Sicot that all would be revealed the following day, if only he could be allowed to sleep. He requested a lawyer, stipulating that whoever was to represent him must be a woman. He promised Sicot that he wouldn't be disappointed by what he had to tell him. Sicot pressed but finally acquiesced.

Weidmann was placed in cell number three of the Saint-Pierre prison adjoining the Versailles Courthouse, a squat three-story stone-and-brick building ten minutes' walk from the entrance to the Palace. His was the same cell once occupied by Bluebeard Landru.

He had use of a straw mattress, a washbasin, a table and bench, and a toilet. The warden assigned him a cellmate, a car thief named Petit-Jean, who'd been instructed to learn whatever he could about Weidmann in exchange for a reduced sentence—and to make sure Weidmann didn't kill himself.

Three lawyers were assigned to represent Weidmann. Renée Jardin was the lone female attorney in the Versailles bar association. She spoke German. At forty this was the biggest break of her career. She would work alongside Robert Planty, thirty-nine, the dashing and well-respected head of the local bar association, married to a woman said to be the most beautiful in Versailles, and also conversant in German; and Jean Raoult, who at twenty-seven already had his own practice.

On first meeting the following morning Weidmann rose to offer Jardin his seat. He apologized that he had no money to pay for her services. He was taken from his cell to the courthouse, wearing prison-issued blue cotton work fatigues. Bourquin, Primborgne, Sicot, and Poignant escorted him in a protective ring. Dozens of reporters waited at the entrance. Weidmann and the officers pressed through the scrum to climb a staircase to reach Magistrate Berry's chambers, to a symphony of pops and fizzles from hot flashbulbs. Weidmann was shown to a comfortable leather chair and handed a cigarette. A brazier warmed his feet. His handcuffs were removed. The magistrate was ready to listen, the stenographer to record.

He stopped pretending he spoke only German and now talked to them in his accented French, complaining that he'd never been in a jail with worse food. The prison cook had smiled and stuck his thumb in his soup at the previous evening's dinner. He was bothered by the sounds coming from the other cells and called the damp conditions unacceptable. (The Saint-Pierre prison actually offered the relative comfort of central heating.) German prisons were far superior and their inmates far better behaved, he said. To one observer he seemed less a prisoner than a tourist complaining about a poorly run hotel.

During an hours-long examination he calmly gave his confession, starting with a muddled account of the Lesobre murder. Weidmann said that he'd killed him for the money, figuring that real estate agents would carry a lot of cash, and that he'd chosen the first agency he'd seen walking the streets of Saint-Cloud. After killing Lesobre and taking his wallet, he'd kept his lighter because he liked the look of it. He said that a friend named Fritz Frommer had been a witness to the murder, and then he alluded to a third accomplice, an unnamed "American gangster," but then later retracted those statements. He eventually admitted killing Fritz Frommer in La Voulzie's kitchen. He'd done it for money. Frommer had three hundred francs on him.

He said that he'd killed an American woman named Jean de Koven after she'd come to his villa. Sicot was blindsided. Of course he knew about the case of the missing American that had made the papers that summer, but neither he nor anyone else on the force had thought to connect her disappearance to the man he was now interrogating.

Weidmann swore that he'd only wanted to kidnap her at first. They'd drunk some milk, smoked a few cigarettes, and nuzzled on the couch in the living room, she lying on her side, he sitting upright, and talked about their respective hopes for the future, he said. And then he'd put his large hands around her neck. He told them:

> I closed my eyes and squeezed until she was dead. I took her into the hallway, I opened her handbag, and I took out some money, cheques, and her passport. I didn't know, when I had the idea to rob her, how much she would have. I found a shovel in the basement, I dug a hole under the porch and I put the body there. The sun was rising. I strangled her again with a cloth napkin and I put one corner of it in her mouth. I don't know why I did that since she was already dead. I took the gloves, hat, and coat she'd left back in the villa, and put them back on her. I left her handbag and camera next to her and covered everything with dirt. I spent a few hours after that wandering around the garden.

No one else had been present at the time. He would lead them to her body if they took him to La Voulzie. Asked why he'd buried her with her belongings, he said he wasn't really sure but offered that maybe it was so that a woman who was sometimes at the villa, named Colette Tricot, wouldn't get jealous.

He explained the methods he'd used to find de Koven, waiting in the lobby of the Hotel Ambassador. No one had been quite right before he'd met her. An older British couple seemed promising until they'd let on that they had no children nor close relatives, meaning no good candidates to pay a ransom. He thought he'd found a victim in a sixtysomething American woman who'd come to Paris for the Exposition despite her fear of large crowds. He'd offered to serve as her guide, and she'd agreed but then begged off at the last moment. He was certain that he'd scared her off, not because of any danger he might pose but because she must have thought he was trying to seduce her and become her paid gigolo. The only woman he'd ever accepted money from was his mother, he told his audience.

Next, he admitted to killing the chauffeur Couffy. He had some interest in Couffy's cash, but more important he'd coveted his car, which he wanted to use so that he could pose as a chauffeur himself, trying to secure long trips down to the coast with clients likely carrying the large sums needed for travel.

And finally, he described the murder of the publicist Leblond. He told them about Roger Million, explaining how he'd met Million and another Frenchman, Jean Blanc, in prison and how they'd come to rent La Voulzie. He said that Million had shot Leblond and that afterward they'd driven the body to leave it by the cemetery in Neuilly.

He showed no remorse when describing these acts. He explained that because "he didn't know these people" he had no regrets, and besides which, "they didn't suffer."

For whatever reason, he said nothing about the murder of the would-be au pair Keller.

He then gave them the vaguest of summaries about his life before coming to Paris. He claimed that he'd fled Germany, under fire from border guards, because he wanted to escape military service and because he wanted to earn money in Paris, perhaps by finding some kind of work at the Expo, with the hope of one day returning to Frankfurt to show his parents that he'd done well. This was the one moment that he showed any kind of deep emotion. He'd let out a little sob and said, to no one in particular, "Provided that my mother will forgive me...Provided that my mother will forgive me." He apologized for his tears. Observers were only left more confused by this break in his placid surface. Was it an act? Did he register normal human feelings?

When asked about his political beliefs, Weidmann only shrugged. Yes, he said, his parents had been members of the Nazi party since 1931. Hitler's color portrait had hung in his house next to Christ on the cross. But he'd never believed in any of that, Nazism, Communism, nothing. People were always trying to get him to pledge to one cause or another, he said, but he didn't see how that would solve anything at all. He supposed he felt German because he'd been born there and lived there. What really made him feel German was Goethe, and Nietzsche, and Schiller. But then, he asked his interrogators, what if he'd been born in America? What if he'd grown up reading not *The Sorrows of Young Werther* but *Leaves of Grass*? Wouldn't he just as easily feel American?

He finished by hinting that he had accomplices who might do something rash and bring "dynamite to the prison" to stop him from talking. After his questioning he privately told Jardin that he'd give some more little clues to Berry when he saw fit, so that Berry could "discover" the rest of the story on his own.

The authorities had by then amassed enough evidence at La Voulzie to confirm Weidmann's already obvious guilt. He'd made makeshift shrines to his victims, displaying their personal objects neatly in a chest of drawers. Detectives found Lesobre's house keys and Leblond's papers. (Weidmann had been wearing Leblond's suspenders when he'd been arrested.) They found de Koven's passport and a few uncashed checks. They found pairs of men's and women's shoes and high-heeled boots, and a wristwatch and a gold signet ring and a woman's blonde wig, all carefully arranged as if they were museum pieces. There were two address books, one belonging to Weidmann and the other to Million. They found five fake IDs, as well as two German passports in Weidmann's name, one expired and one still valid. They also discovered two books on Bluebeard Landru, which Weidmann later said he read to see if they held any tips he might find useful. The inspectors noted that aside from some bloody cloths left soaking in a sink, the villa's interior had been kept spotlessly clean, the white sheets gleaming, the floors perfectly swept.

They'd found telegrams addressed to various people, who would have to be investigated, along with those listed in the address books. This would lead to inconclusive police investigations stretching from Great Britain to Canada to French Indochina.

The inspection of the villa had provided enough evidence to corroborate Weidmann's statements that suggested that Million, Blanc, and Tricot were, at the very least, people of interest. A hunt began for all three.

No bodies were found at La Voulzie. And so, shortly after making his confession, Weidmann was taken to the villa. He was accompanied by his lawyers, as well as the public prosecutor who would eventually lead the case against him, Max Balmary.

Crowds were already milling about the property. Rows of bicycles belonging to people who'd ridden miles to Saint-Cloud were stacked against the gates. The onlookers were allowed to wander freely about the grounds during Weidmann's visit. Reporters captured chilling photographs of children standing a few feet from the killer as he pointed out his crime scenes. The two arresting officers, Bourquin and Poignant, also had starring roles in this performance as they were called on to re-create their dramatic arrest.

Crouching under the front porch stairs, Weidmann led investigators to the body of Jean de Koven, buried beneath two feet of wet red clay. Her body was dirt-caked and doubled over; she was wearing the tartan skirt and cream blouse she'd put on for her date with Siegfried Hunter. Next to her lay a handbag containing a white leather notebook and the camera she'd brought along to take souvenir photos. Weidmann had made a noose out of several cloth napkins tied together. He'd placed the end of this noose in her mouth with such force that he'd knocked one of her teeth loose. Her throat was badly bruised.

From under the stairs Weidmann then led the officers into the cellar's back left corner where he'd stuffed the body of Fritz Frommer.

The bodies were placed into two of the simple wood coffins brought along in anticipation of such discoveries. Renée Jardin would recall that Weidmann appeared to be the only calm person there, holding forth in front of the policemen as if "receiving guests at a party" and at one point wandering over to check on his beloved rosebushes. In several pictures documenting the event he is smiling.

While Weidmann was offering his tour of La Voulzie, Blanc, Tricot, and Million shared a meal in Nantua, three hundred miles away. Before dessert Blanc was called away: His brother had called from Paris, telling him that their names were in the papers as Weidmann's possible accomplices.

Back in Million and Tricot's room that night, Million, clutching his pistol, suggested that the time had come for the three of them to "disappear," without specifying what he meant. Blanc and Tricot convinced him that the only rational option was to get a lawyer and surrender themselves.

After getting rid of all compromising evidence in their possession, they took a train up to Paris. At several stops along the way they whispered to one another about switching course and fleeing to Switzerland before talking themselves out of it. Instead, they huddled together and went over what they would tell the police.

Following a tip, the Tenth Brigade of the Lyon police forces had already been dispatched to Nantua. Failing to find their suspects, they turned to gathering statements from the locals.

Blanc, already trying to distance himself from Million and Tricot even while admitting his involvement in their crimes, was the first to disembark, surrendering at the Paris police headquarters on the Quai des Orfèvres. He said that all he'd done was loan Weidmann some money and help Million launch a lumber business.

A little later at the Versailles Palais de Justice, Million and Tricot simply walked in and announced themselves, accompanied by their lawyer, Henri Géraud. Before the police could shield the suspects from the press, a photographer caught Million looking nonplussed and defiant, a walking sneer. He told the police that he'd been a witness to the murder of the publicity agent Leblond, but only because Weidmann had lied to him. Million said that he and Weidmann had made a "deal" that after robbing Leblond they would let him leave unharmed. Instead, Weidmann had shot the man and driven the body away alone. Tricot admitted only to knowing that Weidmann had killed Leblond and that fear for her own life had kept her from telling anyone.

Early one morning a few days before Christmas two *Paris-Soir* reporters went out to La Voulzie. No police were present to keep them away, as the department lacked the budget to keep men on watch at all hours. In the yard, under snow, the two reporters discovered photographs of a young woman, with writing that seemed to indicate they'd been taken somewhere in Alsace. The reporters sent copies of the photographs to their paper's local editor in Strasbourg. Acting on his own instinct the Strasbourg editor matched it to the photo that a local reader named Keller had previously sent to the paper in search of his missing wife, Jeanine. The editor went to the police.

In Versailles Weidmann was confronted with the photographs of

Jeanine Keller, without revealing that an unidentified body, which they now suspected to be hers, had already been discovered weeks earlier in Fontainebleau. Weidmann in a flat voice admitted to murdering her and told them that she was buried in a grotto in the heart of the forest in Fontainebleau. He added that they would find there a child's shovel wrapped in newspaper and that it would bear Roger Million's prints. When asked why he didn't say anything earlier about Keller he said he'd simply "forgotten" about her when making his earlier confessions.

Just before the year's end Weidmann's parents arrived unannounced at the prison. They'd read about his arrest in the *Frankfurter Zeitung* and had sought the advice of the best lawyer they knew, the same local magistrate who'd gotten Weidmann sent to Preungesheim Prison for his botched kidnapping attempt. The Frankfurt magistrate had connected them with a bombastic and well-known Parisian lawyer, René Floriot, who'd picked the couple up in his car from Gare de l'Est and orchestrated this prison-cell ambush, hoping to use the surprise to wedge his way into becoming part of Weidmann's defense.

Weidmann had been writing to his parents regularly since his arrest, while stipulating that he would only keep communicating with them if they promised never to come see him. Because they'd broken the agreement he refused to see them.

Weidmann's parents had a note sent to their son begging him to retain Floriot as his attorney and expressing doubts about his own choice of Renée Jardin. At Floriot's urging they portrayed Jardin as a publicity hound lacking the experience necessary for the task at hand. Weidmann refused their advice.

The Weidmanns stayed as Floriot's guests in his Paris home for two nights. He arranged for them to give interviews to the press and be photographed by his side.

Weidmann finally allowed his mother to see him on December 30. They talked in Berry's chambers, with an interpreter translating for the lawyers and officers present. Denied a razor as well as the attentions of a barber, he explained that he was ashamed by his several days of facial hair. In the end he still refused to retain Floriot, but he spoke sweetly to his mother throughout the meeting. A few days later he would write her a reconciliatory letter, telling her, "I'll be happy when all of this is over. I'm not scared."

26

A SMALL AND SINISTER EUROPEAN ENTANGLEMENT

Flanner had followed the news of the de Koven disappearance that past summer but hadn't found the unsolved case meaty enough to mention to her readers. Now with Weidmann's arrest and confession she had her opening.

"I almost cabled to ask if you wanted a whole extra crime piece from me on the Jean de Koven (American girl) murder," she wrote to White just before Christmas. "Decided you wouldn't. It's a very specially bloody affair: six bodies so far, greatest mass murder in France since Landru, whose cell the German murderer is now occupying… There are many picturesque strange angles: for a connoisseur, one of the best crimes in the past ten years. Her being an American adds interest here, of course, for us all. I know a girl she knew here. She was a simple, trusting, gabby chaste little American. What an awful thing to go out to tea with a new foreign beau and have him strangle you. He murdered five other people in one month thereafter. A monster, as the French say."

Before White could reply Flanner outlined the Weidmann Affair in a couple of paragraphs of a Paris Letter that ran on the first day of 1938. She ghoulishly compared the mass of onlookers who'd gone out to watch Weidmann leading officers to the dead bodies at La Voulzie to the contemporaneous crowds of "feverish children and their freezing parents" gazing in wonder at the Galeries Lafayette's beloved Christmas displays of mechanical toys and dolls. Both events had caused blocks-long queues requiring police barricades to control. Sketching out Weidmann's background, Flanner noted that he'd worked as a guide and interpreter at the Expo, "until assassinations had taken too much of his time." She closed by focusing on his American victim. "According to those who knew her, Miss de Koven was friendly, confidential, and talkative. Europeans have often criticized Americans for being those things. Rarely, thank heaven, are we killed for them—plus our traveller's checks."

Magistrate Berry had counseled everyone involved with the case to exercise caution when speaking with the press, as he rightly assumed that the Nazis would be watching the proceedings closely. His warning had little effect. French papers and magazines filled with questions and speculation about Weidmann's motives. How had he gotten into France? Was he a madman acting alone, or a trained assassin sent by the Gestapo to destabilize France? Was he a spy whose victims had important secrets? Had he been brainwashed? Was he somehow connected to the Cagoule terrorist cell? If he killed people only for financial gain, why did he ask for such a small ransom amount for de Koven, and why did he pursue victims that he should have known would be traveling with so little cash? The novelist Colette, who wrote about Weidmann's arrest in *Le Journal*, found something fetishistic about his collection of women's shoes and desire to wear the jewelry and other personal effects of his victims. She suggested a sexual angle, with Weidmann, Blanc, and Million "sharing" Tricot and perhaps also the women they killed, which rather than provoking jealousy only solidified their existing homosexual bond.

Flanner in that first Paris Letter on Weidmann mentioned that some of the French reporters were prodding their own readers to consider the accused as the most glaring example of something inherently evil in the German character, to wonder if, as one of them put it, the country's cultural and political environment "has not influenced the Rhineland's sons, seduced by the notion of force, and without the antidote of human idealism." The French press freely called Weidmann a "murderer," "monster," and "assassin" in print. At that time no libel law pressured French journalists to add "alleged" before any of those descriptors when writing about someone accused but not yet convicted of murder.

Flanner restrained herself from adding one more theory to the mix. "I tried to be simple as all get out, about one of the most complicated queer mass murders that ever took place here," she told McKelway after filing the piece. "Funny how mass murders become at once strange, nearly inexplicable; the murdering of one person we all understand though have lacked the courage to compass. When I think of the individuals I really longed to see out of life, I'm relieved I was too timid, then, to tend to them; the last person I really wish were under sod is now in Haiti, the fool, as three thousand whites were massacred this winter, she'll return (second class ticket) in style and safety—and of course massacre is awful. Sometimes individuals seem nearly worse."

Only two weeks after Weidmann's arrest, Flanner decided that the case merited its own standalone piece, and that, like her French colleagues, she could use his story as a way to talk about larger issues.

White encouraged her to work quickly to get ahead of potential competitors. "We hope you will hop to that so we can print it before the big publicity begins again here. It seems to us that the lead should simply introduce Miss de Koven, saying she came to Paris, then one day, etc. and so on. I know you will do a topnotch story on that and hope you will have time to do it immediately."

When she filed, she told White she barely had the strength left to type, since she'd finished in four days a piece "which I'd ordinarily take a whole year or season to (if you'd let me). I hope you like [it]. I've certainly liked doing it." Her writing appeared under the rubric of Annals of Crime, a relatively recent *New Yorker* addition dreamed up by McKelway to be deployed whenever a contributor had a crime-related story deemed worthy of sustained investigation. Titled "American in Paris" and signed as Janet Flanner, it spread across eight pages of the magazine's midsection.

In revisiting the Weidmann case, Flanner now offered the tale's American, French, and German protagonists as representatives of their respective national characters.

> The late Jean De Koven was an average American tourist in Paris but for two exceptions. She never set foot in the Opéra, and she was murdered. In the first four July days of her initial visit to the capital of France, her routine had been classic: she had settled in a quaint little Left Bank hotel near the Place Saint-Germain-des-Prés, she had seen the boulevards by night, had attended the Folies-Bergère, admired the Louvre, and bought a ticket, ironically enough, for Dukas's "Ariadne and Bluebeard" [based on the folktale of the murderous nobleman]. But when the opera's red-and-gold curtain rose, her seat was

> empty—for she was dead and probably already buried under the front porch of a cottage in Saint-Cloud.

To Flanner, de Koven's typically American "weakness" for "sociability with strangers" had sealed her fate. Weidmann, with all his talk of Wagner and great books and his villa near Napoleon and Josephine's chateau, had fed into her overly romanticized, tourist's version of Europe. And maybe in this regard Flanner saw something of her younger, dreamier self. In an earlier time might she, too, have fallen for Siegfried Hunter's offer to show her *la Grande Paris* that most Americans missed seeing?

Weidmann was the ultimate Aryan,

> an exceptionally handsome male in the medieval manner; his features are those of an etching by Holbein of some German *moyen-age* merchant, with an alert, inquiring, open, hungry eye, a well-cartilaged nose terminating in a cold, curious ball like that on the end of a thermometer, and a large, amply delineated classical mouth with adequate lips. The hair rolls free from the forehead in untidy artistic confusion. He looks and acts like a man who, if he hadn't had in his makeup the criminal compartment, would have made a good Gothic citizen.

And she offered Weidmann's crew—Million, Tricot, and Blanc (the "bourgeois boob")—as representative of the French national character for being so easily muscled into passivity by their demented German overlords. In her final summation she suggested:

> Only a typical Frenchman like Million, accustomed to the old apprentice system and his country's gerontocratic

> policy, by which the young always work (at low pay) for their elders, would have participated in such a poor proposition as the Weidmann murders. Only a typical postwar German like Weidmann, unfamiliar with the value of money as the rest of the freer world knows it, would have killed so many people for so little. And only a typical American, like poor Miss De Koven, would have been so sociable, so confidential, or could have seemed so rich. The De Koven case was a small and sinister European entanglement.

Flanner had no doubt that the case would end in Weidmann's execution, for "the French are still a rational-minded race and their law courts show it." They wouldn't be fooled by any "legal nonsense."

McKelway, who edited "American in Paris," commended Flanner on a "swell piece," one that "everybody liked very much indeed... Your copy has been simply splendid lately and both Ross and myself thought [it] was exceptionally clean."

27

I AM THE WOUND AND THE KNIFE

Weidmann's cellmate Petit-Jean was released early in 1938. Weidmann had gotten to enjoy his company for only two weeks. He said that he was happy for Petit-Jean's mother to have him back home but was sad to see him go. Petit-Jean was, to Weidmann, an authentic *parigot*, as native Parisians liked to call themselves, a touch "perverted," and, using the English expression, "a real happy-go-lucky guy." He'd sung old café songs in their cell.

Following Jardin's advice that he do something to occupy his mind, Weidmann started keeping a journal in a red notebook she'd given him. He should tell the story of his life, she suggested, adding that it might help her with her defense.

He scribbled in the notebook with an almost religious fervor. He wrote that he wanted to "leave a faithful portrait of himself," for "until now no one has known me" and that those who said "he is the worst of mankind" were as wrong as those "who said the opposite." He hoped the notebook could be sold to get him enough money to "be better treated." He would speak to a "Madame X" to arrange the sale for a "fabulous sum." (No evidence suggests the existence of such a woman.)

He'd taken to meditating and to talking with God. He read and reread the Bible and *The Imitation of Christ*. Jardin, unnerved by his sudden fervor, tried to arrange for him to be visited by the bishop of Versailles, but Weidmann refused to see any clergymen. He penned tender letters to his mother in which he turned her into the Virgin Mary. Eventually he consented to give confession to the prison chaplain, afterward telling Jardin, "I've cleaned my soul just as I clean my cell, it wasn't so hard."

At the same time Weidmann embraced darker reading material. He asked for anything by Nietzsche and for Baudelaire's *Les Fleurs du mal*. He decided the poet's cursed life mirrored his own, and that certain of Baudelaire's passages had been written just for him. He repeated Baudelaire's words to himself over and over like a mantra: "I am the wound and the knife. The victim and the executioner." He saw himself as a great writer, a misunderstood exile worthy of public embrace. Like Baudelaire, he said, he was a "romantic revolutionary." They shared the same "horror," the same "isolation," the same "black melancholy."

"I only become myself when there's a revolver in my hand," he wrote. "The revolver-God that I lovingly caress in my pocket." He complained of having a "ball" stuck inside his head and called the women who sent him letters "crazy." (From Jardin he'd learned he was receiving fan mail, including marriage proposals.) Being allowed to shave only once a week and shower twice a month he described as barbaric. He would "teach the warden a lesson he'll never forget. All of France will laugh at him. But there's no rush. It can wait until after the trial."

He told Jardin that he now wanted to represent himself, alone against his judgers like Christ. Jardin advised him that in France defendants were barred from appearing in court without counsel. She remarked to a colleague that her client already seemed to be living "in the shadow of death." And yet he was an ideally behaved prisoner. He passed hours each day working alongside other inmates making paper fans and party favors.

Saint-Pierre's warden let him keep two stray cats in his cell as reward for this conduct, one black and the other gray. Weidmann fed them milk purchased from the prison canteen. He was occasionally allowed to walk in the prison's small triangular yard, which was dotted with sycamore trees.

As Jardin observed Weidmann, she decided that delusion, frustration, and shame were the chief motivators behind his crimes. In his mind he'd built himself up into a god and felt he deserved to live as one. That fantasy butted up against the brutal forces of reality, and it resulted in a furious and insatiable raging. The fates had given him great physical gifts and great appetites, a great "passion for living," she surmised, and yet "his physical strength, his intelligence, his good manners and his pleasant looks had brought him nothing." Angry and impulsive after his release from Preungesheim Prison, he'd performed the only acts that made him feel "the power and authority of a boss." He felt "the despotism of the gang leader with nothing but contempt for his crew," she wrote. He felt "the power of the finger on the trigger."

28

THE LAST MIDDLE-WESTERNER

Flanner spent much of early 1938 struggling with sciatica, embarrassed about regular visits to the osteopath, and having to wear woolen socks and a travel blanket to keep her legs warm at the opera. She told White she was prepared to welcome the aging process but only when she was "older"—for now, at forty-five, she had "no patience" for it.

Despite her ailment, which she thought was exacerbated by the cold, she honored her commitment to write the "Ski Letter" she'd promised the magazine, an attempt to offer readers a bit of escapism through a vicarious trip to a stylish European resort. She traveled to Megève in the French Alps, wearing two fur coats and so many layers underneath that she could hardly squeeze through doorways. There she witnessed a strange celestial event that she took as an omen. After a heavy hailstorm, with much thunder and lightning, the sky glowed so red that the local firefighters went out to hunt for the source of the blaze, the only logical explanation for such a sight, but found none. "The heavens are upset," she wrote White, "man's fate not clear."

After Megève she was able to unwind in Cap d'Antibes with James and Helen Thurber, with a stocked wine cellar, a kitchen overseen by one of the Riviera's finest cooks, and a long garden stuffed with flowering mimosa that wound down to the sea. They had "a grand time." She told McKelway that she and James Thurber had a long and "bitter discussion [about] whether Burns or Wordsworth is the better poet. As we both think they're lousy I don't know why the talk ever started."

From there she went to Orgeval. With Noël Murphy she listened to crowds in Vienna chanting "Heil Hitler" as the radio reported on German troops crossing into Austria. After hearing Hitler's speech, she said she couldn't fathom how his throat could stand all that screaming.

Because the Austrian annexation had happened after sundown in France on a Friday, the evening newspapers hadn't caught the news as quickly as the radio had, an example for Flanner of print journalism's shortcomings. Her outlook hadn't been helped by recently learning that most of Paris's eighteen major dailies were failing financially, with some on the brink of bankruptcy just when Parisians most needed to stay current.

"The only noise in the war-laden air was that of static and not of guns, and for the first time the radio, as a vital news purveyor, completely put the newspapers on the back-number shelf," she wrote in her Paris Letter afterward. "French radio listeners, with heavy hearts and often with tears of excitement for tragedies remembered or new ones to come, knew that another Hitlerian *fait accompli* had settled into its permanent historical place." He'd remade the map of Europe over a single weekend, writing a change in "ink which would once have had to be written over a period of years and in blood." The popular prediction among the French was that he would next take over Czechoslovakia "without waiting for the democracies to vote to arm to stop him." She relayed hearing "lots of French talk...of bitter admiration for the man who has been able to put his country where France once was—at the head of the continent of Europe. A weekend of dictatorship has undone a century of democracy." To the French "at the moment democracy looks damnably *démodé*, and even Europe's new map will, they suppose, soon be out of style."

Flanner was not without her own "bitter admiration" for Hitler. Even as he terrified her, she remained enthralled by him. "I laugh when I think how nobody wanted to admit he was clever, a great diplomat, permanent and of vast importance when I wrote my Profile," she told R. A. Hague. "Dorothy Thompson said he was a man without a future. I wish to God that was true. We are all a little worried but not much. Peace is the price of giving him anything on earth he wants—and he wants the earth." In another letter to Hague she wrote, "I guess I'm straddle minded: I'm anti-socialist and pro-Blum; I'm anti-Nazi and think Hitler the most interesting strange man in Europe. He interests me more than one million Chamberlains."

She went to Paris just after the Anschluss and saw little public reaction to the news. It was as if the French were pretending they no longer formed part of the European community, she said. After learning of the complete annexation of a sovereign nation they'd gone to bed "as if nothing had happened," though she admitted that from the French perspective nothing *had* happened, "since war hadn't happened. That is the only thing that counts here." She was certain they wouldn't be stirred to combat even if Hitler did take Czechoslovakia—or "anyhow, not unless England fights first." In her estimation, France was still so bitterly divided that it was just as likely its citizens would wage war among themselves as they would go off to fight the Germans.

In a note to herself, she wrote, "I think the country [France] will go Fascist in some form, but they must have one man to follow;

maybe he isn't even born yet...*People remain pilgrims*; they love to love, they yearn to follow, to believe, to put trust in. It's a human necessity which democracy, ironically, has deprived them of, in seeking to serve everyone." To Hague she wrote that the French looked to be "in a fine mess...everyone in a funk, knowing Fascism could win and work better [than] ever now."

She wondered, in the pages of *The New Yorker*, if all that was left to do in the wake of Hitler's easy Austrian victory was to chronicle the steady decay of European democracy. Britain and France remained functioning democracies—"that's proved by their citizenry's now lambasting the government, jeering its leaders, cheering fallen figures formerly lampooned, mixing idealism, realism, and revenge, and disagreeing with each, all, and themselves, and at the top of their lungs, on Hyde Park soapboxes or in French boulevard cafés"—but when it came to "diplomatic prestige" they'd "just taken a sickening wallop." These were two of the most powerful empires the world had ever known, and yet in the face of authoritarian power they flailed about with the "precious inefficiency that comes from men's having enough liberty to make money, to make gardens, to make a million different odd things—even to make, if they choose, fools or rich rogues of themselves, rather than obediently making machines, military motions, and sacrifices." They were in "no position to compete suddenly with totalitarian competence."

To Flanner no one in France had stood up to offer a logical path forward. The minister of foreign affairs was stalling for time, failing to announce any new policy in reaction to Hitler's maneuverings, which seemed "just as well. Until France gets her insides fixed up, her outsides won't look right no matter what a member of the family says." While stressing that she remained an "impersonal observer," she offered, in a Letter that May, a Cassandra-like statement about the inability of France's government and citizens to prepare for the worst while so distracted by internal strife. "It's melancholy to see how quickly humanity, if left free after its initial success, deserts the early, earnest union that gave its cause strength and squabbles itself to bits."

The beliefs and passions of millions had paled against the whims of a well-placed few, as if they were all still living in the age of kings and emperors. "Everything that is happening in Europe now is happening according to the characters, rather than the politics, of a few leading men. What is taking place here is psychology, not history. History will come later."

She returned to Murphy's farmhouse for what would be an unusually icy spring, threatening crops around France. On Orgeval's prized strawberry bushes she saw not "two buds to a plant."

The American novelist Glenway Westcott recalled a conversation with Flanner at the farmhouse from that time of "narrow hopes and great general dread":

> And now little by little, in allusions amid what we had to say about politics, we were bidding each other an extraordinarily fond and significant kind of farewell. "When are you sailing?" she asked, and I told her. "You know, you're quite right not to stay here," she said. "No one is going to be able to write fiction in France from now on. Do you think you will be able to, even at home, when the war gets going? Oh, I wish I could go home with you. How I envy you, in a way."

But she corrected herself. She did not envy me, she said; it was only her sentimentality and imagination. To stay in France as long as it was humanly possible was her fate. Because it was fate of course she herself did not altogether understand why it was. "But I shall be the last to leave. The last Middle-Westerner on this peninsula of Europe, of Eurasia."

29

HE HAS ABNORMALITIES

That spring of 1938 the court sent in three alienists, or doctors of psychology, to assess Weidmann. Drs. Claude, Génil-Perrin, and Truelle examined him for signs of sexual deviance, careful to look for an inflammation of the testicles, which French scientists at the time believed could cause criminal madness. But aside from balanitis, a minor inflammation of the glans of the penis, his genitals were deemed healthy. He bore no signs of sexually transmitted infection. After some questioning about his sexual history the doctors declared Weidmann "sexually normal." He next underwent an intense physiognomy exam, so that the doctors could see if his head shape and facial features predisposed him to a criminal mentality. They also examined his handwriting.

The three doctors filed a vexing twenty-five-page report. In the words of Dr. Claude, in strictly medical terms they had discovered nothing to permit them to declare Weidmann insane, and yet "some things are beyond the scope of medical detection...Weidmann is not like other men. He has abnormalities."

Scavengers meanwhile continued to pour into La Voulzie to forage for macabre souvenirs during gaps in police surveillance. One local started offering clandestine tours, charging admission. The widow Braux, the villa's owner, accused police officers of using wood from the property's walls to build outdoor fires to heat themselves during their watches. She was struggling financially as she couldn't rent the place. A prospective buyer offered her the very low sum of 125,000 francs for the property, which she accepted reluctantly. But then the Saint-Cloud city council vetoed the transaction when the buyer revealed that he wanted to turn the house into a crime museum.

While the defense and prosecution developed their cases, the French Ministry of Foreign Affairs had its own work to do in preparing for the still unscheduled trial. Ministry officials learned that a French citizen, driven by "patriotism," in his words, had written the court begging them not to focus on Weidmann's German identity during the proceedings, lest this draw ire from France's neighbor and lead to "German troops occupying Versailles." This was only a more extreme version of the ministry's own concerns about the political fallout of putting a German on trial for murder, especially given that two of his victims were Jewish and one of them, Frommer, had also served prison time for his vociferous anti-Nazism.

Saint-Pierre's guards were put on high alert after guards at another French prison learned that one of their own inmates had received a rambling letter from Weidmann in which Weidmann promised to come to see his friend soon "in person." The Saint-Pierre warden took that wording seriously, given that Weidmann had earlier baited him and some guards with talk of accomplices coming to save him. Maybe the Germans were planning to send agents to storm the prison so he could escape? The warden dispatched a larger rotation of armed guards to watch Weidmann's cell, which at nights had previously been guarded only by two unarmed men.

Meanwhile French officials were tending a delicate relationship with their American counterparts. Members of the de Koven family were demanding to come testify. They felt it vital to establish publicly that Jean's "honor had remained intact" before her murder. They'd already spent so much of their meager resources sending Jean's brother Henry to Paris after her disappearance. The family requested that the French state cover full travel and lodging for whenever the trial was set. They were refused.

30

ITSY-BITSY ANTI-NAZI ME

Ever since learning in January 1938 that her sister Hildegarde was pregnant for the first time at nearly forty, Flanner had been "frantic" with worry. Late in that spring she received terrible news. "Hildegarde, my younger sister, lost her baby son a few moments after he was born," she wrote to Katharine White. "He had long eyelashes, the doctor said, and was strong and well but he had fought too hard for his immature inexperienced heart to stand; she had been let lie in labor 40 hours, the accoucheur refused to call in a surgeon for a Caesarian until it was too late. I am heartbroken, so grieved—and angry—that maybe I've told you before, I can't remember, it occupies my thoughts so. Hildegarde is 39, her first child, her last."

Outside the Hotel Bonaparte, the world was falling apart. Inside she found order in the steady drum of the typewriter. The pages, the paragraphs, the sentences. She turned some notes on a recent trip to Glasgow ("the ugliest city in the whole Empire, I'm told") and London at the start of the summer into a dazzling Letter, in which she took comfort in the continuity of the season's rituals of "planting the penny hedge at Whitby, the midsummer bonfires in Cornwall, swan-upping on the Thames...horse, livestock, and flower shows...archery tournaments, Wimbledon...polo, yachting, rowing, and racing events... rural music festivals."

In Letters that June she repeated her by-now-common refrain about how bizarre it felt to live as if one were consciously marching in slow motion toward death without being able to do anything about it. "The European history being made right now is going to make queer reading someday. Indeed, it looks strange to some of us already." She proposed that because Hitler stood so far beyond the pale of what a normal leader looked like, no one was qualified to understand what he wanted in exchange for peace, nor what might spark him toward waging a full war. His "unpredictable mental processes and moves" were "the great and dangerous novelty in Europe today...being unlike anything that the chancelleries have for centuries considered part of the game." And because his "mind is a type that Europe is unfamiliar with, for too long Europe complacently stated that Hitler had no mind at all. Europe is now having a chance to become familiar with it at a moment which, the democracies hope, is not too late."

She passed much of July in Cannes ghostwriting the American publicist and hostess Elsa Maxwell's biography of the socialite Barbara Hutton, which ran in three issues of *Cosmopolitan*. It paid three thousand dollars, a sum so big "I dare not turn it down," as she told White, adding that she hoped to keep the job secret, otherwise "I shall die of embarrassment...My first step toward the bordello." At least collaborating with Maxwell had been fun. She had charm she could "turn on like a fireman's hose," said Flanner. (Maxwell apparently held no grudge from when Flanner had gently mocked her in a 1933 *New Yorker* profile, telling Flanner that her friends had decided she'd "gotten off cheap.") Working "in relays with stenographers, secretaries, chauffeurs, a lot of hooey if you ask me," the two of them banged out thirty thousand words in eight days, with Flanner saying that Maxwell, who worked "like a badger (when she isn't up playing roulette till 5am)," did most of the writing, while she was just "a leech to suck it out of her." Flanner promised White that as soon as she deposited her fee she would go "burn a candle in some church for my little soul to be washed all itsy-bitsy clean again. I couldn't write anything decent which anybody on earth would pay me that much for."

Her body still screaming with pain, she went to see her doctor as soon as she got back to Paris. When he diagnosed a kidney stone she cheered up, since now she could ascribe her past months of depression to a physical rather than mental ailment. "Seventeen years of dry white wine put it there," she told White of her stone. "I'm glad to know it's urinal not cerebral trouble that's the cause." She could also see the logical solution to her problem, which was to change her habits. Telling White she'd switched to a regimen of mostly white meat, "washed down with cider only," which she was sure would "melt" the stone by "some strange magic," she reported feeling much better, and that she wouldn't need to have an operation "IF, the cider works." The alcoholic McKelway, who'd heard that Flanner had improved after dropping wine and hard alcohol, told her, "I am peculiarly able to understand. I also have given up cocktails and wine for a while and I am rather irritated to find that I feel much better."

Flanner couldn't rest. She'd already set aside August for a reporting trip through Central Europe, during which she'd promised to deliver four Letters from four locations in four weeks, or as she'd outlined her plans: "Bayreuth, Prague, Vienna, Buda and I hope I don't help lead a war." She'd proposed, too, in all seriousness, Oslo and the North Pole for the following summer. "Life is always ironic," she told Hague. "Traveling, which I've adored and was too poor to do for years, is more tiring when it's in connection with a job—which pays one's way."

She soon nixed going to Prague, explaining that while she didn't expect any "trouble" there, it would "be the nastiest place to be caught in" if war broke out. "Vienna is next nasty but there is a long route out through the south that offers an exit." She advised the magazine of her contact at the American Consulate in Berlin, in case "anything happens and you need a pilot to find itsy-bitsy anti-nazi me." She anticipated that reporting from Germany would be difficult. "You know that every crack correspondent of Europe is there, sniffing, tracking, collecting and has been there for weeks, that they have built-up relationships, built-up sources of news...I'm a little terrified of the job... nearly decided it was too much." She took comfort in having Noël Murphy to "ford me around and keep me company, no joke on a long lonesome trip."

Before she left she had the chance to enjoy a few perfect evenings in Paris. A small burst of heat made everyone forget the lousy summer, and it brought out the Genêt of old in an especially lyrical Letter.

> Only in the cool, opaque dusk has Paris, after its heated noons, been coming to life again. Then every neighborhood has become its own small village. The restaurants with terraces, big or small, have swarmed with diners; in the sidewalk cafés, beneath awnings and parasols, *garcons* have sweltered till midnight over trayloads of *bocks* and *café liégeois*; at the humble corner bars, the *patron* and the habitués have simply moved their chairs, beer, and radio out into the street and made a comfortable night of it. The younger generation...has been making its particular kind

> of hay while the sun shone. It has flocked to Seine bathhouses...the Seine water in which the swimmers bathe is filtered; male and female beauties loll there every morning; a cabin, towel, and tips come to less than thirty centimes; an inexpensive meal is served at water level.

Still, she had to note that "harvest time has often been war time in Europe...everyone here is keeping an eye on the newspapers."

31

A TOUR OF THE CAVERNE DES BRIGANDS

On a sunny June 16, 1938, Weidmann and Million were taken from their respective cells in Saint-Pierre to offer their conflicting accounts of the murder of Jeanine Keller at the Caverne des Brigands. Twenty-six court officials and two dozen journalists joined them. Whether this group included Flanner is unknown; she mentioned the event briefly in one of her Letters.

Unlike Weidmann's previous trip back to La Voulzie, this time three hundred uniformed officers were there to keep onlookers well back from the action. And yet, many must have passed through the cordon, with permission or not. Pictures from the day are jammed with men and women in civilian clothes. In one, a boy of about thirteen or fourteen can be seen halfway down the entrance to the cave.

The two killers were barred from having any direct contact with each other. They traded glares. Weidmann was asked to re-create their crime. Renée Jardin had brought along her housekeeper to stand in for Jeanine Keller. Weidmann led them to where they'd dumped the shovel used to bury her. Inspection would later reveal that it bore his and Million's fingerprints.

As Million rose to offer his version, Weidmann was left to sit by himself on a rock out of Million's sight line so as not to influence his actions. A few police stood near Weidmann, and yet a French journalist got close enough to ask him a few questions. Weidmann answered them all with mystic riddles. The only thing he revealed of substance was that he was writing his memoirs to make some money to send to his parents. During another quiet moment, Jardin asked him what he was thinking about. "*Meine Mutter*," he answered. He felt bad for making her suffer, he told her. The lawyer asked was she a Catholic, to which he answered yes. Jardin advised him to ease her pain by admitting his remorse, to not die "among the wicked." He repeated that he had no regrets about his crimes, repeating the words of his earlier confession, that he "didn't know" his victims and that they "didn't suffer."

Entrepreneurs among the assembled crowd sold handmade postcards of Weidmann. One of Weidmann's lawyers, Raoult, bought one and took it around to be signed by the prosecuting attorney, some police officers, and finally by the two men accused of murder.

32

HISTORY LOOKS QUEER WHEN YOU'RE STANDING CLOSE TO IT

Flanner set out with Murphy for Bayreuth in early August. Despite having been a regular at its annual music festival, Flanner had never done a Letter from the town. She'd suggested to her editors that it would be "the prize potato for us" that year, as they were putting on a massive Wagner celebration to mark the 125th anniversary of his birth. Flanner assumed it would be their last chance to visit the festival for some time. Perhaps in the rarified environs of Bayreuth she would find some sliver of German logic and civility, some tiny signal to tell her that this might all end with Hitler's being toppled.

She and Murphy were among only a handful of foreigners in attendance. The festival ran Wagner's *Ring* cycle, along with *Tristan* and *Parsifal*, the last featuring the famed French soprano Germaine Lubin, on loan from the Paris Opera. Flanner enjoyed herself. She filed a quizzical Letter from Bayreuth that, while mentioning the new Nazi party headquarters in the town and some of the mild propaganda efforts meant to stir German youth, read on the whole as a straight report on the festival's satisfying musical selections and performers.

"Indeed, it really was lovely Wagner." If she had concerns about how her publicly taking pleasure in the event made her complicit with the Nazi regime, she never voiced them, privately or in print.

White told Ross she thought Flanner's Letter from Bayreuth was "absolutely first rate...She helps keep the tone of the magazine as much as any single person."

Flanner and Murphy went on to Salzburg for more music. Flanner told Hague she wanted to describe the Salzburg festival's "new Nazi season," as "the comparison with the past seasons should be interesting." No foreigners were invited to perform, nor would the music be conducted by the festival's two great stalwarts, Arturo Toscanini and Bruno Walter, who'd been replaced by an inferior "Nazi newcomer," in Flanner's words. In her Letter from Salzburg she remarked that the Viennese Symphony was "functioning here intact for the last time. Its racial purge will occur after its seasonal utility is over, when its best fiddler and cellist, along with a dozen other non-Aryans, apparently all in the strings, will be dismissed." She drew attention to the informal American and the British boycott of Austrian resort towns. She wrote of how some of the Salzburg peasants she'd met had struck her as terrified of trading in any kind of talk related to war, convincing themselves there would be none because this was what Hitler had promised them.

Only once she got to Vienna did she seek to fully address the Nazi persecution of Jews in print. Disgusted by what she saw there, she and Murphy left quickly to cross into Hungary—noting the heavy concrete roadblocks and barbed wire demarking the Czechoslovakian border to the east as they passed—so she could cable her report free of the Nazi censors. She said later that she didn't want to appear paranoid, but that she couldn't ignore what she'd seen in the Austrian capital post-Anschluss. Within hours of getting to Budapest she was sending off a hastily written piece.

Running in *The New Yorker* in mid-September, her Letter from Vienna focused largely on Goebbels's "Eternal Jew" exhibition, just launched in the city after showing in Munich. Posters advertising the event showed a bearded Jew in village garb clutching a palmful of gold with one hand and brandishing a whip and a map marked with a Soviet hammer-and-sickle with the other. These were displayed on "billboard pillars along with ads for American movies, for [the exhibit] is considered one of the summer attractions." In the cavernous Nordwestbahnhalle, crowds hissed at pictures of "degenerates" such as Albert Einstein, Charlie Chaplin (not actually Jewish), and Felix Mendelssohn. The Nazis had designed the exhibit as if it were a crass sales tool, wrote Flanner, making use of "prints, photographs, models, electric signs, graphs, fine typography, and sales talks…not to make consumers buy a product but boycott a race." The displays aimed to mark Jews as the world's secret puppet masters, communist and hypercapitalist at once. Flanner looked closely at some among the thousands of "Austrian Christians" touring the crowded rooms alongside her. "On their faces is a strange expression which pagan faces doubtless wore when watching exhibitions at which Christians were thrown to the lions."

Moving beyond the exhibit to the streets of Vienna, she wrote of stores marked "Aryan Business," decorated with swastikas. While Jewish doctors and lawyers had been barred from practicing, Jewish-owned stores remained open. "We bought non-Aryan stockings in the humble Mariahilf Jewish wholesale district and a non-Aryan washrag in the smart retail Kartnerstrasse." She detected among the Viennese a similar sense of defeatism and nihilism that she'd seen among the French. No matter their individual thoughts about Hitler, they seemed resigned to the idea that "nothing can stop him now." In the same Letter she tried to squeeze in some lighter material, but instead of balancing the piece it rendered it tonally bizarre. "Whipped cream and pastries still flourish in Viennese coffeehouses," she remarked in between documenting the persecution of Jews and making dire Hitler-related predictions. "Sacher's is less well run than when old Frau Sacher made it hum. The famous Kipferl crescent rolls are still white but will probably be an adulterated gray." Vienna had left her bewildered. She closed her Letter: "No one seems to know what will provoke the next great war. This ignorance today is Central Europe's only bliss."

In Budapest Flanner and Murphy checked into the Hotel Ritz. All the affordable rooms were already booked for a Eucharist Congress, she explained to McKelway, feeling guilty about enjoying such luxury on her expense account. "This city is like a slightly South European Berlin," she told him. "It's gayer here, people less stodgy, music in cafes really divine, such musical invention…shops very smart, people lively, and oriental looking." Here again she found the people resigned to a dark future. "The farther east one goes in Europe, the farther east one finds the people fatalistically suppose Hitler will go. In Hungary, for instance, the peasants don't think he'll stop with Czechoslovakia. They think the Führer will push on to Istanbul." Her writing from those weeks, with all its flightiness and ambivalence and paranoia, captured what it must have felt like to be living through that moment, filled with chaos and lies, especially when one's job was to find order and truth.

"History looks queer when you're standing close to it," she wrote from Budapest, "watching where it is coming from and how it's being made."

White judged Flanner's whole series of Central European Letters "superb" and "timely in a ghastly sort of way." She singled out the Vienna Letter as "the best thing I've read in political reporting and general atmosphere on Vienna since the Anschluss" and told Flanner that Ross had said to tell her he agreed. White meanwhile suggested to Ross that "it might repay us to move Janet out of Paris and London oftener."

McKelway wrote her, too. "Honestly, Janet, we're all proud of what you're doing these days and though you may not hear from us about it much we do appreciate it, and we understand the difficulties, too." About her writing on Budapest, he told her "it was a fine letter and we are filing it somewhere for some future historian who may someday write a book about this magazine and its people."

"That was a hard trip into Central Europe," Flanner wrote back to McKelway a few days later. "The psychic voyage into what seemed such a horrible possible new planet of war—it was that which took the strength out of me. Not that I really felt war was imminent as it became only a little later; I was not nearly that prophetic; but the weight of hate was something nearly audible, like any big cart or tumbril driving up closer and closer on a road." She made a similar point to White, describing the "trek" as "hard, physically and mentally, since the mileage was as great as my constant worry about eliminating everything except important portents, provided I could find them, and granted I could couple them on to what truthfully seemed to me to be local facts."

Flanner returned to Paris doubly convinced of the Nazi intent to conquer the world. At the Hotel Bonaparte she was greeted by a letter from Ross. Trying to stick to their usual sardonic tone with an opening joke, he was, under the guise of giving her advice on how to react should she find herself in a conflict zone, also trying to line her up as his war correspondent, flattering her while trying to get her to commit to the future role.

> Speaking of war, and assuming you will be alive to read this, I wish to urge you now that if there's a war or fighting (as there seems to have been today) you are to keep calm. I went through two years of war and had no difficulty in keeping calm most of the time. The civilian population isn't in great danger in a war and one's routine of life isn't more difficult and is changed only by degrees. Don't get panicky, whatever. If there is a war your duty will probably be over there, and your interests. I don't know anyone more competent to write about it. I say this especially after reading your latest letters. They are all of a high degree of excellent. You're one of the best informed people in Europe, and one of its ablest interpreters, undoubtedly.

Flanner had no time for a thoughtful reply. After hearing Hitler's September 26 speech in which he threatened Czechoslovakia with war, challenging the sovereignty of an ally of France and Great Britain, she and Solano gathered up their cash in different currencies (French, British, American), packed a few suitcases, and headed to Orgeval, joining an exodus of cars loaded with belongings, bound for the countryside, coasts, or mountains, or seeking passage further abroad.

The autumn return to school was postponed indefinitely. People were given sandbags to put out fires from any bombing. The American embassy was offering help to its expatriate population in France, distributing food and gas and arranging travel. Two military cruisers were dispatched to Brest on the west coast to ferry Americans home.

Ambassador William C. Bullitt called for all Americans to leave France, but almost all passages on ships were sold out. Flanner and

Solano burned some of their correspondence and buried their jewelry in the yard alongside Murphy's silver. They bought as much fuel as they were allowed, storing it in teakettles and champagne bottles. They bought canned food, matches, and tools. Friends cabled begging them to come home. They'd heard that two and a half million Frenchmen had been mobilized.

"We're all thinking about you a lot these days, and worrying some, as you can imagine," wrote McKelway. "Be careful, won't you? One result of all this may be that if hell breaks loose over there we'll find ourself with a brilliant journalist in New York, which God knows would make <u>us</u> happy."

In her reply Flanner tried to capture the mood in Orgeval: "We were all dazed with fright...It was fear of gas that seemed to horrify us all, I who have been through no war, and the Frenchmen who had been through it and said gas was the worst...It frightened us most in anticipation." She told McKelway of how "the French men were swell; marched off, mildly cursing the Czechs, and got into uniform. Not an ounce of emotion displayed, no tears, no outcry or threats, no street riots, nothing except that thing called a sense of duty. Lots of the clichés one saw coming true, they turned up like verities. I have been as informed by life as I have been worried by death."

On September 30, Neville Chamberlain, Édouard Daladier, Benito Mussolini, and Hitler signed the Munich Agreement, handing the disputed Czechoslovakian Sudetenland to the Germans. Solano and Flanner, sharing the common belief that appeasement meant no war, returned to Paris greatly relieved, alongside millions of others who felt the same. Simone de Beauvoir, for one, wrote of how

> the storm abruptly passed over without having broken, and the Munich Pact was signed; I was delighted, and felt

> not the faintest pang of conscience at my reaction. I felt I had escaped death, now and forever. There was even an element of triumph in my relief. Decidedly, I thought, I was born lucky: no misfortune would ever touch me.

Flanner rushed out to Le Bourget airfield north of Paris, where just over a decade earlier she'd reported on the dramatic nighttime landing that marked the end of Charles Lindbergh's famous solo transatlantic flight from New York's Roosevelt Field. Once again, the airfield was crowded with people—roughly five hundred thousand, and more of them lining the route stretching from the airfield to Paris—who'd come to see another momentous landing. Daladier touched down, returned from Munich. With no illusions about Hitler's true aims, he'd expected to be met by an angry mob, for having abandoned France's obligations to defend its ally. Instead he received a hero's welcome. Flanner saw people weeping at the sight of him, mothers holding up their children to witness the moment. What she nor any other journalist recorded was Daladier's private response to the sight of the joyous crowd on the tarmac. To his top aide he'd whispered: "*Ah, les cons*" (Oh, what idiots).

Flanner reported in an October Letter on that strange stretch of days, when war had "seemed imminent. Now all the French know is that there is peace. In their curious calm, they don't want to know anything else." People had seen that it was possible for "statesmen to think everybody's way out of war." Newspapers sold out as soon as they hit the stands, and in small towns shopkeepers pasted Roosevelt's speech on Munich, translated into French, on their windows so that "passers-by could read, reread, hope, and remember when once the Yanks were coming." She quoted from Léon Blum's hopeful editorial in one of the papers praising Chamberlain and Daladier's work: "War is averted. Man can take up his work again, can again sleep at night, can once more enjoy the beauty of the autumn sun." She closed: "In Paris, nothing is now left of the fear of war except the hooded street lights at night, and the minute blue flames of the curb lanterns to be used during air raids. With danger past, the dimmed streets look very beautiful indeed."

As much as it had rattled her, the experience of living under threat of immediate violence had clarified her thinking. "I would not be able to be a war correspondent," she told McKelway. "All I can write of war would be brief—'I loathe it;' then I would be through. I am like many women I think, a uterine pacifist."

Over the following weeks Flanner chronicled a growing discontent in Paris, as people questioned the logic of the Munich Agreement and weighed its true cost. She told White: "Something has utterly gone out of life here and the people, the high hope of peace has come down to a vague apprehension in which there is no reality because there is no precision except one so great that none dare face it—namely that Hitler will conquer Europe and conquer France. Democracy is no longer new so it is no longer a passionate affair; we all want to use it, not create it...I feel the only respite will come of [Hitler's] dying or being assassinated. It's curious only the Jews and the Germans think they are the Chosen People. I feel different. There is no choice. There is only history."

Talking with Hemingway, who'd come up briefly to Paris from Madrid, did little to ease her anxiety, especially after she'd told him of how much she'd feared a poison gas attack earlier in September. "Hemingway says gas is impracticable and costly. This cheered me till he described, almost with appreciation, the new German bombs, which, having no casing are free for full explosion that actually crumbles a building it strikes and brings up through their throats the intestines of people standing a quarter of a mile away. He's a queer male man; I don't understand war so I don't understand men."

Flanner would also come to question the value of appeasement, though not immediately. "No sooner was the Munich accord made than the critical parliamentary locusts both in Paris and London began nibbling at the peace laurels," she wrote in an October Letter. "The laurels were sad and sparse to begin with—as ragged as an army coming home from the worst war in history. It would have been that kind of war, so it is that kind of peace." Defending Chamberlain and Daladier, she argued that "democracy is not geared to meet crises. To save what remained of the peace of Europe, [they] were forced to act like dictators, indifferent to the constitutions, legislators, and the voters." Reworking the idea she'd voiced earlier to White, she argued that because democracy was an old idea it functioned slowly and deliberately like a "stagecoach," while fascism, born of the twentieth century, could strike with horrible speed. It was a movement that took "its tempo from the airplane." And in this moment of whiplash diplomacy, the fast were exposing the fundamental weakness of the slow.

In the same letter Flanner also warned that, Munich Agreement aside, nothing could undo the fact that the German people were bent on conquest. Unless the French and English readied themselves to match Germany's might "we may see what we still refer to as democracy and liberty slip into mere history." She relayed the common French worry that the labor strife of the previous years had left their country underprepared for war, especially when it came to their air force. The Luftwaffe, on the other hand, was rumored to have huge numbers of modern planes, and German pilots had gained combat experience from missions over Spain. She advised heeding the example of a group called the Union of French Women Decorated by the Legion of Honor, which was recruiting volunteers to shore up France's war preparedness, seeking to fill positions ranging from "*doctoresses*, midwives, and nursemaids down to charwomen, for bomb shelters, and young misses who can ride motorcycles."

After those dark reports she changed tack in a series of November Letters that verged on lighthearted. She extolled Maurice Chevalier's new revue at the Casino and delighted in the Opéra-Comique's marking the centenary of Georges Bizet's birth with a new staging of *Carmen*. This gave her a chance to tell a favorite anecdote: The word "toreador" existed only because Bizet had combined the "torero" and "matador" because he needed a four-syllable word for his marching beat. (Spanish bullfighters still resented being referred to by this neologism.) Such a shift in focus stemmed in part from her relief at the peace, however fleeting, which gave her license to concentrate on things that pleased her. But she was also lacking for political material just then, as diplomatic matters had come to an eerie standstill. She had little in the way of hard news to pass along, and anything she read in the French papers had been heavily censored. The best she could do was to keep making predictions and issue warnings, airing in *The New Yorker* the same concerns she'd made privately to friends. Pointing to the strides Germany had made in rearming while the French were busy fighting among themselves, she saw "reason to suppose that Nazi Germany will be the great engulfing empire of the twenty-first [century]," while all that might be left of the French empire would be "the gift of empty gab."

Busying herself as a way to escape dealing with a frightening reality, Flanner traveled with Murphy to London where Noël was giving a concert. "I hope I do London goodie; I always do hope, I never please me," she told McKelway before she left. "This time, by gad, I'm going to. I feel fine and ready to tweak the lion's tail. Poor appendage.

It's been tweaked so much lately." But her giddiness crashed against the mood of London, as grim and restless as it had been in Paris now that the initial enthusiasm over the Munich Agreement had passed. "When the Premier came home with peace in his pocket," Londoners had felt "lucky rather than secure. Now they don't even feel very lucky...What the public sensibly seeks is action, not talk, and it isn't getting much of either."

What Londoners had to settle for instead were wishful rumors about the enemy's court intrigues: that Hitler had been shot at or fallen deathly ill; that his top lieutenants were trying to kill one another; that Goebbels's wife was set to divorce him. The British public seemed to spend more energy obsessing over the "strange psychology and physiology of the Nazi chiefs, their sublimations, deformities, hospital histories, and phobias," than they ever had about "the degeneracy of [their] own kings." Flanner remarked, too, on how jealous the British had become of Americans, separated from the Nazi threat by an ocean, though it was a jealousy mixed with a desperate longing for rescue. "Never, since our states were founded, has Europe looked toward us with more hope and envy. Ours seems to be the land of the free where men don't have to be brave." She found one bright spot in a cutting-edge production of Shakespeare in modern dress at the Old Vic, "one of the few creative theatres in Europe today," with twenty-four-year-old Alec Guinness as a "sentient, fresh" Hamlet.

Trying to justify her admittedly lackluster London Letters to Hague, she explained that because she hadn't found any other news to report she'd instead tried talking up some of the city's recent cultural events, even though no one there felt especially excited about putting on a new show or exhibit just then. "The truth is politics are the only story afloat in Europe now...So if there's any criticism around the home about the Letter, blame it on Hitler."

She was back in Paris by December, while the German Minister of Foreign Affairs Joachim von Ribbentrop was visiting the French capital, falsely signaling a German desire for diplomatic cooperation by signing a pact alongside his French counterpart. The pact guaranteed the safety of one another's borders and attested to their nations' shared "determination to cooperate in a peaceful spirit on a basis of mutual respect."

Flanner opened the year's final Letter by announcing that Lloyd's of London was "betting 32 to 1 that there will be no war in Europe in 1939." She didn't share the same confidence. Whatever happened, the next twelve months were sure to see Germany expanding while France only grew weaker—"economically, politically, and emotionally." The Munich Agreement had made a mockery of France's historical claims to greatness; the country had revealed itself as "a second-rate power."

W. H. Auden summed up the 1930s as "a low dishonest decade." Flanner looked ahead to its final year with equal disdain. She closed her Letter:

> Not only the visible but the invisible map of the Old World has been altered. The frontiers of what men of good will believed in have been pushed around till nobody knows where they begin or end...Lots of us alive and worrying today will be dead before historians get it all down in black and white for future readers to accept with as little flurry as Gibbon's "Decline and Fall" now arouses. It will be the same sort of story. Until then, we ardently wish you whatever can seem good in the coming *Bonne Année!*

33

THE CELLO

As 1938 drew to a close, Weidmann's trial date had yet to be set. The more Jardin worked on the case, the more keenly she felt her relative lack of experience. Weidmann's parents were still trying to convince their son to replace her with their choice, Floriot. Finally Jardin arranged, with Weidmann's cooperation, to hand over the case to the superstar attorney Vincent de Moro-Giafferi, a colorful Corsican who liked to be addressed simply as Moro. His smooth baritone voice had also earned him a nickname, "the Cello." Jardin would stay on as co-counsel.

Moro, sixty-one, ranked not only as France's most famous defense lawyer but also as one of its leading antifascist crusaders, with a glittering list of accomplishments: the youngest person to ever join the Paris bar when he'd started his career at twenty; a highly decorated veteran of the Great War, wounded at Verdun; elected to the French National Assembly by age thirty. Weidmann was not the first multiple murderer he'd met. He'd gone from a national luminary to an international one while defending Henri "Bluebeard" Landru. It was the first case Moro ever lost, but his performance had been electrifying. Several high-profile clients followed. Other lawyers went to watch Moro's trials, hoping to mimic the unconventional but irrefutable logic and emotional intensity of his arguments, which he made at length without consulting his notes, thanks to a photographic memory. Even his would-be competitor Floriot was a fan, saying that for every word you said Moro had twenty in return. He wore heels to make up for his shortness but was nonetheless an imposing presence in front of the jury with his bulk, big ears, nose, and walrus mustache. Outside of work he enjoyed a comfortable life removed from those of the people he represented, a collector of wine, pipes, Chinese erotica, rare books, and antique weapons. He was said to start each day with a fencing lesson, and in his younger days had dueled several times with swords and once with pistols.

His taking over the defense brought even more attention to Weidmann's case in Germany, where Moro was already a marked man. In 1933, after being barred from defending the Bulgarian Communist (and future leader of Bulgaria) Georgi Dimitrov, who'd been arrested by the Nazis and implicated in the trumped-up Reichstag fire, Moro had launched a well-publicized mock trial in Paris. During those proceedings, which ran in parallel to those in Germany, he'd gone on the offensive, accusing Hermann Goering in absentia of lying and corruption, shouting, "I want the world to hear it: the assassin, the arsonist, the author of the Reichstag crime, it's you, Goering!" A few months after taking on the Weidmann case Moro would also start work on the defense of the young Jewish assassin Herschel Grynszpan, whose killing of the diplomat Ernst vom Rath at the German embassy in Paris that November would be used by the Nazis as the pretext for Kristallnacht. (That case would never go to trial, as the Germans would invade France before it could get underway.)

Moro's involvement complicated public perceptions of the Weidmann Affair. It was harder to frame Weidmann as a rabid Nazi if such a noted antifascist as Moro was willing to work with him. In truth Moro loathed Weidmann, just as he'd loathed Bluebeard Landru before him. Unlike the other lawyers on the defense team, each of whom had in some way been charmed by their client, Moro avoided talking with him directly. Instead, he sent his son to act as messenger. He thought that Weidmann was only playing at his intellectualism and derisively referred to him as "Goethe-Schiller," a play on his literary pretensions.

Moro opposed the death penalty as fiercely as he did fascism. His lone goal in defending such an obviously guilty murderer was to save him from the guillotine while using the trial to further reveal the horridness of Nazi Germany. He would soon come up with his main defense strategy, one as cynical as it was brilliant.

34

NOTHING TO WRITE EXCEPT HATRED FOR ALL

Nineteen thirty-nine opened to the aftermath of a blizzard so cold the Paris pawnshops were ordered to return all overcoats they held in hock to their original owners. Grinning skiers glided along the Champs-Élysées. Paris seemed gripped by a strange energy. Huge crowds escaped from the weather and into the bucolic fantasies of the city's top attraction, Disney's *Snow White*, which met with nightly standing ovations. The cafés had never felt so vibrant. Prices for food and drink had never been so high. People huddled around their radios for hours, often finding that the events that most directly affected their lives had taken place somewhere far away and in a foreign tongue. In the morning a pugnacious speech out of Washington would raise everyone's hopes. By nightfall a conciliatory one from Berlin would terrify through what was left unsaid. "These are queer, mixed times," wrote Flanner.

To her all that mattered were Hitler's words and actions. "Everything else is just a little daily round [of] movies, politics, food, politics, the corner café, and politics," she told McKelway.

In the year's first Paris Letter she offered Napoleon as the ideal candidate to advise the French on handling the Germans just then because, like Hitler, "he, too, planned to carve a map of Europe, to meddle with Africa, boss the Italians, twist the British lion's tail, and bite a piece of the Russian bear." She added that Britain's current government didn't seem up to furnishing another Wellington to defeat the new would-be world conqueror.

In the same Letter, as she chided Europe's democracies for their past blindness, she could just as easily have been describing her own guilt over taking so long to fully wake to the horrors that engulfed her.

> Maybe the only good thing about 1939 is that even if the democracies don't know where they're going, they can now see clearly where they stand. The wishful thinking of the past six years—choosing to believe that Hitler was only funny, that the Nazis were slipping, that their whole setup was a bluff—has, since Munich, given way before undesired reality. [Germany] has been able to afford the costliest war machine of our time...and apparently the only bluff was England's and France's promise to stand by their allies.

She scrambled to adapt as her work brought her to the Ministry of Foreign Affairs on the Quai d'Orsay as often as it once had to the Louvre or the Brasserie Lipp. Nearly all of her Letters from the first months of 1939 open by discussing some kind of military conflict, whether ongoing or potential. Trying to survey the complex and quickly changing landscape while clinging to the Genêt tone yielded tangled sentences. "Since French pessimists aren't ninnies," read one, "the independent sections of the Paris press have contained black suspicions that Germany was bolstering Slovakia's separatists and aiming to neutralize Poland as a means of giving the Rome-Berlin-Axis greater freedom and fuller strength to ask for whatever it was going to ask for next."

While still anxious about sounding too much like a warmonger, on the page she was much angrier. She now openly sympathized with those who argued that appeasement had always been an insufficient stopgap, doomed to fail from the start. In what must have ranked as some of the most dire words yet printed in *The New Yorker*, she wrote, a few weeks into 1939, "No one alive today can know which side's dead men will win the war, if there is one."

She abandoned all hope of Hitler's being an aberration, of his being a madman who held his people hostage and would soon be overthrown or assassinated. She told McKelway that she considered Hitler the purest expression of the desires of a "ferocious" people "out of their century...medieval, with a lust for combat, conquest, capture and seduction," who'd chosen their messiah and were proud of that choice. He meant it when he said that Germany would "fight if needed for what he considers her glory or vital space or virile expression or stuff-and-strut-room or whatever. Unfortunately I think the Germans are finally consolidating around Hitler with a feeling that he will indeed get all he can without war, but has been so successful a leader that if he does ask for war, they should honor his talent by complying...his followers have the purpose of lunatics—so far—I can't help but think they will crack somehow, somewhere, but it may be too late to save the surface of the rest of us."

As her feelings toward Germany calcified, Flanner came closer to taking a public stance against fascism in Spain. She complained in a

January Letter that it had been left to France's "modest artisans and working people" to organize aid efforts to Spain, deducting portions from their factory pay, running charity bazaars and union drives, and passing the hat, while the rich and middle classes did little to help their western neighbors. She championed the American Diana Sheean's efforts to connect French donors with Spanish recipients in need. (She omitted mention of her own connection to the cause, as she'd quietly joined Sheean's committee to raise money and send relief packages to Spanish Republican women and children.) And, unexpectedly for someone who so hated communism, she commended a socialist campaign that had raised enough to send twenty tons of flour to the Spanish border and added that Parisian communists had already sent 150 tons of other foods. "With the middle class of France constantly wailing that, as a species they are being slowly extinguished, like the mammoths, it might be practical for them to note that they are doing nothing to help their kind in nearby Iberian regions."

In private correspondence she tried to distance herself from what she'd written (even while convincing herself of its rightness), as though she'd betrayed her sense of journalistic integrity by drawing attention to the plight of a weakened people. "I sound [in the Letter] as if I'd gone wildly Red," she told McKelway. "God knows I'd like to push Stalin in the Baltic and Adolf after him. But the Right parties and people here don't do anything. They just sit and fuss at the Left's activities without ever admitting they are Right...The Anglo-America committee is Dinah's and we're all on it and I was shanghaied into putting a piece in because the 100,000 franc drive was actually news here."

A few weeks later Flanner wrote to her editors to arrange the year's travel plans around covering whatever places and events they felt were most pressing. She was still willing to report from Nazi Germany, writing only "Germany?" without mentioning any concern apart from the fact that "Mrs. Noel Murphy won't chauffeur me around this summer in her Ford 8 which will be a great drawback to my general methods of getting knowledge. She's redoing her house and broke." Italy, meanwhile, seemed out of the question. "I've not been elaborate in my insults to Italy but I haven't been any too tactful and Jim Thurber wrote a grand nasty anti-dago piccc for which, if I am identified with the magazine, I would come in for a share of blame if I asked for an Italian visa."

She also took the opportunity to remind Ross, via McKelway, that whatever changes the year brought, if a full-scale European war was among them, *The New Yorker* would have to find someone else to cover it.

> I hope it's clear, that despite Ross writing me that one gets used to air raids and long-range guns swatting Paris and has quite a fine time in a war, I shall not enjoy it, I can tell you right now. I mean I shall not stay to be a war correspondent in Paris. I may stay around the edge for a bit because I am ashamed to run too openly, with the millions who can not run at all. But I so bitterly loathe war, I so feel that nothing is worth it and all is lost in it—and jolly well near all will be lost in this next one—that I would have nothing to write except hatred for all, I fear.

In response McKelway suggested an easy assignment writing about the French Riviera. Ross, who'd enjoyed some great runs of luck and misfortune at Monte Carlo's tables in his time, had long been interested in a Genêt Letter from Monaco.

But when the time came to leave for the coast Flanner found herself unwilling to go. She cabled McKelway.

"Would you prefer I go to French border and get Spanish refugee story rather than go Riviera? Riviera seems pallid news now unless Mussolini decides to kidnap Cannes or Nice."

Flanner had become increasingly obsessed by the Spanish Civil War, as it became ever more apparent that what was at stake in the battle for Spain was also what was at stake for Europe and beyond. How could she go off to write about Monaco and the Riviera when such a story was unfolding on the opposite side of France's southern coast?

McKelway passed along her request to Ross, telling him, "I'd like to read her version of what's going on at the border." Ross approved.

Flanner cabled back to say she would drive down with Solano, "who speaks Spanish. I hope we don't give our shirts and socks away and walk about naked and sobbing. I really can't imagine what made me suggest this painful trip except that I was really ashamed to palm off the Riviera at such a moment."

Even while anticipating that the trip would be difficult, she was in no way prepared for what was to come.

35

A JUDGMENT AT VERSAILLES

A February hearing set Weidmann's trial for March. Between the prosecution and defense there would be sixteen lawyers working. Seventy-four witnesses would testify. Eight doctors would offer their diagnoses. Nearly sixty pounds' worth of tightly typed documents detailed the evidence amassed against Weidmann. Given how absolutely those documents established his guilt, the only real questions left for the court were whether or not he'd been mentally ill when carrying out his crimes, and if so, whether France's duty was to kill or care for this sick foreigner on its soil.

The jurors were pulled from suburbs around Versailles. They included a pharmacist, an industrialist, a gardener, an accountant, a mechanic, a few men who lived on the income of properties, and two who had the same jobs as two of the victims: a chauffeur and a real estate agent. Most were in their fifties or sixties. As with any jury in a *cour d'assises* (court of Assizes), the French courts that heard serious crimes, this body was comprised only of men.

A team of carpenters and masons got to work transforming the

Versailles Palais de Justice's main courtroom into an international media center, with telephone booths and desks for reporters to file their stories. The yellowed walls received a fresh coat of paint. To Renée Jardin the renovated room looked "just as ugly and dilapidated as always."

The chief of police distributed a ten-page manual instructing his officers and court employees on how to handle the expected crowds. Two custodians were reassigned to work as ushers, to preempt disputes over seats. As both men and women would be seated in the gallery, positioned higher than the legal workers seated on the room's opposite side, it was partially sealed off with a blue curtain to "preserve the sobriety of a court that would otherwise be faced by the distracting revelations of very short skirts," as the manual informed the staff.

The presiding judge, Edouard Laemlé, advised counsel that the trial should last no longer than three weeks, since by April all resources would need to be devoted to Versailles's role as host of the National Congress to elect the next president of the French Republic.

Additional police officers were posted outside of the Saint-Pierre prison day and night. Anyone claiming to be a member of the force would have his identity scrupulously checked unless already well-known to the officers on duty. No new prisoners could be admitted without the warden first getting approval from the examining magistrate. Any prisoners set to be freed in the coming weeks were barred from communicating with Weidmann, lest they convey any messages to the outside that could influence the trial or its press coverage.

From New York the de Koven family again petitioned the French state to pay for them to come participate in the trial. French officials agreed to cover only Ida Sackheim's travel (steamship, second class), since she was the only family member who could be of any use—although the court had already decided that it wasn't vital for her to give testimony in person as she'd already been questioned at length and had presented a written account of meeting Weidmann and receiving the ransom letters.

The approval to travel reached Sackheim only after weeks of back-and-forth across dozens of pages of memos involving magistrates and diplomats. By then it was too late. The de Koven family would stay in New York, waiting to hear whether justice would be served.

36

A LETTER FROM PERPIGNAN

In mid-February Flanner and Solano reached Perpignan, just off the Mediterranean coast close to the Spanish border. As they approached, Flanner admired the fine blue sky and the almond trees blooming an incandescent pink. And then the scene came into sharp relief: the first humanitarian disaster she'd ever witnessed.

Nancy Cunard, there reporting on the crisis for the *Manchester Guardian*, had primed her on the latest developments. Perpignan had been a launching site for members of the International Brigades, the tens of thousands of volunteers who'd come from nearly fifty countries to fight for the Republican cause, roughly half of them affiliated with the Communist Party, most with little or no combat experience. After reaching Paris, hub of the Brigades' clandestine network and its main recruiting site, they would take the train to Perpignan to be smuggled into Spain overnight through the treacherous passes of the Pyrenees. Now Perpignan was a holding pen, and the bodies flowed in the opposite direction.

Spanish Republicans had looked to France for refuge after the fall of

Barcelona and other crushing losses in late January. German and Italian aircraft supporting Franco's forces had bombed Barcelona's port to oblivion the previous March, hampering chances for maritime escape. The French government had long anticipated the coming Spanish exodus by land and yet refused to fully prepare for it. At first the French denied the Spanish Republican government's request to take in fleeing women, children, injured, and elderly, and sent in a new wave of French soldiers to protect the frontier. A few days later, overwhelmed officials opened the border to all but active men and those of fighting age. And then, finally, to avoid a mass slaughter of the pinned Republican rearguard, France allowed retreating troops to cross.

Over the span of a week nearly half a million Spanish refugees had come through, most of them on foot: mothers with sickly babies, shepherds and schoolmasters, doctors, dockworkers, orphans, mounted soldiers, and eventually the president of the defeated Republic himself, all of them possessing only what they carried. French soldiers, stationed no more than five meters apart, kept the cordon moving along from the border to hastily built concentration camps. They'd confiscated all weapons, sometimes having to tear rifles from the grips of unyielding Spanish fighters. Cunard, who'd hoped to cross into Spain but could get no farther than Perpignan and its surrounding villages, described the sight: "On the mountains each side they come, so that the whole landscape seems to be moving,"

By the time Flanner and Solano reached the coast Franco had closed the border. They toured several camps in Perpignan and other French border towns. They passed thousands of now-stateless people waiting in the bracing wind behind barbed wire as French bureaucrats decided how and where their lives would play out. Everywhere they looked "smoke hung like a flat, low second sky over the scene." People were burning whatever they could to keep warm. "It's a sad story here," she wrote McKelway. She couldn't think of "anything in modern history" with which it could be compared.

Flanner learned of families forcibly broken up and spread among disparate regions as fighting-age men were siphoned into different camps from those housing women, children, the elderly, and the wounded. Wherever one ended up there was sure to be a shortage of food, water, and shelter. Some of the refugees were so hungry they dared to cross back into Spain looking for sheep for milk and slaughter. Camp officials advised refugees to return to Spain and surrender, hoping to cut down on their numbers, or suggested they join the French Foreign Legion. Conditions were so horrible that many would do just that. Some died from exposure. Others from the lingering effects of their journeys, dodging bombardments and the strafing machine guns of enemy aircraft as they trekked toward the snowy mountain passes. Masses died of simple neglect, unable to receive timely medical care. A few hanged themselves from trees with their flannel belts.

Outnumbering the region's local population, the Spanish refugees were made to feel unwanted and unwelcomed. Some of the defeated Spanish soldiers later said that they'd been surprised that the French hadn't greeted them as war heroes as they'd crossed. As George Orwell had written a few months earlier about the Republican cause, "here at last, apparently, was democracy standing up to Fascism." They soon realized how naïve they'd been. French notables including, improbably, the Catholic archbishop of Paris, had urged French citizens in pamphlets and posters to "accept the honor of relieving the frightful misery" of their guests. But elected officials were too scared of the political fallout to release the tremendous funds needed to address the situation, and the right-wing press, already fed up with French immigration policies and now set to foaming at the prospect of an invasion of Spanish "Reds," gave them no reason to hurry. Some locals did act generously toward the refugees. So did relief workers who'd rushed to the area. Many government workers and soldiers tried their best under grueling circumstances. But by and large the French treated the new arrivals, hailing from all over Spain, diverse in background and allegiance, as a single, uniformly dangerous horde. They were marked as criminals, as terrorists.

When filing her Letter from Perpignan a week later, Flanner decided against trying to explain the ideological abstractions that had led to the crisis. She tried only, in sobering detail, to chronicle the effects of this "exodus...without precedent." She'd been writing about politics for a few years, but always at a remove. This was the first time she'd directly covered a military conflict, seen firsthand the rage and desperation in the faces of the people who'd fired and been fired upon. She told McKelway she was "counting on him" to get her as much column space as she needed to tell her story, and he came through.

She opened with her disgust at seeing the refugees "living largely as prisoners of war," after having entered this land as "homeless guests." Readers were confronted with anguished scenes of Spanish women and children lining frigid, muddy streets in flimsy clothes, "hungry, exhausted, and in a panic"; of men sleeping in the sand while others stood in a snaking line to drink from a single trickling spigot, a wait that could take a day; of rations sullied by the unforgiving winds that whipped sand and dust into a dark cloud "that turned the pale sun into a red harvest moon"; of colonial troops from Senegal in their blood-colored fezzes, glaring at the refugees and being watched in turn by French officers. Men wandered aimlessly "under the surveillance of the Garde Mobile, who shooed them around like chickens when they spread out too thickly...most of the men had brought a blanket, their sole possession, and wore it all day like a giant scarf over their shoulders. There was no shelter. The refugees sat, slept, and waited on the brown ground."

People told her about all that they'd left behind in the final stages of their crossing through the foothills: trucks, carts, clothing, personal papers, and "thousands of slowly moving, deserted Catalonian mules and horses, herding together in hunger, idleness, and misery, and constantly edging with strange sociability, toward human habitation." Even in the face of such inhumanity, she tried to remain diplomatic, noting that this emergency was causing pain for the French as well as the Spanish, if in different portions. Though "bad water is general and dysentery is commonplace in all camps," she sought out some measure of hope at one camp's hospital, "excellently" overseen and staffed by the refugees themselves, and which "seemed well run and didn't smell." The patients' "grizzled" faces made her think of Goya. She commended the work of a group of Quakers who were doing "intelligent, unsentimental work" helping to care for refugee children.

The piece ends with the strange paradox of a German among this group, a man who'd volunteered to fight for the International Brigades and had asked Flanner to send a postcard home, which he'd written in French for fear of censors stopping it from reaching Germany. "Dear Family: Since several days I find myself in France and I find myself in good health and now I find myself in a concentration camp."

Leaving Perpignan, sick with *E. coli*, Flanner worried that Cunard, her fellow witness to this disaster and a woman who cared so deeply for the Republican cause, would never recover from her disillusionment. She was right. "Drink...has nothing to do with my case," Cunard would write to Flanner from a sanatorium two decades later, broken, emaciated, declared insane, "but Fascism has...Damn Spain and all its doings. It is because of that—(I *think*) I am here." Lamenting the waste her life had been, Cunard wrote: "What else have I been or done that was worthwhile?—Oh for one month I wrote the truth about the exodus into France from Spain in 1939."

Flanner had once told White that she'd "done nothing for the Spanish war (I am not a 'cause' person)," maintaining that "it's my policy to do my 'giving' personally, not to organizations." White experienced such giving firsthand the previous year, when she'd asked Flanner to find out the date and location of the rumored death of the son of Bill Levick, head of *The New Yorker*'s art department, who'd gone to fight alongside the Republicans. Enlisting help from Hemingway, as well as a commander in the Abraham Lincoln Brigade, as the American volunteers were collectively called, and a *New York Times* correspondent in Madrid, Flanner confirmed the young man's death. Through many cables and letters she found out that his burial site likely lay in the northeastern town of Quinto in the province of Zaragoza, where four unidentified Americans had been killed. Levick refused to believe his son numbered among those four, and White reported that the news "put him over the edge"; soon afterward he left his wife, quit the magazine, became a communist sympathizer, and joined the Merchant Marine. Flanner, feeling "very badly about the Levick situation," asked White, "did I help or only harm?...I don't in the least understand men, K, and especially killing men or men who kill men."

Now she'd publicly exposed herself as a "cause" person, after all. Shocked by how searing her anger had been in Perpignan she grew terrified of having put too much of it on the page, of making her support for the Republicans too obvious and thereby spoiling the many years of trust that readers had placed in the Olympian and impassive Genêt. Even before the Letter ran she'd asked McKelway, "Am I staying in the middle of the road all right?...give me some guidelines on currents in New York."

McKelway told her that in New York her piece was considered a triumph, "the first vivid unprejudiced (or at least unprejudiced enough) picture of what was going on" and "really the only decent thing that's been printed in this country on that situation." He wrote:

> Everybody I talk to who has any judgment thinks you have been doing a splendid job in these most difficult times. A good many people over here are screwy about the times, as you must know. In general, the emotional leftists, particularly the Jewish ones, consider everybody a fascist who isn't doing something definite on their side: speaking before writers' congresses or raising money for the Spanish orphans, or writing for the *New Masses*, or god knows what. The real fascists, of course, are practically undiscoverable except in the case of some crack brain...but the Leftists are so articulate that they are dull and therefore a lot of people who are really quite Left at heart are inclined to avoid them when possible and probably get put down as fascists themselves. It's hard to keep any kind of head, much less a level one, and that's what you are doing, causing our vast admiration and sometimes damn near astonishment.

The fall of Catalonia continued to weigh heavily on Flanner, as it would on many others, not only for the suffering it produced but as an early warning of greater suffering to follow. Across the Atlantic, President Roosevelt admitted that the American strategy of imposing an arms embargo for both sides had hurt the Republicans more than the Nationalists, calling it a "grave mistake."

On an immediate practical level, as Flanner explained in *The New Yorker*, the French now had to go about their lives knowing just how quickly bombers could reach Paris (three hours) and the port town of Biarritz (ten minutes) from the German-run flying field outside the Spanish border town of Irun. The French themselves had developed modern aircraft capable of reaching and killing civilians with unprecedented speed and brutality; who knew what Germany's industrialists and chemists and engineers had under wraps on their side? People predicted entire cities might one day be wiped out from above with gas bombs or through some kind of distribution of "germs."

On a more symbolic level, Franco's victory registered as a depressing blow to the soul of liberal democracy, breeding a growing sense of despair and defeatism among those who still cared to defend an institution that seemed to weaken with each passing year. As Albert Camus would later write, the Spanish Civil War taught his generation "that one can be right and yet be beaten, that force can vanquish spirit, and that there are times when courage is not rewarded."

A few days after Flanner left Perpignan, France officially recognized Franco's Nationalist government, appointing the reactionary eighty-three-year-old Marshal Phillipe Pétain, the celebrated Victor of Verdun and an admirer and former teacher of Franco's, as ambassador.

37

THE GOSPEL OF THE MURDERER

The trial opened in Versailles at noon on Monday, March 13, 1939. For the people of France, whose leaders had so clearly failed to heed the threat of German aggression, Weidmann's crimes presented a tangible injustice that they could see righted. Here in the ancient seat of French power was a chance to avenge the evil of a German who'd committed his crimes on French territory, and whose victims included French citizens, a Jewish-American, and a Jewish antifascist who'd fled Nazi persecution.

People lined up overnight to be among the handful of members of the public admitted into the trial's first day. Celebrities such as Maurice Chevalier and high-profile French ministers arrived demanding seats. Few of them could be accommodated. (Jardin had her picture taken with Chevalier.) One woman, who'd read about Weidmann's love of cats, brought three white kittens to the courthouse to bring him luck. A small number of journalists were allowed to attend each day, on a rotating basis. It isn't clear which days Flanner attended in person.

Judge Laemlé, severe in his scarlet robe, bald and clean-shaven, with a long face, thin lips, and sad, hooded eyes ringed by dark circles, called the court to order, presiding as its president, the foremost of the three overseeing judges. He was far from a magnetic personality, but his understated manner served as a necessary balance to the sensationalized atmosphere of the proceedings. He would show himself to be an even-handed and patient master of ceremonies.

Many in attendance defied the rarely enforced ban on cigarette smoking, adding to the stale smell of so many bodies in their robes and uniforms and suits in the small courtroom. "Unfortunately" the lead counsel Moro "had a horror of fresh air," wrote a British journalist, so that whenever "so much as one pane of glass was opened, he cast an indignant look around him, seized a brown woolen muffler and ostentatiously wound it round and round his neck where it looked odd enough above his black robe. The window was at once shut."

Weidmann entered through an inconspicuous door in the wall into the dock where prisoners sat on pews behind and just above their lawyers, facing the jury. He wore a finely tailored navy blue suit, with a pale blue shirt and tie, his brilliantined hair slicked back. Those who knew him only from press photographs of a strapping and swarthy man were shocked to see how pale and thin he'd gone with his year and a half of waiting.

A woman stood up in her seat to get a look, and to wave to him, but was shamed into sitting back down by the cry of the young widow of Raymond Lesobre, which to one observer "sounded like the rending of a piece of silk." More than once during the trial the ushers would have to shout to the gallery for silence.

Weidmann looked calm, almost sleepy, a man who knew he was already dead. To the novelist Colette, there on that first day, his pleasant, symmetrical features made him even more horrifying as he sat serenely in the dock. The most unsettling criminals frighten us not by openly displaying what makes them "bestial and grossly terrifying," she argued, but through all the ways they appear to be somewhat—but not quite—like the rest of us.

Alongside Weidmann, separated from one another by officers of the Garde Mobile, were the bewildered Jean Blanc, flushing red behind rimless glasses; the visibly terrified Roger Million; and Colette Tricot, her face stone-still and unreadable. Reporters who over the previous months had worked so hard to frame Tricot as a vampish femme fatale now confronted a spent-looking woman in a "dowdy hat," with an "expressionless putty face," as one of them wrote. The four prisoners were uncuffed.

Weidmann, following protocol, was asked to stand and identify himself. He surprised everyone by instead admitting his guilt, speaking in a low and deferential voice, and asking to be rid of his lawyers so that he could defend himself. "I offer you all I can offer," he said. "My life."

The judge advised Weidmann that he was required to be represented by a lawyer, but could change counsel, if he wished. He declined.

Over the following days, the defense and the prosecution, along with a third group of lawyers representing the civil interests of the victims' families, all tried to make sense of crimes that apparently held no meaning for the man who'd committed them. They struggled to give shape to the meandering drift of Weidmann's days in Saint-Cloud. Getting to the truth proved especially difficult given that the four defendants couldn't agree among themselves about what happened. "Weidmann lied to Million, Million lied to Blanc, Blanc to

Colette [Tricot] who, for her part, lied to each of the three of them," wrote one French reporter. And any witness who'd come into contact with this crew was likely to have been lied to by at least one, if not all four, of them.

After his opening outburst, Weidmann seemed to shrink back into himself, answering any questions put to him in a quiet, deadpan voice, as though trying to make clear how little any of the sounds coming out of his mouth now mattered to him, since they changed nothing about what he'd done or what would happen to him. With each day he was "moving farther and farther away from the rest of us," wrote Colette. And yet he strove to answer as fully and completely as he could and with seemingly no motivation to protect himself.

Sometimes his desire to answer as plainly as he could led to testimony that struck the audience as cold and robotic, as if he were "a stranger to himself." He did not rant and rave like other "caged beasts...his marked trait was his softness."

When asked about the failed attempt to kidnap the Baltimore textile man Michael Stein, he answered only that he remembered Million saying it had ruined their Bastille Day. When asked how he'd been so careless as to leave Arthur Schott's calling card at the scene of Lesobre's murder, he shrugged and said that he'd just forgotten about it, in a tone suggesting that he was asking the jury to forgive him not for the murder but for being so thoughtless and sloppy, which provoked jeers from the crowd. He yawned often, seemed forever about to doze off.

Asked directly about why he killed one victim, Fritz Frommer, Weidmann answered, "Because he was carrying money."

During questioning about the murder of Jean de Koven the prosecution produced, in a big glass jar, the three feet of stained linen that he'd used to gag her. The lawyer explained to the court how the linen had been removed from deep down de Koven's throat. Weidmann offered no reaction to the theatrics.

Only when questioned about the murder of the young entrepreneur Leblond, the one killing he didn't carry out directly, did he change course. He asked to address Leblond's ex-wife directly. He begged for her forgiveness, explaining that seeing her had made him realize the true horror of his crimes. He waited in a too-long, heavy silence before continuing: "The only thing I want to regain is my faith, because I want to set myself right with God." He knew, he said, that any forgiveness "would come not on earth but from God alone." Acknowledging that the five other murders "were his," he swore that Million had been the one to shoot her ex-husband. He said he didn't wish to cause the Million family any unnecessary pain, so that if he accused Million of something, it could only be because it was true.

At the end of his speech his body spasmed, his head dropped into his folded arms, and he sobbed. Colette said it was as if he'd fainted; "he just wasn't there." People remarked that a few women in the audience sighed deeply, perhaps even passionately, at this display.

Over the course of the trial Flanner developed a begrudging admiration for Weidmann's unflinching determination to establish an ordered and comprehensive record of everything he and the others had done, offering correctives for any moments when the testimonies of his codefendants conflicted with one another. Because his guilt had never been in question, this set him apart from the other defendants, who were still scrambling to save themselves, lending weight to everything he said. The more he spoke, the more Flanner thought the room belonged to him. He'd "offered a truthfulness so impressive and solicitous that he, the criminal, has gradually assumed the role of a judge and has become the arbiter in the desperate conflicts among the three other prisoners, the regiment of bibbed lawyers, and the crowd of weeping bereaved, black-swathed relatives, all of whom (whenever it was useful to them) have accepted the murderer's 'Yes' and 'No,' or even the taciturn nod of his head, as gospel." And she found those few moments when he deviated from his straightforward answering of questions to make some grand emotional "Rousseau-like" confession absolutely "sensational."

The trial's most dramatic performance was still to come, though not from Weidmann.

38

THE BLOOD IN HIS VEINS AND THE CLIMATE OF HIS DAYS

On the afternoon of March 29, Moro delivered his closing arguments by bursting into an oratory that would span several hours. Everyone in the room was immediately gripped by this "tubby little man with the face of an eagle, the voice of an angel, [and] the vanity of a peacock," as one observer wrote.

"Do me the honor of understanding that I have considered the difficulty of my task," he began. "If, in the course of these proceedings, the stubbornness of the defense has struck you as excessive, place the blame solely with me, an old lawyer whose hair has gone white in the occasionally honorable service of hopeless causes, who never loves his noble profession so much as when he feels the barriers around him multiplying and growing right up until the impossible happens."

He hadn't come to argue the facts, he said. The facts were "obvious" and he had no wish to challenge them. He was there only to "stand against the scaffold, whose blade offers neither remedy, nor lesson, nor example to others; against the executioner's axe, which does nothing but spray guilty blood onto the sickly curious crowds, teaching nothing but cruelty." He noted how many other countries around the world had abolished the death penalty, with nothing to make them regret their decisions. He drew on Victor Hugo, who described the death penalty as the "special and eternal sign of barbarity."

Why not simply give in to our desire for retaliation, shut the door, draw the blinds, and turn the courtroom into a "slaughterhouse?," asked Moro.

Because the French people would not lower themselves to that kind of depravity, especially not now in this time when people stood so eager to slaughter each other.

"Without ignoring the heated times in which we live, rather by being inspired by the current climate, I invoke the rights of a civilization that merges with the genius of our race, and which will live as long as it lives, but which would risk perishing with it if, to humanity's misfortune, its flame is ever extinguished."

And so, even in defiance of the wishes of the guilty party, "who holds his head in his bloody hands and offers it to you as in a ritual sacrifice, to be purified through punishment, I dare say to you: Do not kill this man." For in the end, "Who has the right to punish him? God himself, if he exists, wouldn't dare to exercise that right against this fallen creature."

He argued that executing the mentally ill would one day seem as strange a practice as when hundreds of years ago people executed animals for their supposed crimes.

And Weidmann was most definitely mentally ill. Moro asked why the doctors who'd come to testify hadn't sought to do their primary duty, which was to try to cure this patient, rather than kill him. He, Moro, seemed to be the only one who wanted to understand his sickness, to find out how it took root in his "flesh." The doctors, who'd felt they'd done their work by labeling this complicated, bizarre man as merely abnormal, could not be trusted.

Moro reminded the jury that he'd asked for an independent medical assessment to challenge their findings, which the court had denied him, even though he could draw on an abundance of precedents to show that criminal cases regularly drew on the testimony of independent experts. And he reminded them that he'd called on several esteemed graphologists both in France and beyond to study Weidmann's handwriting and that each one had declared him a psychopath. He argued that graphology was more empirically accurate than psychology, a field that one of the examining alienists himself had once described as a mostly "literary" pursuit. (Moro knew how far he was overreaching here. When he'd called one of these graphologists to the stand, the gallery laughed at the man's pseudoscientific babble.)

Drawing on records from his incarcerations in Frankfurt, Moro noted that an examining physician found that the young Weidmann showed no reaction to a series of pinpricks on the right side of the body (while his left showed normal sensitivity). Making his own medical assessment, Moro suggested that lacking physical response to pain on one side of the body was an obvious sign of "hysteria." A former teacher said Weidmann suffered from delusions of grandeur. The alienist at Preungesheim Prison had diagnosed him as a "born criminal." Weidmann's paternal grandfather had been a career criminal, and was said to have died in an insane asylum. Moro hinted that this grandfather might have killed his own wife.

Using a book on mental illness written by one of the experts who'd testified for the prosecution as a guide, he suggested that some people were simply born emotionally disturbed. Weidmann, he argued, from his very origin had been "perverted…even in the act of his creation, in his mother's womb, in the crib." He cautioned that because Weidmann spoke French so eloquently, because he was so obviously intelligent, it was easy to be tricked into thinking he was sane.

When this line of reasoning prompted some chatter in the courtroom Moro turned round swiftly to face those guilty of distracting him. "Don't let it disturb you, gentlemen," he said, smiling, "that I am pleading for a man's life while you talk."

Judge Laemlé called for order.

Finally, Moro came to his most daring argument. Drawing again on the Preungesheim Prison examination, Moro proposed that Weidmann's "milieu," the environment in which he was raised, had exacerbated his existing hereditary disposition for evil. Germany was "monstrous." And monsters beget more monsters. "The blood in his veins and the climate of his days collaborated to produce the work that is Weidmann." His body held in it the rage of an entire nation.

"Don't be led to believe that Weidmann's crimes came from nowhere," he continued. "I choose my words carefully: These are German crimes."

Moro explained that as a former combatant he knew the Germans well. He'd met them face-to-face on the battlefield. He respected them for their courage. But while the French "genius derives from our kindness, the German genius derives from its brutality." By tracing a potted history of Germany and offering superficial tours of German mythology and philosophy, he framed them as a militant and nihilistic people. One had to admit that "the political actions of a nation reflect the consciousness of the people who people it," and that the German "spirit" had always been brutal and violent. He noted that Weidmann had told a doctor that his strongest childhood memory was of seeing the summary execution of a Spartacist rebel, his head bashed in by a rifle before a cheering crowd. "To fanaticize a people, under the idea [that the world understands no other justice but force], to repeat that idea, to prove it, over centuries, to generations who follow and admire that idea, is to teach something very foreign to us [in France], which is barbarism."

Moro highlighted Nietzsche's passages preaching the need to rise above conventional morality and glorify the "horrible beauty" of the criminal act. A child exposed to the philosophy of Nietzsche, told that God is dead and the time had come for the Superman to reign, was guided along a "certain path." Was it not Nietzsche who in *Thus Spake Zarathustra* taught Germans of the killer who killed not to steal but because he "thirsted for the happiness of the knife," and so only robbed the people he murdered to provide some kind of explanation for his crimes, for he was so ashamed of his madness?

Did this not explain Weidmann's actions perfectly?

And so, he said, "I plead for a child who has been hearing about blood for as long as he can remember. I plead for a child who was taught 'Might makes right.' I plead for a child who was told 'Be the strongest, if presented with an obstacle, break it, crush it, trample it.'"

Finally, he turned to the current moment of German aggression. (The jurors, who weren't sequestered but returned home each night, would have learned that over the course of the trial Nazi tanks had taken what remained of Czechoslovakia.) Weidmann had seen the rise of a "new regime," said Moro, without naming it, and under this regime he'd seen "ten thousand political assassinations or suicides... palaces destroyed, flags desecrated, the deification of those who'd once been abhorred." He would not mention any current German leaders by name, he said, but whoever led Germany led a nation that knew nothing other than "blood." So it had been "since the Middle Ages." And weren't we all as individuals simply "tributaries flowing into the river of a distant and murky past?" Weren't we all formed or deformed by our ancestors? He paraphrased Ecclesiastes: "Our fathers have eaten sour grapes, and our teeth are set on edge."

What, in the end, was Weidmann's true crime? "Being born."

Moro closed by asking the jurors to pity the defendant, driven not by sentimentality but "by reason, emitting from the depths of one's soul." He asked them to "show mercy not because he is him, but because you are you." By sparing the life of this misshapen product of a monstrous regime, they would show the world what they thought of themselves as Frenchmen in the face of German savagery. This jury could represent "something greater" than the community on whose behalf it had been called on to perform. Because Weidmann was German, because of his particular mental makeup, "so foreign from ours," because he was being tried in France, the nation of the Rights of Man and of the Citizen, this jury alone had the chance to stand in for all of civilized humanity.

> I ask you, my countrymen, tasked with judging this fallen creature of such a different race, in front of the world and in the face of that vain and constant clamoring for blood, bread, and circuses, to deliver the magnificent and haughty spectacle of a justice whose true greatness lies in its evenness, in its carefulness, and in its mercifulness.

The courtroom burst into applause, quickly shouted down by Laemlé.

Moro's performance drew the kinds of raves in the press normally reserved for a Jean Gabin or a Clark Gable. He was hailed as a "modern-day Sisyphus." A "legal demigod." He was "one of the world's most dazzling actors."

39

I HOPE TO HEAVEN MOM DOESN'T SEE IT

The jurors were given sandwiches and beer as they deliberated. After a trial of three weeks, they reached their verdict in fifteen hours. Judge Laemlé then submitted them collectively to a six-hour barrage of eighty yes-or-no questions so that the record could show without doubt that each member had agreed on every item of their decision.

Late on Friday night, March 31, 1939, the foreman read the verdict, placing his hand on his heart. Tricot was acquitted of all charges. Blanc received twenty months for harboring criminals. Weidmann and Million were sentenced to death by guillotine.

People hooted and yelled. Million looked as if he'd been punched in the stomach. He screamed, protesting his innocence, saying that he'd only ever been Weidmann's "instrument." The crowd violently shouted him down. He fainted. His lawyer lashed out, calling the spectators cannibals before regaining his usual dignified composure. And then he grasped his revivified client's hands, looked into his tear-stained face, and told him, "Courage."

When the noise died down Weidmann was asked if he had any final words. He stood, shook his head, and sat down again. He smiled silently at the jury and thanked his lawyers, shaking their hands.

Weidmann and Million were led to the basement of Saint-Pierre, death row. Weidmann glanced up at the courtroom clock, which showed midnight as he passed, and laughed to himself.

Following tradition, the executions were to take place in public, outside the prison gates, satisfying the public desire to watch justice being carried out, to experience "the ultimate expression of Law," as Victor Hugo once described the guillotine. "He who sees it shudders in the most confounding dismay. All social questions achieve their finality around that blade."

❧

As part of his ruling Judge Laemlé also ordered that 120,000 francs be paid to the de Koven family in civil damages.

The family's attorney promptly cabled to decline what he described as "blood money," adding that his client's only demand was that the court officially declare Jean's "good repute." In the same cable the de Kovens' attorney questioned whether the body the family had buried two years earlier in New York had actually belonged to Jean, as they'd never been sent any of her personal belongings. Some family members still believed she was alive, held hostage somewhere. He wondered if the French authorities hadn't been looking for an easy solution to the mystery of her disappearance, hadn't covered up their failures by convincing Weidmann, already on the hook for the other murders, to claim that the body under the stairs had been Jean's, to help them solve their problem.

❧

For Flanner, Weidmann's trial had proven "to be, psychologically, the strangest *procés* recorded in French criminal history," as she wrote in *The New Yorker.* Not because of its outcome, for "that he would escape the death sentence was expected by no one, not even Weidmann." What had surprised her about this arduous trial—so full of talk and countertalk, expertise and counterexpertise, of quick unguarded outbursts of truth and of winding monologues of calculated lies—was that none of the evidence or testimony or arguments had brought anyone closer to understanding the defendant or what drove him to do what he did. His evil would remain forever incomprehensible.

What she did understand was the eternal human desire to make coherent stories out of such enigmas. She'd loved watching her French colleagues attack the Weidmann Affair with that special "mixture of malice, insight, libel, philosophy, and inaccurate reporting which constitutes the genius of the fourth estate here." Though he was no more than "a futile Faustian character" he'd "inspired" some of the best crime writing France had enjoyed in decades. Even amid Hitler's invasion of Czechoslovakia, Franco's victories in Spain, and Britain's recent pledge to protect Polish independence, Weidmann kept appearing on the front page. To Flanner the public desire to understand the event had become a force exponentially greater than the event itself, and in the end all the expert opinions and polemics had only made the mystery of Weidmann that much more impenetrable.

Attempts to politicize the case inside and outside the courtroom had not landed with the jury nor the public with as much force as had been promised or feared. A monster was a monster, wherever he came from. "It is indicative of the rational attitude of the French during this moment of acute nationalistic tension that Weidmann's being a German is not considered an additional crime," she wrote.

Just as the trial closed, the *News Chronicle of London* serialized all of

Flanner's writing on Weidmann in three installments, with a caption calling her a "brilliant" correspondent who'd produced "one of the best crime articles of our time." Flanner told McKelway she was upset that *The New Yorker* wasn't properly credited as the original publisher of her pieces and wondered if she should complain.

"Outside of the sappy reference to my being the *New Yorker*'s correspondent the magazine is not referred to in installments two and three though my name is bannered (with the word murder beneath, I hope to heaven mom doesn't see it)."

40

FANTASTIC AND UNREAL AS IT MAY SEEM

Flanner went to stay at Orgeval that spring. She paid to have an extra bathroom installed at the farmhouse, conscious of how much time she was spending there, and concerned, too, about Murphy's money troubles.

She and Murphy passed the greater part of each day with the radio at full volume and newspapers in different languages splayed out on various tables. In New York the German-American Bund had just rented out Madison Square Garden for what was advertised as a "Mass Demonstration for True Americanism"—in truth a Nazi rally on American soil. A massive banner, white with red lettering, hung from the first balcony, reading "Stop Jewish Domination of Christian Americans." When Dorothy Thompson heckled one of the aspiring demagogues on the podium, the crowd of roughly twenty thousand chanted "Throw her out!" before policemen removed her to the safety of the press box.

Flanner and Murphy dealt with the moment's anxieties by tending to their friendships with greater care. The young English portraitist

Francis Rose, one of Gertrude Stein's protégés, joined them for a few days. (Flanner had praised Rose's "curious," occasionally "bizarre" work in her Letters.) He'd come in theory to paint a mural on some plaster boards for one of the dining room walls, but more so because the three of them felt an especially strong need for communion just then, like so many other fearful people across Europe. Any excuse to gather would do. From the farmhouse Flanner penned melancholy letters. "Did I tell you this one from Berlin? It's very sad," she wrote McKelway. "A Jew came in the travel office and asked for a ticket. 'Where to?' they asked. 'Oh, just a ticket,' he said. They brought him a globe of the world which he spun slowly, looking it over. 'Haven't you any other places besides these I could buy a ticket to?,' he asked. Sad and funny and sad."

The New Yorker had meanwhile grown ever hungrier for her work. Her Letters now started running weekly. As she dashed between her base in Orgeval and Paris and London that spring she came closer to accepting the inevitability of full-out war in Europe, even as a part of her continued to kick against that realization. "Events seem worsening. Still I have high hopes if heavy heart," she cabled McKelway. Watching the French and English trying to figure each other out, as they anticipated needing to unite against their common enemy, she joked in *The New Yorker* that the Germans had produced the first-ever absence of anti-English sentiment in France. She predicted that any warfare involving France would only be "incidental to the main struggle...between the old empire of England and the new Empire of Germany." And she'd grasped the wider geopolitical stakes of smaller conflicts that the European press still largely insisted on treating as regional skirmishes. "Fantastic and unreal as it may seem," she warned her readers, "the fate of France and England...rests on what may soon happen to Rumania, or nearly any other Balkan state,

Poland, Greece, Syria, Palestine, Tunisia, Switzerland, Holland, Denmark, Morocco, the Suez Canal, or, what is more impressive still, the Rock of Gibraltar."

Flanner made such declarations with increasing clarity and confidence, while hewing as closely as possible to her role as a conveyor of public opinion and of the educated guesses of her well-placed French and British sources. McKelway noticed a difference in her writing. "It seems to me that you have made great progress this last year in cleanliness of copy. Do you feel that we are doing less to it? We feel all the time that there is less necessity to fool with it, and this, of course, is your fault."

Flanner agreed that something had eased up in her work just as the material she was writing about grew bleaker. She even thought a few of her recent London Letters had been half-decent. "I feel relaxed and more knowledgeable, finally," she told McKelway. "I stepped out a lot," she said about her most recent London trip. "One has to there, to get notions, the papers tell one nothing except what is admitted; one has to move around, talk, listen, conclude—conclude what?"

Feeling charged by the work she'd been producing, she decided she would stay in Europe to cover whatever conflict was coming, at least for as long she could bear it. Her latest plan was to stay on at Orgeval if and when war did break out, while allowing that "if things get bad" she would "try to come home on a warship or whatever they will be taking us off on," as she told McKelway. Solano would join her when it came time to leave. But Murphy would not. "She feels she can't leave, that [this] is her home; she is a fatalist and has great physical courage and vitality and strength."

Murphy had always told Flanner she would pass the rest of her life in France. She refused to quit the place where her husband was buried. She would defend the country she loved, would battle fascism however and wherever she could because this was the morally correct thing to do. Flanner, who by then had seen her share of German military drills and aerial displays, held no illusions about her own limitations if the Wehrmacht crossed into France, however much she cared for Murphy and wanted to be with her. She was no fighter.

Just as Flanner was writing to McKelway as if war might be only days away, Roosevelt issued a call for a nonviolent resolution in cables sent directly to Hitler and Mussolini. Flanner threw out the Paris Letter she was about to file and wrote a new one in hours to reflect the French reaction. "Maybe the hope of peace aroused this afternoon by President Roosevelt's appeal…won't last, but it exists tonight, and to anyone living in Paris the night seems lovely and filled with relief."

And yet the same Letter also described Parisians receiving their first gas masks. In Flanner's neighborhood they could be had for free, packed in their neat khaki cases, at the municipal center near the Saint-Sulpice church. One first had to show proof of residence. Married women needed only their wedding certificates, while "old maids had to show receipts from their landlords proving they had paid their last quarter's rent and were thus legal human beings." People doubted the masks' real usefulness as they hung improperly on all but the most perfectly shaped heads.

By the end of April, the optimism sparked by the Roosevelt letters had disappeared. Germany occupied Czechoslovakia, violating the Munich Agreement, and Italy had annexed Albania. Flanner looked to the British as the great check against such aggression but saw only a "dawdling" government. "A reign of efficiently getting nothing done seems in full force [in Britain], of making sure nothing will be done, that the stupid will be in power and protected, that talent and energy are frowned on as poor taste and that pompous conceit should be the shape of Minister's minds, when they are not emptied gas bags incapable of inflation, even under necessity."

Several times over the next weeks she had to scurry to send rewrites after a fast-moving diplomatic situation "sunk" a story she'd just cabled. After (ultimately unfounded) rumors of conscription in England negated something she'd just filed, she complained about it to McKelway, who forwarded it on to Ross.

"Rather hysterical on subject of civilian danger in war," Ross wrote back to McKelway. "She ought to be reassured but I'm afraid it can't be done."

McKelway wrote to Flanner: "You've really done wonderfully through the continued crises; I wish there were some way we could be closer to you and be more reassuring but I can't think how."

All through spring Flanner hunted for moments of glamour and delight for the Letters. Just seeing someone still devoted to the pursuit of happiness felt like a small miracle, an act of defiance.

She praised those Parisians who'd decided "that until there is bloody belligerence everybody had better go about his business or pleasure while either is left." She found defiance in the faces of three thousand fans of "*le Jazz hot*" who piled into the modernist splendor of the Palais de Chaillot's underground auditorium to hear Duke Ellington and his orchestra, even if the concert was a bust, hampered by poor acoustics and a ragged-looking band in wrinkled suits, no longer the snappy young men in pristine white tuxedos from their last visit when the audience had demanded fifteen encores. Defiance was in the long gazes of the connoisseurs at the tiny Pierre Colle gallery, "glad of a chance to look at something more beautiful than the new map of Central Europe," standing before the wondrous works of "Frida Kahlo Rivera" (then little-known next to her husband, Diego), who made pictures "as beautiful as pomegranates in a dream," the surprise hit of this showing of Mexican art. It was in the wistful sighs of ballet lovers soaking in the nostalgic reveries of a retrospective exhibition at the Louvre of costumes and décor for Sergei Diaghilev's Ballets Russes, showcasing the work of artists whose fame had grown enormously since their time creating curtains, outfits, and posters for the company, from Cocteau to Matisse to Picasso. Though here, too, the realities of the present tinged this "pleasant lapse into the past" with melancholy, for the Ballets Russes were emblematic of "*les beaux jours*, the days of civilized, uncensored pleasures, of new musicians and artists [who] formed fresh pictures and gave new sounds to a familiar world the days of the early nineteen twenties, when politicians as well as hedonists thought a permanent, peaceful age had been born. With such memories in mind, it's not strange that balletomanes were saddened by the show. It was enough to make the angels weep."

41

THIS MISERABLE BEAUTIFUL WORLD

Now that he'd been condemned to death Weidmann was kept chained in his cell "like a bear," as Renée Jardin later wrote. The guards kept the lights on all night and had him under permanent watch out of concern he might beat the guillotine to its goal. Even so he slept well. And in his waking hours he ate meals that could have fed five men. The warden was happy to give him as much food as he wanted and kept him supplied with coffee and cigarettes. He read constantly, mainly from *The Imitation of Christ*, repeating its spiritual instructions to himself over and over.

As the days were getting warmer, the guards opened as many windows as they could without sacrificing security. From the radio of a nearby café Weidmann sometimes heard his name.

Jardin had never had a client sentenced to death. Moro had seen several. They'd started working on an appeal as soon as the trial had ended. Albert Lebrun had just been reelected president of France, and Moro thought he might grant Weidmann clemency as a symbolic act to start his new term at the head of so divided a nation.

When Moro tried to discuss the appeal with Weidmann, he answered, "Thank you, sir, but I'm already far away from all of that."

He wrote to Moro on the last day of May:

> I don't want to leave this miserable beautiful world without expressing my gratitude one final time. You can't possibly know what you've given me with your arguments. It is simply the hope, the tiniest hope but of infinite value to me, that I might be somewhat less guilty than I believe myself to be. That I might hope for some small measure of indulgence on the day when I must stand before the Master of everyone and of everything. And I owe that hope to you. Why say more? You know me and you understand me. Let me shake your hand firmly and without any extra ado say that I remain your very grateful client.
>
> *Eugen Weidmann, Versailles, 31.V.1939*

In early June Moro and Jardin hand-delivered two letters to President Lebrun at the Élysée Palace. The first was from Weidmann, asking Lebrun to spare not his own life, but that of Million. He explained that Million was young and impressionable and that he had manipulated him to do the things that he'd done. (Weidmann's lawyers had tried to talk him out of writing this letter, which hurt his own appeal, but he couldn't be moved.) The second was a letter from Fanny Weidmann begging that her son be spared the guillotine, for he was ill and needed care.

Lebrun glanced at the letters, left them on the desk, let Jardin get in a few words, asked no questions, and said nothing in response.

Outside the Palace, Jardin asked Moro if she would be required to attend Weidmann's execution. He answered that this was the duty of any lawyer.

Five days later, on June 15, Weidmann's appeal was officially denied. On the same day, Million received a stay of execution, his sentence reduced to a life of hard labor in prison. (In 1946 this sentence would be further reduced to twenty years of hard labor.)

On learning that his appeal had failed, as he'd wanted, Weidmann penned a long letter to his mother on the theme of redemption. He asked her to attend Mass and to take communion on the day of his death. He told her that he longed to listen to Wagner as the blade fell.

Weidmann's execution on June 17 was filmed from at least two different angles. Several newspapers ran large photographs of the scaffold, of Weidmann on his way to meet it, and of the moment of decapitation.

Weidmann's body was taken to be buried in an unmarked grave at the Gonards cemetery in Versailles, which also housed the tomb of Bluebeard Landru.

Hours after Weidmann's execution, the French government called for a report on the behavior of the crowd at the event and on the dissemination of photographs of the killing. The French penal code was changed a few days later. Executions would no longer take place in public but in prison courtyards, witnessed only by the authorities and official invitees.

And so, even while he'd been executed "clumsily," Weidmann in death became "a more important criminal than he realized," wrote Flanner in *The New Yorker* that July. He went down "in French judicial history as the last to lose his head while morbid crowds gaped, and as a criminal whose popularity was so great that it changed the law...the *kermesse* scenes in the small town of Versailles the night before Weidmann's punishment were considered too scandalous."

Opponents of the death penalty welcomed this change as the beginning of the end of capital punishment in France. Absent its public spectacle, the state could no longer argue that it served as a significant deterrent to would-be criminals. And yet the government report on Weidmann's execution hadn't been prompted by any official outrage about the practice itself, but only the way it had been witnessed and then represented in the press. The guillotine would remain in use for thirty more years.

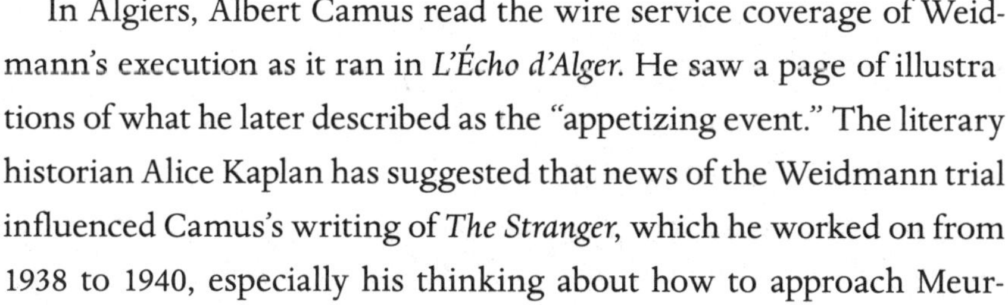

In Algiers, Albert Camus read the wire service coverage of Weidmann's execution as it ran in *L'Écho d'Alger*. He saw a page of illustrations of what he later described as the "appetizing event." The literary historian Alice Kaplan has suggested that news of the Weidmann trial influenced Camus's writing of *The Stranger*, which he worked on from 1938 to 1940, especially his thinking about how to approach Meursault's execution. *The Stranger*'s final line is:

> For everything to be consummated, for me to feel less alone, I had only to wish that there be a large crowd of spectators the day of my execution and that they greet me with cries of hate.

42

THANKS FOR MONEY. WHAT A STRANGE WAR.

At the beginning of summer Flanner booked travel to California for October. She wanted to be with her mother as she underwent surgery and then to return to Paris by early 1940. She'd been fighting for the leave for more than a year. Ross and McKelway approved the travel but made it known that they weren't happy about her plan to be away from Europe just at the moment when all "hell may be a'poppin, either politically or otherwise," as McKelway told her.

The deeper into summer she got, the more Flanner saw Parisians diving into their pleasure, as if unaware or unafraid or both. For a moment Paris came back to her as the glittering dream city she'd once conjured. She tried, briefly and desperately, to write that city back into existence. "Paris has suddenly been having a fit of prosperity, gaiety, and hospitality," she wrote in a July Letter.

> There have been money and music in the air, with people enjoying the first good time since the bad time started at Munich last summer. There have been magnificent costume balls and parties, with dancers footing it till early breakfast...There have been formal dinner parties in stately houses; there have been al-fresco fetes...there have been garden parties that couldn't be held in the garden but were not dampened in spirit by the rain...It has taken the threat of war to make the French loosen up and have a really swell and civilized good time.

She covered the city's Bastille Day parade, which that year fell on the 150th anniversary of the French Revolution. A giant spectacle had been planned years in advance. Now the event held even more significance. The French government and populist press had been stirring up patriotic fervor for months. The British were invited for the first time ever to celebrate alongside the French and sent uniformed men to march in step with French troops.

No longer fearful of warmongering but openly trying to elicit pro-French and British sentiment, Flanner beamed at the sight of citizens proud of their democracies and of those who'd vowed to protect them. She described the cheers that had greeted British and French planes flying in formation over the Eiffel Tower. Two hundred RAF bombers had made what was dubbed a training run but was in truth a show of force, which took the aircraft across to western France and down dangerously close to the Spanish border before returning home "to roost" that same night. The cloudless day had been ideal for "marching and flying," with the night giving way to stars as "a background for fireworks and street dancing." Japanese lanterns hung over the café terraces. People waltzed to accordion music in the open squares while others rode on the roofs of taxis to take in the scene. "The crowds on the sidewalk, the greatest seen in Paris for years, were enthusiastic, noisy, and satisfied. They shouted 'Ooray' for the magnificently modulated marching of the English soldiers, they shouted for all their own, faster-stepping troops, and they burst into pandemonium at the appearance of the famous and fierce Foreign Legion, on whom few of the French had even laid eyes before."

Following the parade, she returned to Orgeval, where friends continued to pile into Murphy's farmhouse. She passed a few long nights talking with Pauline Pfeiffer Hemingway, who was as concerned about her disintegrating marriage as she was about anything else going on at that moment.

Each new arrival brought some fresh rumor or prediction, "as you bring candy to your hostess," said Margaret Anderson, one among the many visitors that summer. *There won't be a war, after all. Mussolini is grievously ill. The common Germans are rebelling against Hitler.* One houseguest arrived swearing that the Germans would bomb France that very night.

By then Flanner had heard so much empty war-related chat that she thought she'd developed an immunity to it. "The higher the source for gossip, often the crazier it turns out to be," she told McKelway; "more full of real ignorance and pretentious wish-fulfillment and bigotry and hope." And yet she and Murphy started covering the farmhouse's windows at night with blue paper so no light could be detected. They stocked up on supplies, following the maximum government allotments for aspirin, iodine, sugar, soap, toothpaste, matches, and the precious one candle per day.

As the brilliance of July gave way to a stormy August, the days swerved wildly from dark with cloudbursts, hail, and lightning to turning chokingly hot. Flanner crammed in as much writing as she could before leaving, highly conscious of not moving quickly enough for the times. "Any news dispatched from Europe to America these days can be false by the time it is put to print," she warned her readers. Alongside her Letters she filed a balanced piece on German women living under Nazism, which would appear in the September issue of *Woman's Home Companion.*

In early August she drove with Murphy to Strasbourg to do a Letter on the region of Alsace-Lorraine along the border with Germany. "Wonderful country to ride about in," she told McKelway. "Found an intelligent official willing to talk...and found the best Moselle wine towns by habit." She drove around vineyards "and drank glasses by the oleanders blooming by the inns." It felt like a working holiday, she said. "Such fun." She closed her letter to McKelway with a sentiment that perhaps struck its American recipient as strange, coming from Europe in the summer of 1939. "Wish you were here too." She might just have been looking for something tender to say to her colleague, who had his own struggles, undergoing various treatments for what we would now call severe bipolar disorder while also navigating a chaotic romantic life. (McKelway would marry five times.)

Just as she filed the Strasbourg Letter, Flanner learned of Hitler and Stalin's nonaggression pact, giving Germany free rein to invade Poland unopposed, and forcing Britain and France to respond.

Flanner hurried to Paris to cover the scene as the French awaited general mobilization. She cabled *The New Yorker*: "Trouble expected this weekend but I still hope for some strange salvation. Am leaving Paris to stay in country near Saint Germain. Address me care Noel Murphy Orgeval Seine-et-Oise. Don't destroy Strasbourg Letter can be revamped later."

"Where's Orgeval?" someone from *The New Yorker* scribbled on a memo to Ross.

The next day Flanner sent another cable: "Still praying for a rabbit out of the hat." And the day after: "Nobody here knows if war or peace." She went back to Paris so she could cable her entire Letter, which couldn't be done in Orgeval. This was far more costly than mailing it, but she wanted to get her report out quickly.

Her Letter, which ran in the September 2 issue, described the hectic movements at the Gare de l'Est, from which men were headed "for the northern frontier fortresses," as well as the efforts to shuffle artworks out of the Louvre "in case war is to be an inevitable part of history." She conveyed the sense of shock and betrayal at seeing fascism and communism, the great ideological opposites, somehow join forces. "What Russia has done has been summed up by the French in one classic French phrase, '*Nous sommes cocus* (we've been cuckolded).'" The dread gripping Paris came coupled by a strange tedium in reaction to not knowing what the next days, not to mention years, would bring. "There has been little relieving excitement—nearly no news, no discussion, no facts, no arguments; nothing but waiting and watching men march off to what may be Sunday's, Monday's, or Tuesday's war."

And yet the general mobilization call had not yet come. The German fleet said to be heading to Danzig had not yet been sighted. "Diplomatic circles believe that Roosevelt's insistent messages may have made an impression," she wrote. There was "a faint hope of peace."

The people of Paris were in her view "completely calm." They'd grown used to the air raid sirens and the town criers urging them to avoid the use of headlamps and houselights at night. Putting herself in the mind of the hypothetical Frenchman about to be called up, she wrote, "If it's got to come, let's stop living in this grotesque suspense and get it over with once and for all." She suggested that "because French soil has not yet been violated, patriotism has not yet come into play. Few Frenchmen are thrilled to go forth and die on the Somme as usual—this time for Danzig. Yet all the French seem united in understanding that this war, if it comes, is about the theory of living and its eventual practice."

By the time her Letter ran, Germany had already invaded Poland, employing their blitzkrieg strategy of a heavy, fast offensive of armored units backed by coordinated air support, focused on striking and then surrounding critical targets.

On the morning of September 3 France and Britain declared war, fulfilling their agreement of mutual assistance with Poland. That evening, off the Scottish coast, a German U-boat torpedoed the British liner *Athenia*, an unarmed civilian ship bound for Montreal, carrying among its more than a thousand passengers several hundred Jewish refugees. One hundred and seventeen people were killed, including several Americans.

Flanner returned to Paris with Solano that same day to report on the reaction to war. It was a Sunday. Aside from air raid drills the city streets were relatively quiet. A few people carried their weekly shopping, using their now-mandatory gas masks to carry their produce. A lot of the stores and restaurants were shuttered. Use of telephones from anywhere other than a private residence was prohibited. Assuming, like many others, that German bombs would soon be falling, she'd hoped to get a last look at her most beloved statues and monuments as she traveled the city. Most of them had already been "sandbagged out of sight."

She and Solano heard Chamberlain on the radio, speaking from the Cabinet Room at Downing Street. "It is the evil things that we shall be fighting against—brute force, bad faith, injustice, oppression and persecution—and against them I am certain that the right will prevail." In solidarity with Poland Chamberlain's broadcast closed with a Chopin polonaise. Margaret Anderson, listening to the same speech, would recall, "The war for me became a victory, known in advance—Chopin over Hitler."

Flanner and Solano went to pay Monsieur Louis advance rent on their rooms at the Bonaparte, up until the following April, assuring him they would be back in Paris by the spring. Monsieur Louis stood at the building's front door and told them that if the Germans "dare to come here, I shall say to them, 'Gentlemen, you may not enter. *Je suis chez moi.*' "

They drove back to Orgeval, joining the masses fleeing the capital.

On that same Sunday, in California, Hildegarde wrote to Harold Ross

> in the hope you may be able to give me news concerning my sister Janet. We received a cable saying she had gone to the country in refuge but we know nothing further nor whether she is trying to return to this country—which, of course, we earnestly trust is so. We presume that her plans would depend largely upon what *The New Yorker* instructs her to do at this moment—in any case we suppose that you may have been in direct and recent touch with her, and we are anxious to have the latest information. Our mother is in the hospital and may have to undergo a major operation. We do not want Janet to be alarmed by this fact, and we confidently expect a successful outcome. But it would be a great help to our mother to have her mind more at rest concerning Janet.

The following day, September 4, Flanner cabled *The New Yorker* to say that for security reasons she'd been barred from cabling her Letters in English. She would keep trying to cable or telegraph as often as she could (and she'd have to write in French), but Orgeval's Western Union office kept shuttering without warning. For now, she would send her reports through Pan America's recently launched Yankee Clipper transatlantic air mail service. She closed her message: "Thanks for money. What a strange war."

McKelway wrote a memo to Ross, clipped to Flanner's just-received message about her difficulties sending cables, as well as the worried letter he'd gotten from Hildegarde. "Flanner is in some kind of panic, obviously," he told Ross. "Attached is my correspondence with her sister about her mother in which sister says mother is not so bad off. In answering Flanner you may want to mention that, as indicating our concern, if in urging her again to calm down and stay."

But by then Ross had already cabled Flanner, care of Murphy: "We here all think your continuing extremely important and urge you find safe place rural France and remain temporarily at least, cabling letter this Sunday and next...Please reply. Love and admiration."

Shortly afterward, Hildegarde got a letter from *The New Yorker* office, telling her that her sister was staying with "Mrs. Noel Murphy" in Orgeval "and doesn't seem unduly distressed. We have made arrangements for her to have plenty of money on call both in London and Paris, in case she should need to get out in a hurry...We are anxious for her to stay there at least temporarily...If we find that Janet wants to come home and is too upset by all that is going on, we will certainly not urge her to stay and will tell her that she undoubtedly can work for us over here to her benefit." It was signed by McKelway, who explained that Ross had asked him to answer on his behalf, since he, McKelway, was "more acquainted with the details, dealing with Janet all the time as I do."

Over the following days in France, banks and train stations and the offices of shipping lines hosted chaotic scenes. French troops dug in along the Maginot Line, the serpentine network of fortifications stretching north from the Swiss border to Luxembourg, meant to ward off attack from the east even while stopping short of Belgium, leaving a fatal gap from its tip at the Belgian border to the Channel. The first wave of the British Expeditionary Force would soon reach the Atlantic coast, with the majority of British soldiers deploying along the Franco-Belgian border. Four and a half million people would eventually be mobilized across the French empire. Large merchant vessels were requisitioned.

On September 6 Flanner went back again to Paris to send her latest Letter by telegraph. The next day from Orgeval she cabled McKelway, advising him that she wasn't sure she could repeat the feat. "Censoring and control of press dispatches change daily. I shall telegraph new letter or supplementary details Sunday if Western Union will accept. Otherwise by mail. Impossible to go to Paris on account of air raids and not enough gas. I will stay at Orgeval safe unless events become worse. Thanks for your cable. I am optimistic."

Her Paris Letter ran in the September 16 issue. "This is a queer war so far—Thank God!" she opened. She related how odd it was that in France the most up-to-date information about the war often came from American radio stations with strong signals, not because they could report things the Europeans couldn't but because they had better equipment and larger staffs.

Veering toward the realm of propaganda that she'd worked so hard to avoid in the past, she relayed the French disappointment in America's declaration of neutrality (many in France had believed that the German sinking of the *Athenia* would play a similar role as the sinking of the *Lusitania* had in finally drawing America into the First World War) and gushed about how American women were helping the French cause, almost certainly drawing on Murphy, Anderson, and other friends as sources. "American women who own automobiles have been aiding the evacuation from Paris of the lame, halt, and blind," she wrote, singling out the heroics of Anne Morgan, J. P. Morgan's daughter, whose committee was "already doing evacuation work in the north, with five American lady car-drivers and four nurses to attend the sick, and...making its first appeal for funds."

Everything Flanner had learned so far about any military maneuvering along the Franco-German border had struck her as "strategically strange." Each side's leaders appeared to be trying to prevent the war from "starting in earnest," reluctant to fully engage. It seemed the only war in history where, even after it had been declared, everyone involved still thought it might be called off. "There is a feeling of dry theory about this entire war, at least until it turns wet with blood."

Without knowing it, she was perfectly capturing the absurd start to what would be known in France as the *drole de guerre* (Phoney War), the stagnant, confounding, and ultimately demoralizing eight-month stretch of conflict without much action (aside from an early, brief, and failed French foray into the Saar region of western Germany), when French soldiers could sit within a few hundred feet of the Germans without orders to fire, lest they goad the enemy into an offensive.

Flanner spent the next few days at Orgeval in limbo, trying to enjoy what was for now a pleasant country life, in love with Murphy though agonizing over the knowledge that they would eventually be separated for some time, and appreciating her deep and enduring bond with Solano, who had also escaped to the farmhouse. They spent "from the first French news at 7 a.m. until the last American broadcast at 11:30 at night" at the shortwave radio, whose promise of whatever garbled scraps of intelligence it might broadcast attracted French officers to the farmhouse, "some of them volunteers of sixty, still gallant and vital with coquetry," as Margaret Anderson recalled. Masses were broadcast for those isolated parishes whose priests had been called up. "Multitudes of French families are now going to church by merely stepping into the parlor and tuning in on the source of their spiritual faith," wrote Flanner.

For someone whose job rested on her ability to provide clear information, she was finding little of it on offer. The Germans and Italians were jamming radio signals from neutral countries, so "to hear what Washington thinks, one is forced to overhear what German miliary bands are playing in Stuttgart or what tenors are singing in Milan… What Hitler really hopes for or is truly fighting for no one knows, as no one on earth knows his odd, dangerous mind," she wrote in a September Letter from Paris (written in and sent from Orgeval). "France is digging in and preparing for any fate. The strained curiosity of an intelligent people awaits more satisfaction and enlightenment than events now offer."

She told readers of how she'd come to depend on a boy, whose father, the local grocer, had just been mobilized. He came twice a week from the town two miles over to knock at the farmhouse window and take their orders, nudging them toward the items he had in stock. If, "like everybody else, what you want is soap…he suggests that you order mustard instead." And the children and wives of grocers and butchers and bakers, who now drove their father's or husband's delivery cars, had also become vital news sources. "We eat their food; we eat their words."

At night Flanner, Solano, Murphy, and Anderson would wander the fields, sometimes discussing their shared worries under the stars. "Would the life we had known in Europe be destroyed?" wrote Anderson, looking back on that summer. "Were we ourselves destined to become catastrophe-people? Could we stay together or would we be separated? Should those who had resources go back to America, try from there to rescue the others?" More often than not they walked in silence, "and looked and listened, measured the peace and order of night. What peace? Stars living and dying."

Flanner described those walks in *The New Yorker.* "Never have nights been more beautiful than these nights of anxiety. In the sky have been shining in trinity the moon, Venus, and Mars. Nature has been more splendid than man."

Ross, directly and via McKelway, repeated his wish that Flanner stay on in France to cover the war. She refused. She'd secured time off to visit her mother and she meant to keep her promise. Solano, too, wanted to leave. Flanner was convinced of the rightness of their decision. She was an American woman who'd written against fascism and could very well be on a German list of targets. And even if she could find the courage to stay and write about violence, she thought she still lacked the skills a good war correspondent required. "I cannot compete with the American newspaper men in Paris, who have not only a vast organization at their command, but also a newshound instinct," she confessed to McKelway. "My being only a commentator puts me in a curious isolated corner." Her problem was that she'd "always written to one side (or behind or around the corner from) the regular news."

At sunrise on September 16, Murphy drove Flanner and Solano toward Bordeaux, where they hoped to find speedy passage for

America. Anderson had driven from Paris the night before—taking her away from her lover Georgette Leblanc, who'd just had surgery for cancer—and escorted them in her own car to the crossroads at the edge of Orgeval. "We were like figures in an old engraving, parting at dawn on dangerous missions, but with motorcars instead of horses standing in the mist," she recalled.

Murphy started up the Ford's engine and drove south, all of the women in tears. They'd packed four suitcases and brought along thirty-five gallons of gasoline in cans. Planes flew above them. Low-lying fog made it a difficult drive. At times they shared the road with lines of rattling tanks painted in camouflage, some garlanded with flowers. Soldiers had written the names of their sweethearts in chalk on the necks of the guns. The women saw artillery being pulled by groups of muscled Percheron stallions. Halfway to Bordeaux they stopped at Tours for more gas but found empty signs on the station's tanks. They managed to beg for four gallons. Securing any more than that required written permission. Rejoining the main road, they passed green buses from Paris sagging under the weight of medical supplies, horse feed, kit bags, and furniture for the barracks.

They arrived, bone-shaken, at Bordeaux. The port city had long been a waystation for travelers to and from Europe. Hemingway had taken his first European steps there, among the American Red Cross ambulance drivers deposited there by the transport ship *Chicago* in the final months of the First World War. In the past weeks fifteen thousand Americans had passed through looking for a way home. Many thousands more came seeking routes to other countries. By the time Flanner and Solano arrived, Bordeaux remained the only French port serving North and South America.

Murphy left them. In the immediate she would go to work with Anne Morgan helping to ferry the disabled out of Paris. She knew the dangers to expect. A few weeks earlier, when her wait in a bank line had been interrupted by an air raid drill, she'd used the moment to write to her sister-in-law Sara Murphy urging her "for heaven's sake" to get Sara's daughter Honoria out of Paris and back to America as fast as possible, while also hoping—vainly, as Honoria refused to leave Europe without her mother—that Sara would then come back to help. (When Sara and Honoria Murphy finally had left from Le Havre on the coast of Normandy a few days after France declared war, they found their ship, the *George Washington*, had just been repainted with a massive Stars and Stripes to remind enemy bombers of its American, rather than French or British, provenance.)

Flanner and Solano checked in to Bordeaux's Hotel Majestic and tried to settle into some kind of life. They couldn't find places on any ships. Military planes flew overhead while the people below panicked and fought in the streets. Blackouts threw the city into darkness each night. Flanner was sure the Majestic would be bombed. She felt numb.

The city was packed. Some people passed the time drinking, others watched movies, others prayed. Seats, beds, pews: all were crammed with bodies. Any place dealing in mail or news or travel had a line morning and night. Bordeaux was now a city of strangers, some "going there for the first time and perhaps seeing France for the last time, people moving away from the war, people arriving to take their part in it, people safely hibernating, people being evacuated, people of all stations and colors, from all nation and dependencies." The army had put many of the area's men to work harvesting and storing the grapes from what had been a bountiful summer, preparing for the eventuality that French citizens might not have access to Bordeaux's yields for some summers to come.

Flanner lauded the staff of the American consulate for functioning "admirably, patiently, and paternally," and waiving regular bureaucratic requirements for travel. But finding a sailing was the greater task. The United States Lines office was in "total confusion" as people poured in from all over France after failing to get out of the other main ports of Cherbourg or Le Havre in the north. The police barred entry to the building. People had been camped on the sidewalk outside for a week, waiting for the company to honor the return tickets that they'd bought months earlier, back in their hometowns.

Flanner cabled a Letter from Bordeaux at the end of September. Russia had just invaded Poland, an about-turn as staggering as the Russian-German pact had been a few weeks earlier. In "grim shock," Flanner wondered about the "psychological possibilities" of this abrupt shift in policy. She couldn't figure out what Germany and Russia were playing at, nor how deep this "opportunist union of Europe's two ideological enemies" truly went. She offered no prediction. She was on firmer ground in the Letter's second half as she conjured Graham Greene in describing Americans, French officers, and "rich Brazilians" whiling away their time at the terrace bar of an upscale hotel, overlooking an avenue flooded with loitering lower-class drinkers. She spotted, among those waiting for passage, her hero Arturo Toscanini, already in exile from Italy and soon to be returning to New York, as well as the Trinidadian-American flying ace known as "the Black Eagle," Hubert Fauntleroy Julian, who planned "to fly something for someone in the war if he can get things fixed up in Harlem first."

In her next Letter from Bordeaux, Flanner wrote that she'd learned the name of the man people believed to be the first French soldier killed in these hostilities, Clément Sarantyn, a twenty-nine-year-old sergeant who fell in the short-lived Saar offensive. His was a lovely name and one "easy to recall...before the millions of other names are perhaps finally turned in. All over France, in the parish churches and...town squares, the war memorials and names of the last war still look so new, so little weathered, so freshly carved that French sculpture would seem to have no need for more so soon."

After three weeks at the Hotel Majestic Flanner and Solano boarded the SS *Washington* on October 5, 1939, scheduled to dock at New York's Pier 59 a week later. Before leaving she'd received a cable from Ross, advising her that he was sending her colleague A. J. Liebling on a plane to Paris as her "substitute," and that she should immediately send Liebling a list of all her sources and any other "inside dope."

Flanner watched France, Spain, Portugal, disappearing. Solano stood on the deck beside her. Noël Murphy was likely in her Ford somewhere between Orgeval and Paris. Flanner's future with each woman remained uncertain.

She had no address, no professional direction, little money. She was leaving what she knew to be the biggest story of her lifetime. She was leaving millions with no ships to board and no piers that would ever welcome them. She had been a foreign correspondent. She had been a foreigner. She had been in France to observe and explain it for American pleasure. She had never been French. She had always been an American.

Her Letter from France, filed a few hours before stepping onto the *Washington*, ran in *The New Yorker* during her crossing.

> This period has brought about the greatest, most terrible, and most destructive migration of modern times, a

> movement of men, women, and children trekking across Europe in flight from other men, women, and children, hurrying because there have been bombs in the air or because there will be bombs in the air, running with their bundles or sitting stagnant in slow trains, sleeping in strangers' garrets or haymows, and eating bitter bread anywhere because they are democrats or Jews or Christians or libertarians or just plain people, trying to save their sanity, their children, and what is left of their lives. Whether they go north, south, east, or west, they head toward poverty.

These men, women, and children had been displaced by a war that with all its absurdities, paradoxes, and delicate patchworks of allegiance and rivalry was still, to her eye "really a commonplace war, since it is simply a fight for liberty. It is only because of its potential size that it may, alas, prove to be civilization's ruin." She signed off as Genêt. A long, painful time would pass before she signed that name again. Now she was only Janet Flanner.

43

PARIS, GERMANY

As the Wehrmacht took Paris in June 1940, a group of Gestapo agents went to search the Versailles Palais de Justice for Weidmann's case files. They destroyed the few documents they could find and then went hunting for Weidmann's lawyers and for his executioner.

They located one of the defense attorneys, Raoult. He'd understood the value of his Weidmann documents and had already hidden them in his son's toy box before the Germans arrived. They searched his house but failed to look there. The files survived. A search of the home of the lawyer Planty also revealed nothing.

Weidmann's executioner, Jules-Henri Desfourneaux, had little to offer the questioning agents. He would continue his work through the war. As a public servant of Vichy France, he would cut off the heads of several members of the French Resistance.

Vincent de Moro-Giafferi knew that his name would be high on the list of French targets and had fled his apartment at 27, Avenue Kléber before Paris fell. The Germans tore up the property, removing every single object they found. Moro would manage to always stay one step ahead of the Nazis and Vichy officials for the duration of the war, first in the south of France and then in Corsica.

Renée Jardin actively collaborated with the Nazis during the war. She convinced the Germans, who'd learned that Weidmann had kept a prison diary, that no such diary existed.

Only a quarter century later—after the deaths of Moro, Planty, and Raoult—would Jardin publish her annotated reproduction of the small red book that was in the envelope Weidmann had given her on the morning of his death.

Coda

HARSH INTELLIGENCE AND BEAUTIFUL SPOILS

Following the liberation of Paris in August 1944, Flanner returned to France for *The New Yorker*, traveling as an enlistee in the Women's Army Corps (WAC). William Shawn threw her a send-off at the office, to which she wore her WAC-issued field jacket and olive skirt, "to get the shock over with." Her colleagues "approved" of the uniform, "even declared [it] becoming."

She told Ross she planned to write on the search for looted artworks and other cultural treasures, and the punishment of the Nazis and their French collaborators. She was once again, as she had two decades earlier, going to Paris for "Beauty, with a capital B," now paired with writing about Justice with a capital J.

She had passed the war working in the worst office in *The New Yorker's* headquarters on Forty-Third Street. She slept poorly, smoked endlessly. Her hair came out in clumps. Noël Murphy, writing to Flanner just after the fall of France in June 1940, had given her a directive:

"Wake the Americans up." Flanner became a loud voice for American involvement in the war, bucking the consensus at that time, pre–Pearl Harbor, which favored nonintervention. She argued that the world's democracies had to send the message that any sovereign nation's borders couldn't be breached without dire consequences for the invader. She gave a series of public lectures, seeking to engage Americans in the war effort. "We must be ready with the deep feeling and the real conviction that democracy is worth dying for, as our ancestors did," she told her audiences.

At a cocktail party in the summer of 1940 she met Natalia Danesi Murray, ten years younger than Flanner, beautiful and dark with a beguiling voice, and divorced from the New York head of the William Morris Agency. She worked as an Italian-language broadcaster for NBC, which beamed shortwave reports into Europe. Flanner visited her often on Fire Island, where Murray kept a cottage. They frequented a rundown hotel called Duffy's because it had a jukebox and small dance floor. It was there, Murray's son wrote, that "my mother and Janet had danced together, had drunk a lot, had toasted their hatred of dictators together, and had fallen in love."

Flanner saw in the Italian-born Murray some of the European vitality she'd once known in France. By the end of their first summer together they'd moved into a rented duplex they called the Chicken Coop at the top of a building at Fifty-Eighth and Madison. Solano, who despised Murray, described this period as the time when "everything changed nearly down to the roots of life." But Solano soon met a sculptor named Elizabeth Jenks Clark, and they settled together in New Jersey. Solano and Flanner kept up their regular and intimate correspondence.

For *The New Yorker* Flanner filed informative pieces such as "Paris, Germany," about life in occupied Paris, drawing on contacts in France including the American ambassador Bullitt, whom she'd profiled before the war. She also wrote about French collaboration with the Germans, dangerous subject matter at the time. She wanted to get the truth out into the open, so that people could judge events and act accordingly, following their conscience about whether to engage with Germany for the abstract cause of democracy rather than out of specific allegiance to France. In another piece she offered a rousing account of the growing French Resistance and one of the earliest American profiles of the man she saw as the great hope for France, Charles de Gaulle, at a time when he was still a relatively obscure figure, internationally. Rather than looking for anything humorous about de Gaulle or his public persona, as she would have instinctively done before the war, she instead wove a straightforward account of a heroic leader.

Her best wartime work was a massive four-part profile of Marshal Phillipe Pétain, the octogenarian head of Vichy France, into which she wove a deeply researched history of Third Republic France, in particular the events leading to war and collaboration. "Printing this will probably be a milestone in American journalism," Ross told her in 1944. "I don't know what our debutant subscribers and the younger married set will think about this, but our savant clientele will be profoundly impressed and a great many other adults, for the series has a surge to it that makes it almost a romantic adventure piece. I now think your time was well spent and that probably you'll be offered a chair of French History at some Middle Western University."

In the spring of 1944, at the request of the US government, Flanner wrote a pocket guide to France for soldiers prepping for D-Day. Shortly after finishing it, she decided it was time for her to get back to Europe.

Murray, wanting to stay close to Flanner and eager to contribute to the American effort in the European theater of war, had left her broadcasting career to train at the OWI (Office of War Information), becoming a captain in Special Services in its Psychological Warfare Branch. She and Flanner had separated with loose plans to reconnect as soon as possible. "She wondered where we would meet and when," recalled Murray. "She felt cut in pieces by geography: New York, Paris, Rome." Solano, though happy in New Jersey, told Flanner that she, too, longed to join her abroad, ideally within the year. Meanwhile, the first person Flanner wanted to find once she reached France was Noël Murphy.

Terrified of flying and set to cross the Atlantic for the first time ever by plane, she felt she had "nothing in my head but work, worry, and dull confusion," plagued by survivor's guilt, and unsure of how best to serve as a journalist. In early November 1944 she took off for a flight to London that started out with "a handsome orange moon" and bright stars before giving way to "blue sunshine and bluer ocean." She was the lone woman among the passengers and to her surprise the one with the steeliest nerves. "I am as calm as a bird in flight. No fear. I was calmer than all the men!"

During her stopover in London she shared fish and chips in Soho with Nancy Cunard, who'd been working there as a translator, and was "still angry at the world of course." A few months earlier, begging her to come to France, Cunard had relayed what it felt like to be in the thick of the conflict: "Great love and much of it. Excitement, tragedy, danger, beauty, huge walks, climbing, dawns and nights, and WINE and TOBACCO, and REAL values."

As soon as Flanner reached Paris she took the electric train to the "comic" Saint-Germain-en-Laye train station a few miles from Orgeval, passing the cemetery where Noël Murphy's husband was buried, fortunate that her track hadn't numbered among the many across France that had been blown up at the hands of either the Germans, the Allies, or the Resistance. Noël met her at the train at dusk in the pouring rain. She looked thin and bent "as any peasant after four year's labor in mud and wind," her hands rough from work. And yet for someone who'd so often been ill, she seemed healthier than ever, which Murphy attributed to regular hours, hard work, vegetables from her garden, and sour milk from her cow, Salomé. Although bombs had fallen nearby and Germans had camped on a neighboring property, the farmhouse, too, remained in good shape. The old cats Flanner had once doted on now had grandchildren.

It was an awkward reunion. After her letter in June 1940 and a one-sentence note a few weeks later saying she was safe, Murphy had stopped writing to Flanner altogether. ("Noel is incommunicado to you," Cunard had written to Flanner in 1940; "that is worst of ALL things, save death.") Murphy had learned from Hemingway that Flanner had met someone new in America. She accepted "without question like a hind that is beaten [the] fact that I have an Italian friend," Flanner told Solano, adding that Murphy never let on if she knew how deeply that friendship ran. "What a coward I am, but how can I deliver that blow [from] which she so obviously cowers in order not to receive?"

Flanner and Murphy's own connection remained strong, though she was baffled by Murphy's almost beatific detachment from all that she'd experienced during the war, including a brief imprisonment. "How can I hate anyone?" Murphy answered in reaction to Flanner's surprise at her relatively forgiving views on the enemy; "everyone is so awful." Flanner assumed Murphy's love of German culture had somehow deranged her. "I am not interested in anybody preferring German lieder to US Kentucky hillbilly songs," she wrote to Solano. "I am interested in knowing in which time which race has organized, fantastically, to represent an alliance with evil." She wondered how the same woman who'd often shocked her with her past "brutality" had morphed into "the nicest woman in France, so good, so gentle, undemanding." (Murphy would be accused of active collaboration; Flanner refused to believe she'd gone that far.) She recognized that Murphy had been the one who'd had to deal with Nazis on her doorstep, and for that reason she pushed the issue no further.

After three days Flanner returned to Paris, having hitchhiked on an army Jeep from Orgeval, a practice she would repeat many times as she spent parts of each week with Murphy. Canadian soldiers were the ones who stopped most often to pick her up.

The French capital had been spared heavy bombing by both the Germans and the Allies, and while many public sculptures had been looted and many walls and streets had been left pockmarked by gunfire, most of the city's major monuments and buildings remained unharmed. Flanner went to see the Grand Palais, badly damaged in a firefight, and the National Archives, so shaken by shelling that hundreds of its windows had shattered. Tens of thousands of books had been lost to a fire at the Palais Bourbon, where German troops had entrenched themselves in the final stages of the city's liberation. The city was filthy from neglect. Much of the Tuileries Gardens had been dug up for trenches, strewn with barbed wire and abandoned artillery. Flanner found the city "shabby" and its inhabitants "rude and sad."

Calling on the proprietors of the now "utterly decrepit" Hotel Bonaparte, Flanner found Madame Mélanie dying of breast cancer, heavily drugged, and "talking feverishly." Monsieur Louis said little and cried often. The gossip was that he rented out a couple of the rooms by the hour. Flanner told Solano that a German had taken over her old place while an American woman, a "semi trollop," had occupied Flanner's. "I can never sleep in that bed." The French friends she'd reconnected with all looked "completely deteriorated." "Dear God is all Europe ill and dying?," Flanner wrote to Solano. Flanner saw the whole "sadness of this Continent" mirrored in people's "private lives, in their smaller complete sadness."

After seeing the Bonaparte she felt doubly thankful for having been placed across the river with several other foreign journalists at the aptly named Hotel Scribe, until recently the Paris base for Nazi propaganda officers, now headquarters of the Allied press corps. There she and her colleagues tracked the war's progress on giant maps pasted to a conference room wall, and shared access to telegraphs, telephones, and an in-house radio studio. She and the few other female correspondents were advised not to go out in public unless in uniform, "for safety" as "foreign ladies."

She felt out of place among the several-hundred-strong corps, most far younger than her, and almost all of them men. But she soon became a popular figure, treated as a kind of mascot and praised for her ability to drink as hard as anyone there. She favored dry martinis. Hemingway joined her often in the hotel's basement bar, usually deep into the night, and snuck up in the mornings to use her bath. Sometimes they visited their old haunt, the Deux Magots, where Hemingway, "in a rumbling whisper," read her some poems he was working on. She thought the poems—most likely ones written for Mary Walsh, soon to become Hemingway's fourth wife—told the "truth of a decade," she wrote to Solano. "I've seen a lot of him & love him far more than ever." The two were photographed at the Deux Magots resplendent in their heavy uniforms, her hair snow white, his streaked with silver, their respective thick eyeglasses on the table, a cigarette between her fingers, various half-gone drinks in front of them. In the picture they are huddled close enough to touch. He looks down at his words on the paper; she looks off into the distance, forehead creased, strong chin jutting out. There is a heaviness about the pair. They look closer to seventy than to her fifty-two and his forty-four.

Beyond the hotel and the cafés Flanner found Paris embroiled in a period of recriminations and revenge. Gone was the elation of the first months after the liberation, when American and British flags flew in tandem with the *tricolore* from seemingly every window, strangers came up to embrace soldiers, and the metros were packed with people eager to throw themselves back into the routines of daily life. All around her she saw "dishonesty, fear—all from Nazis yes, but before was here, fear of losing money value, losing greed, comfort as they call it, indifferent to voice of mind, only body."

France no longer executed criminals like Eugen Weidmann publicly. But summary executions had become a common occurrence. Acting sometimes spontaneously and sometimes with careful planning, people shot their fellow citizens dead in the street without trial, for the crime of collaboration. This was the so-called *épuration sauvage* (wild purge), the first chaotic stage that preceded the more codified purging done in courts. Women accused of giving comfort to the enemy (known as "horizontal collaboration") had their heads shaved in public squares and were sometimes marched naked down the streets afterward, sometimes assaulted, and in some cases beaten to death by the crowds. "You have no idea how strangely things have turned out here," she told Solano. "Nothing not even treachery or collaboration is anything like the same in shape, form or intensity as I fancied it in New York."

Surveying the French capital, so familiar and so foreign at once, she felt as if she were looking at a "picture of something now fallen to the bottom of a well, with water clouding the image and mud despoiling the color." Even while walking its streets she felt "homesick" for Paris, since the city she knew no longer existed. "I continue to feel I shall fall awake soon, as one falls asleep, a process of nature, and when I fall awake, nothing which has happened will be true," she told Solano. "So must the people of Europe feel, and they have had to hope to awake for five years."

On December 15, 1944, she filed her first Letter from Paris in five years.

She covered food rationing, the black market, the national sense of shame and tepid optimism, de Gaulle and the functions of the new government, the deaths of friends and strangers, and "the cleaning up of the collaborationists." She got into it without any ado, writing declarative sentences as if she'd never left: "The good and bad that lie at the base of French life are now being temporarily pressed to the top," she wrote in the opening paragraph. The country had entered a necessarily violent period of rejuvenation, another cycle in its modern history of revolution, one requiring an unwavering, even brutal, sense of purpose. "As *Combat*, a former underground newspaper that has assumed great importance here, has just declared, this is the time, in France, for harsh intelligence." After the "great national deviation from morality as the result of the French people's contact with the Nazi doctrines and of the French people's unhappy, defeated, introverted contact with itself...what France needs most, now that she clearly has a leader without a past, is not the salvation offered by any one political party but a revival of morality, to be practiced alike by the governing and the governed."

The piece ran signed by Genêt. Neither Flanner nor Ross had

thought about what byline to use in advance. Ross cabled her just before the Letter ran: "Used Genet signature with earnest conviction that it sounds triumphant note at this moment." She said she was happy he felt that way and told him that he'd acted as a "supreme editor in chief" in making the call unilaterally. She was, however, "disgusted" that William Shawn, whom she normally adored, had rewritten the Letter to "smooth" over her "acute sharp angry tone," and that he'd changed her use of "We" to an "I," which "I never used in fifteen years at the job."

At the Hotel Scribe, as Flanner and a few colleagues passed Christmas Eve of 1944 over a dinner of goose and champagne bought from the army post exchange, and a good bottle of "prewar gin," everyone was talking about the final push in Europe. About 150 miles to the east in the freezing forests of Ardennes, Allied troops were waging what would be the last large offensive campaign on the Western Front, the Battle of the Bulge. Even when complete victory felt so near at hand Flanner remained pessimistic. "I do not see how the upper class minds, the anti-democrat brains which have shown such stupidity in the decades just past, have enough intelligence to force onto the world what they want today, yet such seems the case," she wrote to Murray. "Everywhere the true democrat forces seem pushed down as if they were dogs" while the entrenched class of elites "with its selfish habit of privilege, its contempt for all those beneath" remained as powerful as ever. As she looked at France in "complete paralysis," she asked if even in defeat Germany and all the other anti-democratic "enemies" had somehow "won, as usual." She said that she had long "been in love with democracy, the words of some men, like Lincoln, have been like love letters to me. But [democracy] is not a good lover anymore, it is somewhat senile & very rich & its mood is Saturday night, not a long arcadian perspective. This is the century of Saturday night, in America at least."

After her initial burst of writing she simply stopped. She wondered if she'd lost the ability to feel altogether, admitting to Solano that she couldn't even bring herself to cry. She failed to hit a deadline for the first time in her career.

It was Hemingway who gave her the push she realized she needed. He suggested she go out to La Rochelle, an active combat zone, to see firsthand how war was waged. A Scottish army captain took her there in his Jeep. She arrived wearing an officer's khaki-and-green field uniform, accented by her own choice of pink pants, the red fur-lined cowboy boots ("my wild west boots!," she called them) gifted to her from the editor of British *Vogue*, and matching mittens. She brought the soldiers chocolate, cigarettes, tea, soup, and gloves. She stayed for five days, getting close enough to talk with active combatants and put herself at risk of being hit by enemy fire.

But back in Paris she didn't know how to translate the experience into a Letter. She told Solano that Hemingway advised her to write "it the way you saw it, dog (his new name for all)—There is never any other story," to which she'd answered that it felt as if she hadn't seen anything. "That is always all," he'd said back to her. She said this was the finest writing advice she'd ever received.

While in the past she'd often complained about the rigors of traveling for her work now she wanted to be everywhere at once, to see as much of the war and its effects as she could. Citing her potential usefulness in helping to communicate with locals and prisoners in French and German, as well as her knowledge of European political history, she bargained for access to areas that other enlistees in the WAC couldn't reach. She slept in simple military cots or on the floor of whatever press camp she was stationed in, in a borrowed sleeping bag. She tried to manage her drinking, though going more than a few days without alcohol made her feel "nervous and tight."

In a Letter from Cologne she reported on the aftermath of its fall to the Allied forces, after being bombed beyond recognition over the course of more than two hundred aerial raids. She'd used the piece to illuminate Germany's mistreatment of its prisoners, who'd finally been liberated from the city's Gestapo prison. "During their first half hour's delirium of freedom and fresh air, [they] acted like lunatics—sobbing, falling down on the cobblestones of the courtyard, wagging their heads, and holding their temples, where they had most often been beaten. From the nose of one French boy the blood spurted in a pale-pink, excited, pulsing jet." Ross advised Flanner to keep "this piece in mind as an example of how simple it is to scoop the world, even if a flock of other journalists have the same facts and the same opportunities...You have told me...what the Germans *are* in Cologne...The war is going to be over and forgotten before any number of real atrocity stories are printed, I'm afraid, unless the *New Yorker* gets around to doing something."

After Cologne, Flanner flew to Wiesbaden, where she interviewed a young French woman who had been arrested after being anonymously denounced for her role in the French Resistance and recently released from Ravensbrück, the women's concentration camp. Flanner wrote her piece on Ravensbrück that same night, and the next morning pressed the wary army censors to let it through relatively intact. Flanner confronted readers with the image of a survivor whose "torso now seemed to consist of only her broad shoulder bones" and who spoke of starvation and lashings and medical torture and forced labor and other "constant and humiliating horrors" the woman was too traumatized to name, and of the mass murder of Jews.

From there Flanner flew to Weimar to ride by Jeep toward Buchenwald a few days after its liberation. A young survivor led her around the grounds, showing her the gallows, the crematorium outside of which she saw naked corpses stacked not far from the tidy flower gardens kept by Nazi officers. "I wish nothing had happened that has happened in all our lives," she wrote to Solano.

"The news from the concentration camps seemed to me the most important news of all the years of the war," she wrote to Murray. "With the...emergences of dead and dying, what lay behind the war, vaguely perceived but not so important as the military figure of Nazi might, suddenly became the great, horrible, shocking protagonist. It must never be forgotten." She echoed the sentiment nearly word for word in *The New Yorker.* Over the following months Flanner would try to trace the fates of prisoners of the camps for their American friends and relatives.

After Buchenwald she woke at nights screaming. She'd seen "wicked *proof*" of the pointlessness of "governments, politics, religion, God, and even man himself." And yet at the same time she felt a renewed sense of purpose as one who could expose a broad audience to what she'd witnessed. "You'd not know me," she told Murray. "I fly around like an elderly white crow; I have a fine Nazi pistol; I stand journeys which slay the younger women. I am trying to watch, learn, think, decide as to what will happen to this wicked Europe."

She was back in Paris for the final days of the war in Europe. "Death to tyrants," she wrote after Mussolini's summary execution and Hitler's suicide. "What rejoicing. How feeble the mere headlines Mussolini Dead, Hitler Dead...the Bible alone with its terrible paeans of praise for the dead enemy are suited to the hearts now light with joy because of death...Curse them both."

All she could think to do on V-E Day was to go visit Monsieur Louis at the Bonaparte. "We drank Armagnac of an old vintage in an osier case, smelling of our peculiar basement, we drank to victory, to you, to the departed," she wrote to Solano. "We both wept."

"Physically war stops, mentally it now begins," she told Murray. They saw one another a few weeks later, spending a few June days in Rome before traveling on to Capri, and Naples. Their time in Italy, "living in the luxury of love and private surroundings…in happiness, in beauty, in scenes of art, in ripe figs, yellow wine and yellow sun," rejuvenated Flanner's long-dormant aestheticism, which she'd feared she'd lost for good. She set off on what was perhaps the most brilliant and productive period of her entire half-century career.

In the fall of 1945, Flanner traveled through Germany, gathering material and conducting interviews to write a series of pieces she would collectively title "The Beautiful Spoils." It would be about how the Nazis had organized their massive operation to systematically loot or destroy countless works of art and cultural artifacts across Europe, and would end with a profile of the sixty-odd volunteers of the Monuments, Fine Arts, and Archives section of the Allied Forces, tasked with mitigating wartime damage to culturally valuable sites and recovering stolen art; they were known as the Monuments Men.

She meanwhile arranged to go to Nuremberg to cover the international military tribunals set to open that November, where twenty-two Nazi leaders would stand trial. She'd planned to attend a day of the proceedings and write up a single Letter as she focused on her research into looted art. But the drama and historical significance of the trial gripped her. She would file five Letters from Nuremberg even as she traveled around Germany and France to complete her three long "Beautiful Spoils" pieces, alongside several Letters from Paris and elsewhere.

The Allied powers had chosen Nuremberg, then under American occupation, both because of the symbolic weight of its having hosted the annual Nazi rallies, and because although bombed beyond recognition it was one of the few cities in Germany with a courthouse still standing. Charging the Nazis for the mass murder of Jews and other persecuted groups was only one facet of the proceedings. The tribunal's driving goals were to establish a public record of what the Nazis had done and to set internationally recognized standards by which future war criminals would be judged, so that such atrocities would never be repeated.

Flanner was assigned to live in a castle just beyond the city with forty other women: reporters, legal clerks, stenographers. They shared a single bathroom, with one bath, a toilet, and two male urinals. When the official overseeing the villa said that the women were being difficult as they complained about the conditions, Flanner responded that giving women urinals would indeed make them difficult. Flanner joked in a letter to Murray that the Russian women hogged the bathroom by going in groups, as if extending communist ideology to their basic needs.

On the trial's first day, as American Supreme Court associate justice Robert H. Jackson read sixty-five pages of charges, people in the courtroom heard what was for the vast majority of them a new word, coined in 1944 by the Polish Jewish lawyer Raphael Lemkin: genocide. The 160 journalists gathered there to hear the charges were "momentarily the world's largest news group in one place covering one event," noted Flanner.

She turned fifty-four in Nuremberg, enjoying what she called "a ripe period" in her life. She felt she was on "a small Allied island of hope, sanity, and justice surrounded by the sullen, Valhalla-minded Germans and their ruined town." Fellow reporters would remember her typing away in the Nuremberg pressroom deep into the night, as if she never slept. "I have never worked harder," she told Murray. "I have been really not normal."

Attuned to all matters of performance and spectacle, her eye was drawn to all the different ways in which the players involved in the trial presented themselves. She was most fascinated by Goering, who she thought delivered a "bravura" performance, showing himself to be far more cunning than Jackson and the other prosecutors. "Everybody in court had suffered, one way or another, from Göring's mind, but few had ever before sat and listened to it work," she wrote in *The New Yorker*. "He was malicious and disturbing." His testimony "amounted to an alarmingly serious lecture given by an active, if captive, historian on the most cynical military period in Europe's history." Talking over the muffled explosions of dynamite from beyond the courthouse, as the Allies worked to clear Nuremberg's rubble, he laid out the Nazi plans to conquer the Mediterranean, take Suez, and trick Russia into fighting England, going country by country with cold logic. "It seemed as if I were listening to the words, to the idea, the moment indeed, when IF—the gigantic IF was being reported upon, by which they might have won," Flanner told Solano.

She understood how angry some of their friends would be that she "called Goering intelligent" in print, she told Murray. "But he is; he was formidable on the stand in his own right and seemed even more dangerous because of the stupidity of our Jackson." Unlike many of her peers she was careful not to be blinded by patriotism in reporting on how the Americans were handling the proceedings. She pointed out how American prosecutors showed film footage from Belsen, Dachau, and Buchenwald while levying charges against the Nazi wars of aggression in Czechoslovakia and Austria, not the countries where these camps were located, and argued that by reading and rereading the same evidence ad nauseam, they were only weakening their case. "Our lawyers have succeeded in making the world's most completely planned and horribly melodramatic war dull and incoherent."

But critiques of prosecutorial strategy aside, her overarching goal with the Nuremberg Letters was to leave an explicit record of what the world had suffered at the hands of the Nazis and to outline the ultimately heroic Allied efforts to charge multiple defendants with the novel charge of crimes against humanity, in a case without any true precedent. And she didn't flinch when describing the evidence of atrocities presented during the trial, as when the courtroom was shown snapshots taken by Nazi soldiers that included "in addition to a German police dog eating a living man, and a starved pig eating a man, wife, and child while bystanding Germans pointed and laughed—a child who had been decapitated and several adult heads without bodies. It must have been spring down there. Beside the heads the German soldiers had stuck signs on which they had scribbled, 'Spring Fruit!'"

She rightly anticipated that the tribunal would fail to stamp out Nazi ideology, noting that even as the trial went on there were people in England bidding furiously to buy items from von Ribbentrop's London embassy furnishings at auction. She quoted a German professor who said that "the worst of Nazism is that parts of it are now organized, instead of unorganized, kinds of thinking, and all over the world many people still have such thoughts."

When the last of the Nuremberg Letters ran, Ross, along with his own congratulations, told her that the publisher Alfred Knopf had called it the finest reporting he'd seen on the trial. Katharine White added that the work was "magnificent and makes me proud that *The New Yorker* has you in Europe."

That October of 1946, twelve of the twenty-two defendants were sentenced to death by hanging, which took place in the prison's gymnasium two weeks later. (Goering would escape execution by swallowing a cyanide pill.) Albert Speer, the architect who'd designed the fairgrounds not far from where the trial took place, was among those who escaped execution in favor of multiyear prison terms. Many would see those sentences shortened. There would be twelve more trials at Nuremberg. Most of the criminals convicted there would be released by the end of the 1950s.

Flanner had by then told Noël Murphy how intimately she'd entwined her life with Natalia Murray, and Murphy hadn't taken it well. Meanwhile Murray complained that she felt like one of Flanner's three wives, alongside Solano and Murphy. Flanner shot back that she also had "a husband, *The New Yorker*." She admitted that her heart ached "for the pain I give you & me, for the pain I give Noel and even Solita." But at the same time she asked what was so wrong about wanting to stay connected "with those one has loved, when one loves again?"

Murray floated the idea of moving to Paris, but Flanner forbade it, for the sake of Murphy, who tolerated their relationship but swore that if Murray came to Paris she would cut Flanner completely from her life. "I feel a foreigner everywhere," Flanner told Murray. "Unsatisfying, polygamist, neither Christian nor pagan, neither good friend nor loyal lover, neither bold enough for my desires nor harsh enough to be responsible for my acts." She toyed with quitting the magazine altogether to appease Murray, but couldn't see surviving mentally or financially without her job. The best she could manage was to ask for periodic breaks so that they could be temporarily reunited, while making endless promises to return permanently to New York and to their life together.

Finally in May 1947, Murray gave Flanner a list of demands that would have to be met or she would leave her for good. A few days later, Murray, hearing no response to this ultimatum, then sent a letter of final parting, telling Flanner that she was now free to pursue her work without the burden of their relationship.

Flanner wrote back, "I think that I seem to have felt you ebbing away...because my contact with reality has been slipping away; it is more difficult each day for me to know who or what I am...my distress...is general, like a landslide, like an earthquake or like being drowned...You are my last horizon, your figure, your shoulders, your straight waist, your shapely legs, all of you standing against a scene that is the last thing my eyes in love will ever see. You are my last portrait of the heart."

She wondered whether "being a woman loving women has also helped tear me and my life and my brain to bits...I would rather see a young girl dead than go through the struggles against society, for self-control, for peace and for the mad kindly tender joy only such love brings; it is a love which truly understands the beloved because there is no different ratio of reaction or character as between men and women. I feel it is the most equal and therefore the most powerful in its imaginative bliss and pain."

She promised to be a better partner. But she told Murray that if she was to share her life with her it had to be a life filled with writing. "If I am not alive enough to work I am not alive enough to love or to be loved." She closed: "I feel shaken, ill, an old frame of nerves, trembling with decisions, hopes, experiences, patterns, and delicacies," and marked the letter with a bright red kiss.

The letter touched Murray. She and Flanner recognized that they would always love one another, even while at an impasse on where and how to do so. Writing the letter had clarified for Flanner that no matter how much she would continue to hurt Murray by being away from her, she knew she didn't want to return permanently to her old life in New York. She would once again settle permanently in Paris, alone. She would keep writing her Letters.

"I do NOT think I will be back," she told Murray. "I am too fascinated by Europe and its activities."

One night in the spring of 1948, Janet Flanner was made a knight of the Légion d'honneur. She wasn't there to have the ceremonial red ribbon pinned to her chest in recognition of her years of service to France. She'd earlier received the invitation to an event at the Quai d'Orsay, but had figured it was just another party of some official nature and felt too busy in her work to attend.

The evening she was officially knighted Flanner spent at the farmhouse in Orgeval, writing up another Letter for *The New Yorker.*

ACKNOWLEDGMENTS

I would like to acknowledge the work of everyone at the Library of Congress, the New York Public Library, the Bibliothèque nationale de France, the Archives départementales des Yvelines, the American Library in Paris, the University of British Columbia Library, and the Vancouver Public Library, as well as the communities that support these vital institutions. I'm indebted to Brenda Wineapple's work on Janet Flanner and to Roger Colombani's on Eugen Weidmann. Thank you to the many friends, mentors, and students at UBC, NYU, USC, Stanford, and in France who helped to shape my understanding of the city of Paris and its history. I'm very grateful for funding from the Canada Council of the Arts and the BC Arts Council.

Eternal gratitude to Kimberly Burns, Bob Castillo, Monica Cervantes, Audrey Chapuis, Mags Chmielarczyk, Henry Daughton, J. P. Daughton, Dan Edelstein, Erin Files, Matt Fox-Amato, Chris Friedrichs, Adam Gopnik, Pico Iyer, David Kuhn, Mark Long, Amy Reading, Lucy Sante, Vanessa Schwartz, Morgan Spehar, Allison Warren, and Tobias Wolff. And to Ayelet, Daylan, Eleanor, Jeremy, Jon, and Poppy.

A very special thank-you to my wonderful agent, Becky Sweren, to Maddie Caldwell for being my editorial partner, and to Amar Deol for taking this to the finish line.

Thank you to my loves: Laura, Lucinda, and Eloise.

NOTES

In recounting Weidmann's crimes, capture, trial, and execution, I've drawn on 2,435 pages of archival documentation concerning "L'Affaire Weidmann," housed in the Archives départementales des Yvelines, folders 2U-905-1 and 2U-905-2. These documents include testimonies collected by the authorities during their investigations before and after Weidmann's arrest; court transcripts and related documents; detailed narratives about the actions of Weidmann and his associates created for the court's use; as well as other related ephemera. I've drawn on these documents too frequently to cite them on a sentence-by-sentence basis in the notes. I've also made frequent use of Renée Jardin Birnie's annotated publication of Weidmann's prison notebook, *Le Cahier Rouge d'Eugène Weidmann*, and of Janet Flanner's coverage of the Weidmann case across several pieces in *The New Yorker.* Any time I've drawn on sources outside of the archival collection, the prison notebook, or Flanner's reportage, I've noted it with an endnote. I've also provided an endnote whenever quoting directly from Weidmann's words in the notebook, as recorded by Jardin, all translations my own. Contemporary reporting on the case sometimes contained claims that differed from these archival sources, either due to journalists having incomplete or faulty information or because they were outright fabricating stories. Secondary sources about Weidmann also offer differing accounts of what actually happened. I've tried my best to sift through all the primary and secondary documentation to create a narrative that is as faithful to the truth as can be achieved, and I would hope that anyone retracing my steps in the archives would agree with my decisions. In cases where an outside source differed from information I found in the Yvelines archival records, I've given preference to the archival records in my interpretation of events.

Throughout the book, any text within quotation marks comes from a primary or secondary document. I did not make statements about Flanner's or Weidmann's psychological motivations without sufficient archival material to back my claims, drawing most often on Flanner's correspondence and Weidmann's prison notebook, respectively. I've used "perhaps," "likely," and "might" when it felt necessary to do so. I trust readers can deduce my degree of certainty about any given claim made within this text by its supporting endnote.

THE LAST PUBLIC EXECUTION IN FRANCE

1 The time and place: David H. Walker, *Outrage and Insight: Modern French Writers and the "Fait Divers"* (Berg, 1995), 106.

3 "I'm ready": Renée Jardin Birnie, *Le Cahier Rouge d'Eugène Weidmann* (Gallimard, 1968), 230.

3 It was like a scene: Dominique Lanzalavi, *Vincent de Moro Giafferi* (Albiana, 2011), 126.

4 "No," he said: Jardin Birnie, *Cahier*, 235. A slightly different wording is quoted in "Weidmann a expié ce matin a 4 h. 32," *Paris-Soir*, June 18, 1939.

5 "Everything was contradictory": Alice Kaplan, *Looking for the Stranger: Albert Camus and the Life of a Literary Classic* (University of Chicago Press, 2016), 52. Kaplan quotes from "Weidmann a été décapité," *L'Écho d'Alger*, June 18, 1939, which in turn was quoting from the wire service. I use Kaplan's words because of the eloquence of her

translation. On Weidmann's execution, see also Roger Colombani, *L'Affaire Weidmann* (Albin Michel, 1989), 309–313; "France Guillotine's Head of Murder Ring," *New York Times*, June 17, 1939.

5 "He met his end": Janet Flanner (as Genêt), "Letter from Paris," *The New Yorker*, July 15, 1939. Flanner's contributions to *The New Yorker* will hereafter be cited in shorthand as FNY, followed by the date of publication.

6 To write, she said: John Bainbridge, *Another Way of Living* (Holt, Rinehart, and Winston, 1968), 14.

1: IT IS ALL I HAVE, DARLING

7 Her friend Jane Grant: Jane Grant to Janet Flanner, June 1925, Jane C. Grant Papers, University of Oregon, Box 1, Folder 3. Hereafter Janet Flanner as letter writer or recipient will be cited as JF.

8 The letters were just: Jane Grant, *Ross, "The New Yorker," and Me* (Reynal, 1966), 223.

8 "He wants anecdotal": Jane Grant to JF, Grant Papers.

9 Flanner once said: Bainbridge, *Another*, 15.

9 They offered the state's: Brenda Wineapple, *Genêt: A Biography of Janet Flanner* (University of Nebraska Press, 1992), 3.

9 It was in the office: Wineapple, *Genêt*, 26.

9 "Business things": Mary McCarthy, "Conversation Piece," *New York Times*, November 21, 1965.

10 "I was too old": McCarthy, "Conversation."

10 To some people: Wineapple, *Genêt*, 31–32.

10 To others, she claimed: McCarthy, "Conversation"; William Murray, *Janet, My Mother, and Me* (Simon and Schuster, 2000), 39.

10 She told her mother: Ray E. Boomhower, "Janet Flanner," entry, Indiana Journalism Hall of Fame, citing an undated Flanner interview with *The International Herald Tribune*.

10 "I suffered so": McCarthy, "Conversation."

10 After briefly teaching: Alden Whitman, "Janet Flanner, Reporter in Paris for *The New Yorker*, Dies at 86," *New York Times*, November 8, 1978.

10 "That's where I saw": McCarthy, "Conversation."

11 When Rehm reported: Wineapple, *Genêt*, 38.

12 She abandoned Sarah Wilkinson: JF to Stanley Walker, July 19, 1936, *New Yorker* Records, New York Public Library, box 251. Hereafter, documents located in the *New Yorker* Records will be designated as NYR, followed by the box number. Luita Dean Spangler, "On her mouth you kiss your own: Lesbian conversations in exile, 1924–1936" (unpublished dissertation, University of New Hampshire, Durham, 1992), 44; Wineapple, *Genêt*, 48.

12 Recalling those years: Wineapple, *Genêt*, 45.

12 Around this time: Wineapple, *Genêt*, 52.

12 More than a half century later: Janet Flanner, *Darlinghissima: Letters to a Friend*, ed. Natalia Danesi Murray (Random House, 1985), 486.

13 And though women had won: Malcolm Cowley, *Exile's Return* (The Bodley Head, 1951), 6.

13 "Feeling like aliens": Cowley, *Exile's Return*, 6, 74. I've used versions of Cowley's quote to make similar points in Mark Braude, *Making Monte Carlo: A History of Speculation and Spectacle* (Simon and Schuster, 2016) and *Kiki Man Ray: Art, Love, and Rivalry in 1920s Paris* (Norton, 2022). When providing historical context on Paris in the twenties in this chapter I similarly draw on arguments and evidence from these two previous books.

13 She said later that Solano: Wineapple, *Genêt*, 53.

13 She felt bad: Wineapple, *Genêt*, 53.

13 "Nothing you could have done": George "Eddie" Rehm to JF, December 18 [ca. 1950s], Janet Flanner and Solita Solano Papers, Library of Congress (hereafter LOC).

14 She sold off: Wineapple, *Genêt*, 54.

14 First came three months: JF to Solita Solano (hereafter SS), April 14, 1973, LOC.

14 The Café de Flore: Janet Flanner, *Paris Was Yesterday 1925–1939*, ed. Irving Drutman (Harvest, 1988), xxii.

15 And they woke: FNY, March 3, 1972.

15 One of their friends: George Davis to SS, August 11, 1949, LOC.

15 For twenty cents: Solita Solano, "The Hotel Bonaparte" (unpublished draft of a short memoir), LOC.

15 The Bonaparte was "our ideal": Solano, "Hotel Bonaparte."

16 Flanner brought a single: Wineapple, *Genêt*, 63.

16 "I wanted to be Miss Henry James": Shari Benstock, *Women of the Left Bank: Paris, 1900–1940* (University of Texas Press, 1986), 105.

16 As a large, liberal, and modern city: Ronald Weber, *News of Paris: American Journalists in the City of Light Between the Wars* (Ivan R. Dee, 2006), 5.

16 "Do not like California": Murray, *Janet*, 42.

17 American critics: Franklin P. Adams, "The Conning Tower," *New York World*, October 9, 1924; W. R. Benét, *Saturday Review of Literature*, November 1, 1924.

17 "Janet's book is racing": Wineapple, *Genêt*, 70.

17 She told her that: Wineapple, *Genêt*, 70.

18 "I thought Paris": Bainbridge, *Another*, 18.

18 She would watch: Flanner, *Paris Was Yesterday*, xxii.

18 Her favorite views: Flanner, *Paris Was Yesterday*, xxii.

18 She reveled: Flanner, *Paris Was Yesterday*, xxi.

18 Solano, a friend of Putnam's: Wineapple, *Genêt*, 94.

18 While encouraging Flanner: George Putnam to JF, December 15, 1924, LOC.

19 "Is your magazine": Grant, *Ross*, 223.

2: THE DIAGNOSIS

21 This could be done rationally: Richard J. Evans, *The Coming of the Third Reich* (Penguin Press, 2005), 36–37.

3: AN OVERSIZED MINNOW LEARNING HOW TO SWIM

22 "It was all very giddy": Murray, *Janet*, 40; Wineapple, *Genêt*, 45; F. Scott Fitzgerald, "My Lost City," in *The Crack Up* (New Directions, 1945).

23 Grant refused: Susan Henry, *Anonymous in Their Own Names: Doris E. Fleischman, Ruth Hale, and Jane Grant* (Vanderbilt University Press, 2012); Thomas Kunkel, *Genius in Disguise: Harold Ross of "The New Yorker"* (Random House, 1995), 59.

23 She later said: McCarthy, "Conversation."

23 Still, even from her: Grant, *Ross*, 7.

23 When America entered the war: Kunkel, *Genius*, 44.

23 In Paris he met: Kunkel, *Genius*, 58.

23 When the war ended: Grant, *Ross*, 31.

24 He had little regard: Ben Yagoda, *About Town: "The New Yorker" and the World It Made* (Da Capo, 2000), 37.

24 He once asked: Charles McGrath, "How Harold Ross Created *The New Yorker*," *The New Yorker*, February 12, 1995.

24 Ross knew him: Kunkel, *Genius*, 60.

24 A friend in publishing: Kunkel, *Genius*, 94.

25 Fleischmann convinced the people: Kunkel, *Genius*, 112.

25 Launching the magazine: Kunkel, *Genius*, 89.

25 Meanwhile printing and postage: Yagoda, *About Town*, 28.

25 The genteel Luce: Amy Reading, *The World She Edited: Katharine S. White at "The New Yorker"* (Mariner Books, 2024), 118.

25 With the rise of a national: Kunkel, *Genius*, 88.

26 And he wagered: "Prospectus—*The New Yorker*" (1924), Manuscripts and Archives Division, The New York Public Library.

26 If *Vogue* and *Vanity Fair*: Judith Yaross Lee, *Defining "New Yorker" Humor* (University Press of Mississippi, 2000), 84.

27 Anonymity also kept: Grant, *Ross*, 9; Kunkel, *Genius*, 100.

27 "I am looking to you": Jane Grant to JF, Grant Papers.

27 The first issues: Yagoda, *About Town*, 40.

27 The future *New Yorker*: James Thurber, "The Years with Ross," *The Atlantic*, January 1958.

27 Flanner would be one: Yagoda, *About Town*, 44.

28 He gave Ross: Kunkel, *Genius*, 102.

28 Despite the pressure: Yagoda, *About Town*, 73.

28 "Too many people": Janet Flanner, Introduction to Grant, *Ross*.

28 Her Letter's main point: FNY, October 10, 1925.

28 Her early Letters: Wineapple, *Genêt*, 99.

29 They exercised "critical judgment": Bainbridge, *Another*, 21.

29 In any case, she thought "flâneuse": Wineapple, *Genêt*, 98.

30 "The French can't pronounce": FNY, October 10, 1925.

30 On the annual St. Hubert's Hunt: FNY, December 19, 1925.

30 They were "chatty and instructive": Benstock, *Women*, 105.

30 She promised to send her mother: Wineapple, *Genêt*, 98.

30 "Hardly any of us": Wineapple, *Genêt*, 75.

30 "We knew where": Wineapple, *Genêt*, 59.

30 She and Solano had freed: Wineapple, *Genêt*, 69.

31 They spoke of "our *quartier*": Solano, handwritten annotation of scrapbook image, LOC.

4: A YOUNG MAN ALONE ON A MOUNTAINTOP

32 The same questions she'd asked him: Colombani, *L'Affaire*, 62.

32 His mother had warned him: Colombani, *L'Affaire*, 61.

33 Wagner showed him: I borrowed "troglodyte world" from Paul Fussell, *The Great War and Modern Memory* (Oxford University Press, 2013).

33 It seemed that all the while: Alex Ross, *The Rest Is Noise* (Picador, 2008), 209.

5: HOTEL BONAPARTE

34 By crossing the Atlantic: Wineapple, *Genêt*, 75.

34 "That's why, in longing": Murray, *Janet*, 42.

34 She might have known: Wineapple, *Genêt*, 75. I am indebted to Wineapple's research, interviews, and insights in untangling Flanner family relations.

35 They figured out that because: Wineapple, *Genêt*, 105.

35 Only once settled: Bainbridge, *Another*, 16.

35 "Hedonism, in its proper sense": Bainbridge, *Another*, 24.

35 One friend recalled: Hank O'Neal, *"Life Is Painful, Nasty & Short—In My Case It Has Only Been Painful and Nasty": Djuna Barnes, 1978–1981: An Informal Memoir* (Paragon House, 1990), 139.

35 Notoriously seductive: Solano, "Hotel Bonaparte"; Wineapple, *Genêt*, 85.

35 The scene could bewilder: William Carlos Williams, *The Autobiography of William Carlos Williams* (New Directions, 1967), 229–230. Spangler, "On her mouth" pointed me to this passage in Williams's memoir.

36 "Three pairs of white gloves": Kathryn C. Hulme, *Undiscovered Country* (Little, Brown, 1966), 38–39.

36 Solano said that Barnes: Solano, "Hotel Bonaparte."

36 In the villages: Simone de Beauvoir, *The Second Sex* (Vintage, 2011), 201–203.

36 Abortion was illegal: Mary-Louise Roberts, *Civilization Without Sexes: Reconstructing Gender in Postwar France 1917–1927* (University of Chicago Press, 1994), 63.

36 "I like all the people": Diana Souhami, *No Modernism Without Lesbians* (Bloomsbury, 2020), 295.

36 And as one Montparnasse: Jimmie "the Barman" [James Charters] and Morrill Cody, *This Must Be The Place: Memoirs of Montparnasse* (Collier, 1989), 5.

37 Flanner was "magnetically handsome": Solano, "Hotel Bonaparte."

37 And in her smooth, deep voice: Bainbridge, *Another*, 15.

37 Her "diction and delivery": Yagoda, *About Town*, 407.

37 Flanner wrote of her "lovely little figure": Handwritten note from Flanner added to Solano, "Hotel Bonaparte."

37 Flanner said the French: Flanner, *Paris Was Yesterday*, xii.

37 First they would share: Wineapple, *Genêt*, 62.

37 For the equivalent of an American quarter: Flanner, *Paris Was Yesterday*, xiii.

38 They trekked across: Flanner, *Paris Was Yesterday*, xi.

38 Or they popped down: FNY, March 3, 1972.

38 Or they dashed off: Wineapple, *Genêt*, 67.

38 Flanner and Solano sought it out: FNY, March 3, 1972.

39 Flanner discovered the two: Bainbridge, *Another*, 22.

39 If mornings often began: Wineapple, *Genêt*, 82,

39 There they mixed: Simone de Beauvoir, *The Prime of Life* (World Publishing, 1962), 350.

39 With each passing day: Solano, "Hotel Bonaparte."

39 And France, in the rush: Brooke L. Blower, *Becoming Americans in Paris: Transatlantic Politics and Culture Between the World Wars* (Oxford University Press, 2011), 8.

39 Some among the few thousand: Blower, *Becoming*, 6.

40 Several Black GIs: Tyler Stovall, *Paris Noir: African Americans in the City of Light* (Houghton Mifflin, 1996).

40 But the biggest: FNY, March 3, 1972.

40 It was easier than ever: Paul Fussell, *Abroad: British Literary Traveling Between the Wars* (Oxford University Press, 1994), 72.

40 But finances: Herbert Lottman, *Man Ray's Montparnasse* (Harry N. Abrams, 2001), 110.

40 "We were a literary lot": Flanner, *Paris Was Yesterday*, vii.

40 While boasting of their escape: Blower, *Becoming*, 7.

40 They preferred bars like the Dome: Humphrey Carpenter, *Geniuses Together: American Writers in Paris in the 1920s* (Unwin Hyman, 1987), 96.

40 And in the end: Blower, *Becoming*, 2.

40 For Hemingway: Malcolm Cowley, *A Second Flowering: Works and Days of the Lost Generation* (Viking, 1973), 59.

41 She and Solano took: Wineapple, *Genêt*, 62; Murray, *Janet*, 42.

41 Europeans might still believe: Bainbridge, *Another*, 20.

41 "I felt I was living": Flanner, *Paris Was Yesterday*, xvi.

41 "I don't want to know": Flanner, Introduction to Grant, *Ross*, 7.

41 He tended to give: Benstock, *Women*, 106.

41 People said France: Weber, *News of Paris*, 5.

42 She credited the French papers: Wineapple, *Genêt*, 102.

42 "I learned more": Bainbridge, *Another*, 19.

42 She found it easiest: Grant, *Ross*, 224.

42 She wanted to develop: Grant, *Ross*, 224.

42 She found him endearingly odd: Grant, *Ross*, 7–10.

43 "I had the very good fortune": Flanner in *The Writer in America*, directed by Richard O. Moore (Perspective Films, 1975).

43 He demanded excellence: Wineapple, *Genêt*, 102.

43 She ignored his requests: Wineapple, *Genêt*, 104.

43 Flanner and Ross collaborated: Wineapple, *Genêt*, 103.

43 On the state's ceremonial: FNY, May 14, 1927.

43 Thanks to her androgynous: Wineapple, *Genêt*, 102.

43 Even as Flanner felt: Wineapple, *Genêt*, 108.

43 She judged the hit: Flanner, *Paris Was Yesterday*, 3–4, 72–73.

44 She said she avoided: Wineapple, *Genêt*, 104.

44 "Let's let other magazines": David Remnick, "*The New Yorker* in the Forties," *The New Yorker*, April 28, 2014.

44 Flanner said that it made: Flanner, *Darlinghissima*, 43.

44 There were only so many: Calvin Tomkins, *Living Well Is the Best Revenge* (Museum of Modern Art, 2013), 30.

44 While Ross and other editors: Harold Ross (hereafter HR) to JF, November 19, 1932, NYR 11.

44 Doda Conrad: Murray, *Janet*, 43.

44 For an inside track: JF to Katharine Sergeant White (hereafter KSW), July 10, 1938, Katharine Sergeant White Papers, Bryn Mawr College (hereafter BM).

45 She made connections: JF to KSW, October 2, 1929, BM.

45 "I always attend": McCarthy, "Conversation."

45 She would clip: Murray, *Janet*, 43.

45 Her job, as she saw it: Whitman, "Janet Flanner."

45 Solano was an experienced: Carlos Baker, *Ernest Hemingway: A Life Story* (Collier Books, 1988), 247.

45 A woman living: Hulme, *Undiscovered Country*, 52.

45 "I trust only": JF to R. A. Hague (hereafter RAH), undated, 1935, NYR 227.

45 She timed her: "Schedule for Paris Letter," June 28, 1931, NYR 157; "Paris Letter Schedule," November 30, 1932, NYR 168.

46 After the dissolution: Anne Chisholm, *Nancy Cunard: A Biography* (Knopf, 1979), 51.

46 She, too, considered Paris: Chisholm, *Cunard*, 51.

46 A friend noted: Chisholm, *Cunard*, 60.

47 "To be in the presence": Chisholm, *Cunard*, 96.

47 They soon spoke: Wineapple, *Genêt*, 79.

47 They would sign off: Chisholm, *Cunard*, 96.

47 The writer William Murray: Murray, *Janet*, 42.

47 Solano wrote in an unpublished: William Patrick Patterson, *Ladies of the Rope: Gurdjieff's Special Left Bank Women's Group* (Arete, 1999), 16.

47 She had the money: Chisholm, *Cunard*, 90.

47 Flanner and Solano borrowed: Solano, "Hotel Bonaparte."

47 She felt she had to guard: Chisholm, *Cunard*, 96.

47 The trio often started: Wineapple, *Genêt*, 80.

47 All sorts of people: Chisholm, *Cunard*, 97.

47 "We were lively and hip": Anita Loos to Solita Solano, April 24, 1974, LOC.

48 Flanner met him: Noel Riley Fitch, *Sylvia Beach and the Lost Generation: A History of Literary Paris in the Twenties and Thirties* (Norton, 1985), 136.

48 "There was something": Bainbridge, *Another*, 19.

48 She was struck: Baker, *Hemingway*, 138.

48 When they hosted: Baker, *Hemingway*, 136.

48 Flanner thought him drawn: JF to Carlos Baker, December 7, 1966, LOC.

48 Hemingway told Flanner: JF to Carlos Baker, December 7, 1966, LOC.

49 They discovered that: Flanner, *Paris Was Yesterday*, viii.

49 "Grand news—your book in print": Nancy Cunard to JF, undated, LOC.

49 Years later Flanner: JF to SS, undated, likely 1974 from context, LOC.

49 A Los Angeles reviewer: *Cubical City* reviews in *Los Angeles Record*, October 30, 1926; *Boston Evening Transcript*, October 30, 1926; *Times Literary Supplement*, December 23, 1926; Lionel G. Short, unclear publication, stamped "New York City," December 18, 1926; unclear publication, stamped "New York City," October 15, 1926; unclear publication, stamped "Tulsa, Okla.," October 30, 1926; *Chicago Post Evening Review*, date unclear. All in Scrapbooks, LOC. Wineapple, *Genêt*, 95, notes Flanner's reaction to the Los Angeles review.

50 Flanner recalled the most: Flanner, undated speech to the American Institute of Arts and Letters, LOC.

50 More recent critics: Rai Peterson, "Janet Flanner's *The Cubical City* and the Life She Left Behind," *e-Rea* 16, no. 2 (2019); Spangler, "On her mouth."

6: TRUE NORTH STRONG AND FREE

51 He would recall: Jardin Birnie, *Cahier*, 58.

51 "His greatest ambitions": Jardin Birnie, *Cahier*, 175.

52 He'd felt marooned: Colombani, *L'Affaire*, 60.

7: BECOMING GENÊT

53 "I know I must": Murray, *Janet*, 45.

53 But the book: Wineapple, *Genêt*, 95.

53 "I need and long": JF to KSW, undated, 1928, NYR 138.

54 Flanner moved more slowly: JF to KSW, August 14, 1935.

54 White would lobby: See, among many possible examples, "Extract of Letter from Mrs. White to Mr. Ross," undated, 1931, NYR 157.

54 She rejected one piece: KSW to JF, May 7, 1929, NYPL.

54 She made no secret: KSW to HR and others, September 8, 1937, BM.

54 About one piece: JF to KSW, July 8, 1930, NYR 150.

54 Filing another Letter: JF to KSW, July 10, 1938, BM.

55 She admitted to White: JF to KSW, October 19, 1938, BM.

55 Replying to one tough-talking letter: JF to KSW, October 27, 1936, NYR 257.

55 Flanner only got to see: Wineapple, *Genêt*, 103.

55 They "shingled my vocabulary": JF to KSW, July 22, 1931, NYR 157.

55 She could tell herself: Wineapple, *Genêt*, 104.

55 She also knew: St. Clair McKelway (hereafter SM) to JF, March 9, 1939, NYR 315.

55 Ross "asks, simply": SM to JF, March 9, 1939, NYR 315.

55 In her first years: JF to KSW, October 25, 1928, NYR 138.

55 But it soon became clear: FNY, March 31, 1928.

56 Genêt's Paris was: FNY, May 26, 1928; FNY, December 19, 1925.

56 On the death: FNY, December 19, 1935.

57 And like an especially: FNY, March 31, 1928.

57 Dresses that season: FNY, November 21, 1925.

58 She would write: FNY, June 11, 1927; Flanner, *Paris Was Yesterday*, 50.

58 She would make: Wineapple, *Genêt*, 100.

58 "It was Paramount Night": FNY, June 11, 1927.

59 Riding the *métro*: Colin Jones, *Paris: Biography of a City* (Penguin Books, 2006), 41.

60 Musicians, writers, painters: Martin Puchner, *Poetry of the Revolution: Marx, Manifestos, and the Avant-Gardes* (Princeton University Press, 2006), 135–136.

60 The rush of immigrants: Blower, *Becoming*, 8–9.

60 A large contingent: Blower, *Becoming*, 9; Jones, *Paris*, 391–392.

60 "The storm had died away": Paul Valéry, *Variety*, trans. Malcolm Cowley (Harcourt, Brace, 1927), 27.

60 "Politics interested very few people": Ilya Ehrenburg, *Truce: 1921–33* (MacGibbon and Kee, 1963), 94.

60 Diplomacy was something done: Ehrenburg, *Truce*, 94–96.

61 It was a short piece: KSW to JF, January 31, 1929, NYR 146.

61 After the issue: JF to KSW, undated, 1929, NYR 146; JF to KSW, undated, 1935, NYR 227.

61 When she did resume: Murray, *Janet*, 45.

61 Late in 1929 she described: Flanner, *Paris Was Yesterday*, 61–62.

62 Recognizing that the market crash: Yagoda, *About Town*.

62 Flanner had gone: JF to HR, November 3, 1932, NYR 11.

62 She would later say: Patrick O'Higgins, "Janet Flanner in Her Own Words," *People*, February 24, 1975.

62 And yet by putting herself: Reading, *The World*, 118; Kunkel, *Genius*, 118–120; Lois Long, "Tables for Two," *The New Yorker*, February 19, 1927; Corey Ford, *The Time of Laughter* (Little, Brown, 1967), 123.

63 Copyeditors joked: Murray, *Janet*, 44.

63 He communicated with her: HR to JF, July 6, 1932, NYR 11.

63 "Who in God's name": Murray, *Janet*, 66.

63 He was "one of the most": JF to KSW, January 8, 1929, NYR 46.

64 "A paper written by capitalists": FNY, April 25, 1930.

64 Coty established "personal contact": FNY, April 25, 1930.

65 She asked Ross: KSW to JF, January 22, 1929, NYR 146.

9: SMOKED PORK, SWEET CABBAGE, AND MOSELLE WINE

68 In the Black Forest: JF to KSW, July 22, 1931, NYR 157.

68 In Berlin they listened: Wineapple, *Genêt*, 119.

68 Flanner praised her intelligence: Wineapple, *Genêt*, 117.

69 They called her: Wineapple, *Genêt*, 116.

69 Hemingway told Flanner: Ernest Hemingway (hereafter EH) to JF, April 18, 1933, LOC.

69 Murphy, in return: Wineapple, *Genêt*, 118.

69 While Flanner was taken: Wineapple, *Genêt*, 119.

69 Flanner admired Murphy working: Back of photo 22-57C, Scrapbooks, LOC; I have also drawn on Flanner's handwritten notes inside her copy of Gertrude Stein's *The Autobiography of Alice B. Toklas*, held in Special Collections at the American Library in Paris.

69 Flanner recalled the grounds: JF to E. J. Clark, ca. 1955, LOC; JF to SS, November 21, 1949, LOC.

69 Djuna Barnes came to suntan: Wineapple, *Genêt*, 121.

70 Stein asked all sorts: Flanner's notes inside her copy of Stein's *Autobiography*.

70 The shares never went back: Murray, *Janet*, 46; Wineapple, *Genêt*, 117.

70 She continued living: Wineapple, *Genêt*, 119.

70 Solano, who'd started writing: Solita Solano, "Both Banks of the Seine," *D.A.C. News*, September 15, 1933, 36.

70 Sometimes Solano and Flanner: See Flanner's inscription to Murphy in a copy of Flanner's *Paris Journal*, vol. 2, *1965–1971*, held in Special Collections at the American Library in Paris.

70 One of Flanner's college friends: Wineapple, *Genêt*, 115.

71 Friends marveled at how Solano: Wineapple, *Genêt*, 119–120.

71 As Flanner spent more: Solano, "Both Banks of the Seine," *D.A.C. News*, February 20, 1932, 50.

71 Their relationship: Margaret Anderson to SS, August 9, 1972, LOC.

71 More than fifty years: Wineapple, *Genêt*, 47.

71 And Solano in her own: John Broderick, Introduction to Solano, "Hotel Bonaparte," LOC.

71 Shortly after meeting Murphy: Murray, *Janet*, 47.

71 She remained unaffected: JF to KSW, July 22, 1931, NYR 157; JF to James Cain, undated, 1931, NYR 157.

72 She was earning well: See JF–KSW correspondence about the matter in several letters in 1930, NYR 150.

72 Despite having a few: JF to James Cain, undated, 1931, NYR 157.

72 Financial crash or no: FNY, March 14, 1931.

10: THE CHAUFFEUR

74 To his parents' shame: Colombani, *L'Affaire*, 53–54.

11: CRACKING UP

75 She would remember: Bainbridge, *Another*, 16–17.

75 There had been so much: McCarthy, "Conversation"; Wineapple, *Genêt*, 23.

76 Flanner accompanied her: Wineapple, *Genêt*, 23.

76 Undoubtedly the city offered: Wineapple, *Genêt*, 24.

76 Above all, she'd discovered: Bainbridge, *Another*, 23.

76 Inflation had so decimated: Wineapple, *Genêt*, 59.

76 She passed bookstalls: Flanner, undated speech for the Institute of Arts and Letters annual meeting in New York, likely late 1950s or early 1960s, Solano and Flanner Papers, LOC.

77 Somewhere in that same city: Flanner, undated speech for the Institute of Arts and Letters annual meeting in New York, likely late 1950s or early 1960s, Solano and Flanner Papers, LOC.

77 Still, she'd returned: Wineapple, *Genêt*, 70.

77 "I should think that": Bainbridge, *Another*, 16.

77 "It's always been swell": JF to SM, January 27, 1939, NYR 315.

77 Berliners, as one writer: Ian Buruma, Introduction to Harry Kessler, *Berlin in Lights: The Diaries of Count Harry Kessler, 1918–1937*, trans. and ed. Charles Kessler (Grove Press, 1999), x.

78 It was the era's contagious, invigorating idea: Henry Miller, *Tropic of Cancer* (Obelisk Press, 1934).

78 In Berlin the "old forms": JF to KSW, October 15, 1931, NYR 157.

78 And she found that energy intoxicating: JF to KSW, July 22, 1931, NYR 157.

78 In a *New Yorker* Letter: FNY, January 9, 1932

79 "Today, Germany, tomorrow, the world": Modris Eksteins, *Rites of Spring: The Great War and the Birth of the Modern Age* (Mariner Books, 2000), 301.

79 "It's like a dream": Eksteins, *Rites*, 301.

79 "Hitler flags everywhere": Solita Solano, "Both Banks of the Rhine," *D.A.C. News*, October 1933.

79 They saw a Jewish boy: JF to RAH, ca. 1935, NYR.

79 A few weeks after: FNY, August 5, 1933.

80 The only other words: FNY, December 23, 1933.

80 E. B. White once joked: Yagoda, *About Town*, 111.

80 Party politics and elections: Frank Sullivan, "The Political Outlook," *The New Yorker*, March 31, 1928.

80 Finally, Flanner was starting: HR to JF, July 6, 1932, NYR 11.

80 She answered that: Wineapple, *Genêt*, 132.

81 "When the necks": JF to HR, August 29, 1932, NYR 168.

81 When her Liberty Bonds: Wineapple, *Genêt*, 132.

81 She took on rewriting: JF to KSW, June 28, 1932, NYR 11.

81 With Ross's permission: HR to JF, September 13, 1932, NYR 168.

82 At one point she fell: JF to KSW, undated, 1933, NYR 168.

82 Ross eventually took pity: "Spaulding" to JF, July 19, 1933, NYR 182.

82 They'd lost interest: Solita Solano, "Both Banks of the Seine," *D.A.C. News*, April 1934, 32.

12: THE STAVISKY AFFAIR

84 Its deputies were meeting: "The Stavisky Scandal," *The Atlantic*, March 1934.

84 Across France, political fixers: Rod Kedward, *France and the French: A Modern History* (Abrams, 2007), 164.

85 The Radical party: Robert O. Paxton, *Vichy France: Old Guard and New Order, 1940–1944* (Columbia University Press, 2001), 38.

85 No one failed: Kedward, *France*, 164; Pierre Pellissier, *6 Février, 1934* (Perrin, 2000), 31–34.

85 The Stavisky family: David Clay Lodge, *Between Two Fires: Europe's Path in the 1930s* (Norton, 1990), 28.

85 Flanner shared the affair's: Jessica Wardhaugh, *In Pursuit of the People: Political Culture in France, 1934–39* (Palgrave Macmillan, 2009), 24.

86 The "Radicals are covered with mud": FNY, February 3, 1934.

86 A joke went round: Kedward, *France*, 152.

86 They'd been called by their radios: Jones, *Paris*, 410.

87 Most of the people: Karen Fiss, *Grand Illusion: The Third Reich, the Paris Exposition, and the Cultural Seduction of France* (University of Chicago Press, 1997), 11.

87 They would breach: Paxton, *Vichy*, 244.

87 Most of the demonstrators: Kedward, *France*, 165; Andrew Hussey, *Paris: The Secret History* (Bloomsbury, 2008), 343; Caroline Campbell, "Women and Gender in the Croix de Feu and the Parti Social Français: Creating a Nationalist Youth Culture, 1927–1939," *Western Society for French History* 36 (2008).

88 The forces of order: Pellissier, *6 Février*, 13.

89 More of the *hirondelles*: Pellissier, *6 Février*, 123.

89 One rioter mounted: Pellissier, *6 Février*, 168.

89 The smell of motor oil: Pellissier, *6 Février*, 139.

90 Meanwhile other units: Pellissier, *6 Février*, 176.

90 A rumor, unfounded: Pellissier, *6 Février*, 126.

91 Some of the injured: Pellissier, *6 Février*, 142–146, 178.

91 He would die: Pellissier, *6 Février*, 148.

91 Five firefighters: Pellissier, *6 Février*, 162.

91 Changing the lyrics: Pellissier, *6 Février*, 165; FNY, February 17, 1934.

92 Roughly 250 wounded: Pellissier, *6 Février*, 170–171, 184.

92 Some rioters reportedly: Pellissier, *6 Février*, 179.

92 He was killed: Pellissier, *6 Février*, 174, 179.

93 Fire crews kept working: Pellissier, *6 Février*, 197.

93 "You would not know Paris!": Fitch, *Sylvia*, 345.

93 "People observed each other": Julian Jackson, *The Popular Front in France: Defending Democracy, 1934–38* (Cambridge University Press, 1998), 16.

94 "What a time": KSW to JF, February 8, 1934, NYR 201.

94 As she'd tried making: Wineapple, *Genêt*, 135.

94 "By beautiful accident": FNY, February 17, 1934.

94 Two city buses: Pellissier, *6 Février*, 97.

94 "The odd thing here": JF to KSW, February 14, 1934, NYR 201.

95 "AVOID DANGER": *The New Yorker* to JF, February 8, 1934, NYR 201.

95 In her next five Letters: FNY, March 31, 1934.

95 While contemporary coverage: "The Stavisky Scandal," *The Atlantic*, March 1934.

95 She maintained: FNY, July 7, 1934.

95 "Am worried": KSW to JF, March 22, 1934, NYR 201.

95 The Stavisky scandal: Flanner, undated speech to the American Institute of Arts and Letters, LOC.

14: HELL ON WHEELS

100 "Gertrude Stein Has Arrived": Megan Gambino, "When Gertrude Stein Toured America," *Smithsonian*, October 13, 2011; KSW to JF, June 22, 1934, NYR 201.

100 Amid the frenzy: EH to JF, April 8, 1933, LOC.

100 At first, she'd assumed: Wineapple, *Genêt*, 77.

100 Flanner didn't take: Wineapple, *Genêt*, 78; Flanner in Moore, *The Writer in America*.

100 Alice B. Toklas: Wineapple, *Genêt*, 77–78.

101 "The press is instinctively": JF to KSW, October 5, 1934, NYR 205.

101 She meanwhile told Stein: Andrea Weiss, *Paris Was a Woman* (Harper San Francisco, 1995), 94–95.

101 In truth Flanner expected: Annalisa Zox-Weaver, *Women Modernists and Fascism* (Cambridge University Press, 2011), 125.

Zox-Weaver's research suggests that Flanner might have tried writing a Stein profile at some point in the 1930s and that it was rejected.

101 And more important: JF to KSW, May 9, 1935, NYR 227.

101 Though he'd started: "Of All Things," *The New Yorker*, February 21, 1925.

101 Better they should cover: HR memo, n.d. [probably late 1920s], NYR 2.

101 When he was pitched: HR to Uthai Vincent Wilcox, April 30, 1930, NYR.

102 If Americans wanted: Benstock, *Women*, 126.

102 As William Shawn explained: Kunkel, *Genius*, 18.

102 The journalist Mary Heaton Vorse: Mary Heaton Vorse, "Unter Dem Hakenkreuz," *The New Yorker*, July 1, 1933.

102 To one of her editors: JF to Wharton, June 14, 1933, NYR 182.

102 She'd mocked one attempt: Wineapple, *Genêt*, 131.

102 She claimed at that time: Wineapple, *Genêt*, 146.

103 he "seemed not to notice it": Flanner, undated Arts and Letters Speech, LOC; Bainbridge, *Another*, 22.

103 "GIVE ME ANY HINTS": JF to RAH, undated, 1935, NYR 227.

103 Just before proposing: JF to KSW, February 9, 1935; JF to KSW, January 1, 1935, NYR 227.

103 She had a newfound: KSW to JF, April 18, 1935, NYR 227; *New Yorker* to JF, April 11, 1935, NYR 227.

103 It had been "odd, exciting": JF to KSW, undated, 1935, NYR 227; JF to KSW, undated postcard from London, 1935, NYR 227.

104 By talking with local journalists: JF to KSW, February 9, 1935, NYR 227; JF to KSW, January 31, 1935, NYR 227.

104 She said she couldn't eat: JF to KSW, undated, likely April or May 1935, NYR 227; KSW to JF, April 18, 1935, NYR 227.

104 Capitalizing on the goodwill: KSW to Ross memo, "OK on Hitler," undated (though from context 1934), NYR.

104 Though it would push: KSW to JF, April 26, 1935, NYR 227.

104 Ross knew Flanner: KSW to JF, June 26, 1935, NYR 227.

104 Perhaps, concerned: Zox-Weaver, *Women*, 125.

104 Hitler remained: See, for instance, Wyndham Lewis, *Hitler* (Chatto and Windus, 1931); and John Gunther, "Has Hitler a Mother Complex?" *Vanity Fair*, September 1934.

104 "For God's sake": HR to JF, August 21, 1935, NYR 227.

105 The American Jewish Congress: Louis Anthes, "Publicly Deliberative Drama: The 1934 Mock Trial of Adolf Hitler for 'Crimes Against Civilization,'" *The American Journal of Legal History* 42, no. 4 (1998): 391–410.

105 A German-Jewish refugee: Solano, "Hotel Bonaparte."

105 And then she swiftly: FNY, August 15, 1934.

106 She predicted that this next war: FNY, September 1, 1934.

106 She jumped from that remark: FNY, September 1, 1934.

106 In that especially temperate: FNY, September 15, 1934.

106 With the introduction: FNY, April 27, 1935.

107 In that same Letter: Richard J. Evans, *The Third Reich in Power: 1933–1939* (Penguin Books, 2006), 126.

107 Flanner judged the film: FNY, April 27, 1935.

107 Now, in September 1935: JF to KSW, May 9, 1935, NYR 227.

108 The Nazis had banned: Peter Kurth, *American Cassandra: The Life of Dorothy Thompson* (Little, Brown, 1990), 202.

108 Another American correspondent: JF to KSW, June 26, 1935, NYR 227.

108 She rendered a Jewish: Wineapple, *Genêt*, 143.

109 Flanner's fellow correspondent: William L. Shirer, *Berlin Diary* (Knopf, 1941), 16.

109 Flanner's main complaint: JF to KSW, May 9, 1935, NYR 227.

109 Flanner figured that Putzi: JF to KSW, May 9, 1935, NYR 227.

109 Hitler "took special satisfaction": Albert Speer, *Inside the Third Reich: Memoirs*, trans. Richard and Clara Winston (Macmillan, 1970), 59.

109 Flanner was treated: JF to HR, September 30, 1935, NYR 227.

110 "I think your flattering postcards": KSW to JF, September 18, 1935, NYR 227.

110 She avoided interviewing: JF to KSW, May 9, 1935, NYR 227.

110 A young Reuters: JF to KSW, January 28, 1936, NYR 251.

110 "She looked beyond": William Shawn, Introduction to Janet Flanner, *Janet Flanner's World: Uncollected Writings, 1932–1975*, ed. Irving Drutman (Harvest, 1981), xiv.

110 "The great drawback": JF to KSW, October 9, 1935, NYR 227.

111 While she talked: JF to KSW, October 9, 1935, NYR 227.

111 The gathering had started: Fiss, *Grand Illusion*, 176–177.

111 Day and night uniformed: Here I draw directly from William Shirer's recollection from 1934: "The streets, hardly wider than alleys, are a sea of brown and black uniforms," as quoted in Evans, *Third Reich in Power*, 124; see also Shirer, *Berlin Diary*, 5–21, for broader content on the rallies.

112 This "Cathedral of Light": Gitta Sereny, *Albert Speer: His Battle with Truth* (Knopf, 1995), 131.

112 All of it meant to quiet: Evans, *Third Reich in Power*, 121

112 "It's not our place": Fiss, *Grand Illusion*, 7.

113 For the French writer: Fiss, *Grand Illusion*, 177.

113 For William Shirer: Shirer, *Berlin Diary*, 21.

113 And for Janet Flanner: Flanner, *Janet Flanner's World*, 105.

114 Flanner would guard: Flanner and Solano Papers, item 22-36c, LOC.

114 "He is the strangest": JF to KSW, October 9, 1935, NYR 227.

115 In another note: JF to KSW, undated, 1935, NYR 227.

115 She worried about how: JF to HR, September 30, 1935, NYR 227.

115 She took three days: JF to KSW, December 4, 1935, NYR 227.

115 She hated how: JF to KSW, October 9, 1935, NYR 227.

116 She decided she had: JF to KSW, May 31, 1935, NYR 227.

116 While it had been: JF to HR, September 30, 1935, NYR 227.

119 At the same time: Mary Fulbrook, *Reckonings: Legacies of Nazi Persecution and the Quest for Justice* (Oxford University Press, 2018), 36–37.

120 Remarking on his speechmaking: Flanner's three-part Hitler profile can be found in FNY, February 21, 1936; FNY, February 28, 1936; FNY, March 7, 1936.

120 White worried: KSW to JF, June 26, 1935, NYR 227.

120 Flanner shared White's: JF to KSW, February 9, 1935, NYR 227.

15: SHE DOESN'T DO VERY WELL ON THE SLIGHTER SUBJECTS

121 She wanted to see: JF to KSW, August 14, 1935, NYR 227.

121 It "curdled her blood": JF to KSW, October 18, 1935, NYR 227.

121 "Maybe in California": JF to KSW, August 14, 1935, NYR 227.

121 A gossip columnist: Alice Hughes, "A Woman's New York," *The Birmingham News*, April 19, 1936.

122 She was seen: Franklin P. Adams, "The Conning Tower," *Oakland Tribune*, February 9, 1936.

122 In a "Snapshots": "Snapshots of Hollywood," *The Morning Post*, March 11, 1936.

122 Her former employer: "The Girl About Town," *The Indianapolis Star*, March 29, 1936.

122 She'd shown her readers: Zox-Weaver, *Women*, 132; Kunkel, *Genius*, 305.

122 Freelance offers: KSW to HR, March 30, 1936, NYR 20.

122 While she received: See, for instance, Richmond Harris to JF, March 21, 1936, NYR 251.

122 Malcolm Cowley: Wineapple, *Genêt*, 146.

122 Although Raoul Fleischmann: Wineapple, *Genêt*, 146.

122 She told her mother: Wineapple, *Genêt*, 146.

123 To a *New Yorker* staffer: JF to "Miss Terry," undated, likely March 1936, NYR 251.

123 She would often complain: Wineapple, *Genêt*, 146.

123 "Latest is that": JF to KSW, April 27, 1936, NYR 251.

123 She lied to *The Indianapolis Star*: "The Girl About Town," *The Indianapolis Star*, March 29, 1936.

124 As her stature: JF to KSW, undated, 1936, NYR 251.

124 She felt the pull: JF to Miss Terry, undated, likely March 1936, NYR 251.

124 Her way was to read: Murray, *Janet*, 71.

124 "The trouble with me": Murray, *Janet*, 72.

124 Eventually, she threatened to quit: KSW to HR, March 30, 1936, NYR 20.

125 White told Ross: KSW to HR, March 30, 1936, NYR 20.

125 But because this would mean: HR to "Hoyt," April 1, 1936, NYR 20; Wineapple, *Genêt*, 149.

126 "Hildegarde is so intellectual": JF to KSW, February 25 note, NYR 251.

126 She decided she hadn't: Wineapple, *Genêt*, 149.

126 From her ship: JF to KSW, April 1936, NYR 251.

126 Later she cabled Ross: JF to HR, September 2, 1937, NYR 21.

126 Ross had asked her: JF to RAH, undated, Spring 1936, NYR 251.

126 And this time Ross: HR to JF, April 27, 1936, NYR 20.

17: NOT WHO WON, NATURALLY

128 "Thanks exquisite orchids": JF to KSW, April 16, 1936, NYR 251.

128 She critiqued: FNY, July 4, 1936.

129 She wrote with approval: FNY, July 4, 1936.

129 An "odd man": FNY, July 4, 1936; Kedward, *France*, 189.

129 She praised him: FNY, January 9, 1937.

129 The Popular Front's victory: Kedward, *France*, 183.

130 The movement's leader: Luc Sante, *The Other Paris* (Farrar, Straus and Giroux, 2015), 84; Kedward, *France*, 178.

130 He might have been: FNY, January 9, 1937; Kedward, *France*, 178.

130 A heightened awareness: Jackson, *Popular Front*, 8.

130 Striking department-store workers: Charles Rearick, *The French in Love and War* (Yale University Press, 1997), 201.

131 Newspapers ran photos: Kedward, *France*, 204.

131 And yet funding: Kedward, *France*, 187.

131 Flanner noted that the French: FNY, April 24, 1937.

131 When the forty-hour week: JF to RAH, undated, 1937, NYR 274.

131 People also noticed a newfound: Rearick, *The French*, 206.

131 The historian Eric Hobsbawm: Eric Hobsbawm, *Interesting Times: A Twentieth-Century Life* (Pantheon Books, 2002), 322–323.

132 "I hate to go to Germany": JF to HR and RAH, undated, Spring 1936, NYR 251.

132 She'd asked one of her editors: JF to HR and RAH, undated, Spring 1936, NYR 251.

133 Twenty thousand doves: Laura Hillenbrand, *Unbroken: A World War II Story of Survival, Resilience, and Redemption* (Random House, 2010), 32.

133 At that evening's festival: FNY, August 15, 1936.

133 The spectacular displays: FNY, August 1, 1936.

133 "As the newspapers": JF to RAH, July 9, 1936, NYR 251.

133 She wrote, in an issue: FNY, August 1, 1936.

133 At the same time: Weiss, *Paris*, 183.

133 "The past year": FNY, August 1, 1936.

133 "Goering is apparently": FNY, August 1, 1936.

134 She went so far: FNY, October 17, 1936.

134 A few months earlier: FNY, April 15, 1936.

134 Friends wondered: Wineapple, *Genêt*, 149.

134 In trying to justify: JF to RAH, July 29, 1936, NYR 251.

134 She stopped in Salzburg: JF to HR and RAH, undated, Spring 1936, NYR 251.

135 In a jolly postcard: JF to KSW, August 31, 1936, NYR 251.

18: THE CROSSING

136 Frankfurt had one: Evans, *Coming*, 24.

136 The streets were clean: Colombani, *L'Affaire*, 53.

136 Their paper of choice: Colombani, *L'Affaire*, 51–52.

137 They now owned: Colombani, *L'Affaire*, 59.

137 He couldn't abide: Colombani, *L'Affaire*, 62.

19: ALL I AM TRYING TO DO IS WEATHER EVENTS

139 As the Spanish Republic's: Julio Álvarez del Vayo, quoted in Sarah Watling, *Tomorrow Perhaps the Future: Writers, Outsiders, and the Spanish Civil War* (Knopf, 2023), vii.

139 "Paris feels that Spain": FNY, September 19, 1936.

140 Flanner at that time: Wineapple, *Genêt*, 150.

141 The Paris-to-London trip: JF to KSW, December 13, 1937, NYR 274.

141 "NOTHING doing in Paris": JF to RAH, undated, likely October 1937, NYR 251.

141 "Verbal violence": FNY, October 24, 1936.

141 She outlined a book: JF to KSW, undated, 1936, NYR 274.

142 "My brain can't hop": JF to RAH, August 12, 1936, NYR 251.

142 She felt as if: JF to HR, September 4, 1937, NYR 21; JF to RAH, August 12, 1936, NYR 251; Wineapple, *Genêt*, 149.

142 She missed the "domestic feeling": JF to KSW, undated, 1937, NYR 274.

142 She suffered shooting pains: JF to KSW, October 27, 1936.

142 She worked: JF to RAH, September 29, 1936, NYR 251.

142 Most terrible of all: JF to HR, October 14, 1936, NYR 20.

142 "Doctor says": JF to RAH, September 29, 1936, NYR 251.

142 In early December: Flanner schedule, undated, 1936, NYR 251.

143 As Virginia Woolf: Watling, *Tomorrow*, 78.

143 "What the hell?": HR to JF, October 6, 1936, NYR 251.

143 She told White: JF to KSW, undated, 1937, NYR 274.

143 It was "a difficult job": JF to KSW, October 27, 1936, NYR 251.

144 Meanwhile she told White: JF to KSW, November 20, 1936, NYR 251.

144 "One will always": JF to RAH, July 13, 1937, NYR 274.

144 London was a "peculiarly sealed": JF to KSW, November 10, 1936, NYR 251.

144 "I'll be glad": JF to RAH, undated, 1935, NYR 227.

144 And at least: JF to RAH, undated, 1936, NYR 251.

144 Solano, who'd joined: Murray, *Janet*, 35.

144 Ross, White, and others: RAH to JF, October 13, 1936, NYR 251.

144 Flanner spoke openly: JF to RAH, September 7, 1936, NYR 251.

145 "Yes, Janet sounds far too busy": Hildegarde Flanner to SS, January 11, 1937, LOC.

145 F. Scott Fitzgerald: Fitzgerald, "My Lost City."

145 Paris had welcomed: Rearick, *The French*, 127.

146 In Solano's memory: Solano, "Hotel Bonaparte"; Baker, *Hemingway*, 258.

146 In his wandering: EH to JF, 1933, LOC.

146 The magazine had more: Yagoda, *About Town*, 98.

147 By sticking to her usual: Other writers on Flanner have framed her writing in similar terms, including: Jeffrey Gonzalez, "The Metropolitan as Master Subject: Janet Flanner's 'Paris Letters,'" *Mosaic: a Journal for the Interdisciplinary Study of Literature* 43, no. 1 (2010): 41–56; Don Hausdorff, "Politics and Economics: The Emergence of a *New Yorker* Tone," *Studies in American Humor* 3, no. 1 (1984), 74–82; Lindsay Starck, "Janet Flanner's High Class Gossip" and "American Nationalism Between the Wars," *The Journal of Modern Periodical Studies* 7, nos. 1–2 (2016), 1–25.

148 "There's no education": Bainbridge, *Another*, 24.

148 "If you don't go home": Flanner in Moore, *The Writer in America*.

148 She saw her assignment: Flanner, "Day and Night Thoughts" (fragmentary diary), LOC.

20: THE VILLA

149 "High Class Grill": Jacques Lanzmann, *Paris des années 30* (Editions de la Martinière, 1992).

151 The only real difference: F. Tennyson Jesse, *Comments on Cain* (Collier Books, 1964), 111.

21: EVERYTHING'S JUST FINE!

154 In front of her: James D. Herbert, *Paris 1937: Worlds on Exhibition* (Cornell University Press, 1998), 13.

155 Some on the planning committee: Herbert, *Paris 1937*, 6.

155 Many saw the Expo: Shanny Peer, *France on Display: Peasants, Provincials, and Folklore in the 1937 Paris World's Fair* (State University of New York Press, 1998), 6, 22–23.

156 Some of these events: Fiss, *Grand Illusion*, 17, 51–52.

156 In *Mein Kampf*: Fiss, *Grand Illusion*, 15.

156 While complete editions: Fiss, *Grand Illusion*, 15–16.

156 Trade between Germany: Tony Judt, *Postwar: A History of Europe Since 1945* (Penguin Press, 2005), 4.

156 By drawing out French: Fiss, *Grand Illusion*, 14–15, 45.

157 The place was "a gopher hole": JF to KSW, May 1937, NYR 274.

157 Wildcat strikes: Herbert, *Paris 1937*, 29.

157 Two months before: Kedward, *France*, 212; Chris Millington, *Le Massacre de Clichy* (Éditions Critique, 2021).

157 Along with wondering: FNY, March 13, 1937.

157 She asked if anyone: FNY, January 30, 1937.

157 She stressed to her editors: JF to RAH, February 26, 1937, NYR 274.

158 Requesting extra column space: FNY, March 27, 1937.

158 Having heard that ten thousand: JF to RAH, February 26, 1937, NYR 274.

158 She advised visitors: FNY, March 27, 1937.

158 Against a jaunty tune: FNY, October 17, 1936.

158 For heavier fare: FNY, March 27, 1937.

159 While she considered: JF to RAH, March 10, 1937, NYR 274; JF to KSW, May 12, 1937, NYR 274.

159 It housed a transparent: FNY, August 18, 1937.

159 Few who enjoyed: Fiss, *Grand Illusion*, 73–74.

160 Out front of one: FNY, August 18, 1937; film footage at "Pavilion Attractions and Entertainment at the International Exposition in Paris, 1937," United States Holocaust Memorial Museum, https://collections.ushmm.org/search/catalog/irn1003891.

160 Flanner understood that: FNY, June 19, 1937.

161 Its architect: Deyan Sudjic, *Stalin's Architect: Power and Survival in Moscow* (MIT Press, 2022).

161 "The petrol pipe lines": FNY, June 19, 1937.

161 Albert Speer: Fiss, *Grand Illusion*, 60–61.

161 Speer once said: Fiss, *Grand Illusion*, 51, 55, 233; Ute Lemke, "Les touristes allemands du IIIe Reich face à l'autre Allemagne lors de l'Exposition Internationale de Paris (1937)," *Viaggiatori*, September 2018, 155.

162 A mix of Roman temple: Fiss, *Grand Illusion*, 62; FNY, June 19, 1937.

162 After speaking about: Fiss, *Grand Illusion*, 54.

162 Inside, the millions: Herbert and Fiss make a similar point in their respective books.

162 Under titanic chandeliers: Fiss, *Grand Illusion*, 78.

163 In Germany that summer: Fiss, *Grand Illusion*, 76.

163 Meanwhile in Paris: Heinrich Hoffmann, *Deutschland in Paris* (Heinrich Hoffmann Verlag, 1937).

163 One described the experience: Evans, *Third Reich in Power*, 185.

163 Giving interviews: Fiss, *Grand Illusion*, 169.

164 Riefenstahl's win marked: Evans, *Third Reich in Power*, 130.

164 Eighty thousand: Lemke, "Les touristes allemands," 157; Fiss, *Grand Illusion*, 39.

165 When it was finally unveiled: Herbert, *Paris 1937*, 33.

165 A German book: Hoffmann, *Deutschland*.

165 At the Pavilion of Modern Times: Fiss, *Grand Illusion*, 188.

165 "We don't know how": Fiss, *Grand Illusion*, 183.

166 Lebrun said that: Pathé newsreel at "Paris Exhibition Opened (1937)," British Pathé, https://www.britishpathe.com/asset/43948/.

166 Blum had, however: Peer, *France*, 6.

22: AN AMERICAN BALLET TEACHER IN PARIS

175 Some of the headlines: FNY, February 5, 1938.

23: OUR MOVING AND TORMENTED ERA

178 Less than a month: Herrick Chapman, "The Ambiguous Legacy of the Popular Front," *French Politics and Society*, no. 15, 1986, 19–25.

178 Another refrain common: Sante, *The Other Paris*, 4.

178 "I admire him in many ways": JF to KSW, May 12, 1937, NYR 274.

179 "France is more worried": FNY, October 2, 1937.

179 In a scene: Fiss, *Grand Illusion*, 182–183.

180 They were planning: Chris Millington, *The Invention of Terrorism in France, 1904–1939* (Stanford University Press, 2023); Kedward, *France*, 210.

180 Flanner ultimately judged: FNY, October 16, 1937.

180 Privately she admitted: JF to Clifford Orr, undated, 1937, NYR 274.

180 In *The New Yorker*: FNY, August 28, 1937.

181 "I now don't know": JF to KSW, October 9, 1935, BM.

181 The presence of so many: Lemke, "Les touristes allemands," 157.

181 "International expositions illustrate": Peer, *France*, 21; Peer also has an epigraph in her book using the quotation "our moving and tormented era."

182 "Thurber extraordinary": JF to RAH, undated, June or July 1937, NYR 274.

182 But not much later: JF to SM, November 18, 1937, NYR 274.

183 The Munich trip: FNY, September 11, 1937.

183 When filing the piece: JF to RAH, undated, September 1937, NYR 274.

183 There they found momentary: JF to KSW, undated, 1937, NYR 274.

184 She returned "in disgust": JF to RAH, undated, September 1937, NYR 274.

184 "I'm a pessimist": JF to KSW, undated, likely Autumn 1937, NYR 274.

184 And yet privately: JF to RAH, undated, likely January 1937, NYR 274.

184 The best explanation: Wineapple, *Genêt*, 151.

185 They defined themselves: Tony Judt, *The Burden of Responsibility: Blum, Camus, Aron, and the French Twentieth Century* (University of Chicago Press, 1998), 10.

185 Nancy Cunard publicly: Watling, *Tomorrow*, 4–5.

185 Parker and her husband: JF to SM, October 3, 1937, NYR 274.

185 "Several of my Red": JF to KSW, May 1, 1937, NYR 274.

186 In Franklin's dirty room: Baker, *Hemingway*, 301.

186 She pitched her idea: JF to RAH, May 29, 1937, NYR 274.

186 Ross okayed her proposal: RAH to JF, June 15, 1937, NYR 274.

186 Flanner promised "no political": JF to RAH, June 22, 1937, NYR 274.

186 "I have really swell": JF to RAH, May 29, 1937, NYR 274; JF to RAH, June 2, 1937, NYR 274.

187 "Because men are tragically": FNY, August 7, 1937.

187 Hemingway, after reading it: SS to Carlos Baker, December 27, 1966, LOC.

188 "If it's part": JF to "Mr. Rogers," September 9, 1937, NYR 274.

188 She had indeed: HR to JF, August 26, 1931, NYR 21; JF to KSW, undated, 1937, NYR 274.

189 "An editor would say": Bainbridge, *Another*, 22.

189 Flanner passed along: *The New Yorker*'s copy of Ralph Ingersoll to JF, September 15, 1937, NYR 274.

189 White's expertly argued: KSW to JF, October 6, 1937, NYR 274.

190 This would make: KSW to JF, October 8, 1937, NYR 274.

190 Quitting *The New Yorker*: JF to SM, December 27, 1938, NYR 315.

190 Nowhere else could she find: Murray, *Janet*, 72.

24: THE SPREE

192 Blé said he'd asked: FNY, December 29, 1937; different wordings of this exchange are also found in various court documents.

196 Later, after he gave: *Détective*, March 23, 1939.

198 They made a game of it: Jesse, *Comments*, 93.

200 Million's father later testified: James de Coquet, "La septième audience du procès Weidmann fait surgir un nouveau mystère," *Le Figaro*, March 21, 1939.

205 And he rarely removed: Colombani, *L'Affaire*, 13.

25: TO BLUEBEARD'S CELL

210 In the meantime he sent: In some sources "Ange Poignant" is rendered as "Ange Poignard."

211 People said he loved: *Détective*, December 16, 1937.

212 They searched him: Colombani, *L'Affaire*, 6–10.

213 One art lover: Colombani, *L'Affaire*, 19.

213 Soon photographs of the bandaged: Walker, *Outrage*, 103; see, for example, *Le Petit Journal*, December 9, 1937

213 He would recall being struck: Colombani, *L'Affaire*, 22.

214 Sicot pressed but finally: Colombani, *L'Affaire*, 23.

215 The prison cook: Jardin Birnie, *Cahier*, 51.

215 To one observer: Colombani, *L'Affaire*, 46.

215 After killing Lesobre: Colombani, *L'Affaire*, 24.

218 He supposed he felt German: Colombani, *L'Affaire*, 61.

219 This would lead: "5 Nations Seek Murder Clues," *Daily Herald*, January 8, 1939.

220 Renée Jardin would recall: Colombani, *L'Affaire*, 40.

221 Instead, Weidmann had shot: "3 Sought in Killing Give Up in France," *New York Times*, December 11, 1937.

223 A few days later: Jardin Birnie, *Cahier*, 178.

26: A SMALL AND SINISTER EUROPEAN ENTANGLEMENT

224 "I almost cabled": JF to KSW, December 22, 1937, NYR 274.

225 Magistrate Berry had counseled: Colombani, *L'Affaire*, 32.

225 The novelist Colette: Colette, "Assassins," *Le Journal*, December 19, 1937.

226 Flanner in that first: FNY, January 1, 1938.

226 At that time no libel law: Jesse, *Comments*, 103.

226 "I tried to be simple": JF to SM, January 14, 1938, NYR 295.

227 "We hope you will hop": KSW to JF, December 31, 1937, NYR 274.

227 When she filed, she told: JF to KSW, undated, likely early 1938, NYR 295.

228 "Only a typical Frenchman": FNY, February 5, 1938.

229 McKelway, who edited: SM to JF, January 21, 1938, NYR 295.

27: I AM THE WOUND AND THE KNIFE

230 Petit-Jean was, to Weidmann: Jardin Birnie, *Cahier*, 50.

230 He wrote that he wanted: Jardin Birnie, *Cahier*, 51, 60–61, 171–172, 179.

232 He passed hours each day: Jardin Birnie, *Cahier*, 47.

232 He was occasionally allowed: Ambrose Sherwill, *A Fair and Honest Book* (Lulu, 2007), 157.

232 The fates had given him: Jardin Birnie, *Cahier*, 47.

28: THE LAST MIDDLE-WESTERNER

233 She told White: JF to KSW, January 12, 1938 (penciled "1936?" but 1938 from context), BM.

233 "The heavens": JF to KSW, January 12, 1938 (penciled "1936?" but 1938 from context), BM.

234 They had "a grand time": JF to SM, January 14, 1938, NYR 295.

234 Her outlook hadn't been helped: FNY, April 9, 1938.

234 "The only noise": FNY, March 19, 1938.

235 She relayed hearing: FNY, March 26, 1938.

235 "I laugh when I think": JF to RAH, March 9, 1938, NYR 295.

235 "I guess I'm straddle minded": JF to RAH, undated, likely July 1938, NYR 295.

235 After learning of the complete: FNY, March 19, 1938.

235 In a note to herself: Murray, *Janet*, 66.

236 To Hague she wrote: JF to RAH, April 12, 1938, NYR 295.

236 Britain and France remained: FNY, March 19, 1938.

236 These were two: FNY, June 11, 1938.

236 The minister of foreign affairs: FNY, April 9, 1938.

237 "It's melancholy to see": FNY, May 14, 1938.

237 "Everything that is happening": FNY, June 11, 1938.

237 On Orgeval's prized strawberry: FNY, May 14, 1938.

237 "And now little by little": Glenway Westcott, "The Frenchman Six Foot Three," *Harper's*, July 1942. (Westcott has redubbed Janet Flanner as "Linda Brewer.")

29: HE HAS ABNORMALITIES

239 "In the words of Dr. Claude": The doctor's findings were quoted by Vincent de Moro-Giafferi on March 29, 1939, at the Cour d'assise de Versailles, René Bluet stenographer, from Dominique de Moro-Giafferi's personal archives. Moro's remarks are quoted in Lanzalavi, *Vincent*, 120–121. Translation my own.

30: ITSY-BITSY ANTI-NAZI ME

242 Ever since learning: JF to KSW, undated, likely early 1938, NYR 295.

242 "Hildegarde, my younger sister": JF to KSW, July 10, 1938, BM.

242 She turned some notes: JF to RAH, March 9, 1938, NYR 295; FNY, June 28, 1938.

243 "The European history": FNY, June 28, 1938.

243 She passed much of July: JF to KSW, undated, 1933, NYR 168.

244 Working "in relays": JF to KSW, undated, 1933, NYR 168; JF to KSW, July 10, 1938, BM; JF to RAH, August 2, 1938, NYR 295.

244 "I'm glad to know it's urinal": JF to KSW, July 10, 1938, BM.

244 The alcoholic McKelway: SM to JF, August 10, 1938, NYR 295.

244 She'd already set aside: JF to KSW, July 10, 1938, BM.

244 "Life is always ironic": JF to RAH, June 22, 1938, NYR 295.

245 She soon nixed: JF to RAH, August 2, 1938, NYR 295.

245 She advised the magazine: JF to RAH, undated, likely July 1938, NYR 295.

245 "You know that every": JF to RAH, June 22, 1938, NYA 295.

245 She took comfort: JF to RAH, March 9, 1938, NYR 295.

245 "Only in the cool": FNY, August 20, 1938.

32: HISTORY LOOKS QUEER WHEN YOU'RE STANDING CLOSE TO IT

249 She'd suggested to her editors: JF to RAH, March 9, 1938, NYR 295.

250 "Indeed, it really was": FNY, September 3, 1938.

250 White told Ross: HR to JF, quoting White, September 15, 1938, NYR 223.

250 Flanner told Hague: JF to RAH, August 2, 1938, NYR 295.

251 Running in *The New Yorker*: FNY, September 17, 1938.

252 "This city is like": JF to SM, August 22, 1938, NYR 295.

252 "The farther east one goes": FNY, September 24, 1938.

252 "History looks queer": FNY, September 24, 1938.

253 "Honestly, Janet": SM to JF, September 29, 1938, NYR 295.

253 About her writing: Unnamed *New Yorker* editor (very likely SM) to JF, marked November 11, 1938, but likely misdated and should more logically be October, NYR 295.

253 "That was a hard trip": JF to SM, October 12, 1938, NYR 295.

253 She made a similar point: JF to KSW, October 19, 1938, BM.

254 "Speaking of war": HR to JF, September 15, 1938, NYR 23.

254 The autumn return: FNY, October 8, 1938.

255 "We're all thinking about you": SM to JF, September 29, 1938, NYR 295.

255 In her reply: JF to SM, October 12, 1938, NYR 295.

255 "the storm abruptly": de Beauvoir, *The Prime of Life*, 336.

256 To his top aide: Édouard Daladier, *Journal de captivité: 1940-1945* (Calmann-Lévy, 1991), 381.

256 Flanner reported: FNY, October 8, 1938.

257 "I would not be able": JF to SM, October 12, 1938, NYR 295.

257 She told White: JF to KSW, October 19, 1938, BM.

257 "Hemingway says gas": JF to KSW, October 19, 1938, BM.

258 "No sooner was the": FNY, October 22, 1938.

258 She advised heeding: FNY, November 26, 1938.

259 Pointing to the strides: FNY, November 12, 1938.

259 "I hope I do London": JF to RAH, October 27, 1938, NYR 295.

260 "When the Premier": FNY, December 3, 1938.

260 The British public: FNY, December 10, 1938.

260 "Never, since our states": FNY, December 10, 1938.

260 "The truth is politics": JF to RAH, December 7, 1938, NYR 295.

261 Flanner opened the year's: FNY, December 31, 1938.

261 W. H. Auden: W. H. Auden, "September 1, 1939," in *Another Time* (Random House, 1940).

261 "Not only the visible": FNY, December 31, 1938.

34: NOTHING TO WRITE EXCEPT HATRED FOR ALL

265 Nineteen thirty-nine opened to the aftermath: FNY, January 14, 1939; "Blizzard Cuts Off England," *New York Times*, December 27, 1938.

265 "These are queer": FNY, February 18, 1939.

265 "Everything else is just": JF to SM, January 12, 1939, NYR 315.

266 In the year's first: FNY, January 14, 1939.

266 "Since French pessimists": FNY, March 25, 1939.

267 In what must have ranked: FNY, February 2, 1939.

267 She told McKelway: JF to SM, undated, (March?) 1939, NYR 315.

267 She complained in a January: FNY, January 28, 1939.

268 She omitted mention: JF to SM, January 27, 1939, NYR 315.

268 "With the middle class": FNY, January 28, 1939.

268 "I sound": JF to SM, January 12, 1939, NYR 315.

269 She was still willing: JF to SM, January 27, 1939, NYR 315.

270 "Would you prefer": JF to SM, February 7, 1939, NYR 315.

270 McKelway passed along: SM memo, undated, February 1939, NYR 315.

270 Flanner cabled back: JF to SM, February 16, 1939, NYR 315.

35: A JUDGMENT AT VERSAILLES

271 Nearly sixty pounds': "When He Saw His Mother He Wept," *Sunday Pictorial* (London), February 26, 1939.

271 As with any jury: James M. Donovan, *Juries and the Transformation of Criminal Justice in France in the Nineteenth and Twentieth Centuries* (University of North Carolina Press, 2010).

272 To Renée Jardin: Jardin Birnie, *Cahier*, 72.

36: A LETTER FROM PERPIGNAN

274 As they approached: JF to SM, February 16, 1939, NYR 315.

274 After reaching Paris: Antony Beevor, *The Battle for Spain: The Spanish Civil War, 1936–1939* (Penguin Books, 2006), 158–160.

275 Over the span: Watling, *Tomorrow*, 296.

275 French soldiers, stationed: Sharif Gemie, "The Ballad of Bourg-Madame: Memory, Exile, and the Spanish Republican Refugees of the 'Retirada' of 1939," *International Review of Social History* 51, no. 1, 2006, 31.

275 "On the mountains": Nancy Cunard, letter to the editor, *Manchester Guardian*, February 9, 1939; Watling, *Tomorrow*, 294.

275 Everywhere they looked: FNY, March 11, 1939.

275 "It's a sad story here": JF to SM, February 16, 1939, NYR 315.

276 She couldn't think: FNY, March 11, 1939.

276 Some of the refugees: Gemie, "The Ballad," 32.

276 Conditions were so horrible: Beevor, *The Battle*, 412.

276 Masses died of simple neglect: Watling, *Tomorrow*, 296–298.

276 A few hanged: Gemie, "The Ballad," 33.

276 As George Orwell: George Orwell, "Homage to Catalonia," in *Orwell in Spain* (Penguin Books, 2001), 17.

276 French notables including: Beevor, *The Battle*, 382, 412.

277 She told McKelway: JF to SM, February 24, 1939, NYR 315.

277 She opened with her disgust: FNY, March 11, 1939.

278 Leaving Perpignan: Chisholm, *Cunard*, 308–349; JF to SM, undated, (March?) 1939, NYR 315.

278 "Drink…has nothing": Chisholm, *Cunard*, 314.

278 Lamenting the waste: Chisholm, *Cunard*, 316.

279 Flanner had once told: JF to KSW, January 28, 1938 (penciled "1936?" but 1938 from context), BM.

279 Through many cables: KSW note, undated, 1972; JF to KSW, January 12, 1938 (penciled "1936?" but 1938 from context); JF to KSW, January 28, 1938 (penciled "1936?" but 1938 from context), BM.

279 Levick refused to believe: KSW note, 1972; and KSW to JF, January 24, 1938, BM.

279 Flanner, feeling: JF to KSW, January 12, 1938 (penciled "1936?" but 1938 from context), BM.

279 "Am I staying": JF to SM, undated, February 1939, NYR 315.

280 McKelway told her: SM to JF, March 9, 1939, and March 21, 1939, NYR 315.

280 "Everybody I talk to": SM to JF, March 9, 1939, NYR 315.

280 Across the Atlantic: Adam Hochschild, *Spain in Our Hearts: Americans in the Spanish Civil War, 1936–1939* (Mariner Books, 2017).

281 On an immediate: FNY, February 2, 1939.

281 People predicted entire cities: Michael B. Miller, *Shanghai on the Métro: Spies, Intrigue, and the French Between the Wars* (University of California Press, 1994), 15–16.

281 As Albert Camus would later: Albert Camus, *L'éspagne libre* (Calmann-Lévy, 1946), quoted in Hochschild, *Spain in Our Hearts*.

281 A few days after Flanner: Beevor, *The Battle*, 386.

37: THE GOSPEL OF THE MURDERER

282 For the people of France: Walker, *Outrage*, 104.

282 A small number of journalists: Lanzalavi, *Vincent*, 118.

283 "Unfortunately" the lead counsel: Jesse, *Comments*, 105.

283 A woman stood up: Jesse, *Comments*, 104.

284 The most unsettling criminals: Colette, *Le Journal*, April 2, 1939.

284 Alongside Weidmann: Colette, *Le Journal*, March 13, 1939.

284 Reporters who over: Jesse, *Comments*, 110.

284 "Weidmann lied to Million": Coquet, "La septième."

285 With each day: Colette, *Paris-Soir*, March 19, 1939.

285 Sometimes his desire: Léon Worth, *L'Intransigeant*, March 12, 1939.

285 When asked about the failed: Jesse, *Comments*, 119.

285 When asked how he'd been so careless: Jesse, *Comments*, 116.

285 The lawyer explained to the court: Jesse, *Comments*, 126.

286 He waited in a too-long, heavy: *Idem*, March 11, 1939.

286 He knew, he said: Colette, *Paris-Soir*, March 19, 1939.

286 He said he didn't: FNY, April 8, 1939.

286 Colette said it was: Colette, *Paris-Soir*, March 19, 1939.

286 He'd "offered a truthfulness": FNY, April 8, 1939.

38: THE BLOOD IN HIS VEINS AND THE CLIMATE OF HIS DAYS

288 Everyone in the room: Jesse, *Comments*, 104.

288 "Do me the honor": Lanzalavi, *Vincent*, 120.

289 He drew on Victor Hugo: Ève Morisi, *Capital Letters: Hugo, Baudelaire, Camus, and the Death Penalty* (Northwestern University Press, 2020).

291 "Don't let it disturb you": Jesse, *Comments*, 142.

293 He was hailed: *Détective*, April 6, 1939.

293 He was "one": Jesse, *Comments*, 142.

39: I HOPE TO HEAVEN MOM DOESN'T SEE IT

294 His lawyer lashed out: *Détective*, April 6, 1939.

295 Weidmann glanced up: *Détective*, April 6, 1939.

295 Following tradition: Victor Hugo, *Les Misérables* (1862).

295 The family's attorney: "Damages Refused in Dancer's Death," *New York Times*, April 2, 1939.

296 She'd loved watching: FNY, April 8, 1939.

296 Even amid Hitler's: Walker, *Outrage*, 103–104.

296 "It is indicative": FNY, April 8, 1939.

297 "Outside of the sappy": JF to SM, March 27, 1939, NYR 315.

40: FANTASTIC AND UNREAL AS IT MAY SEEM

298 In New York the German-American: Russell Maloney, "Heil Washington," *The New Yorker*, March 4, 1939.

299 Flanner had praised: FNY, August 6, 1938.

299 He'd come in theory: Francis Rose, *Saying Life: The Memoirs of Sir Francis Rose* (Cassell, 1961), 389.

299 "Did I tell you this one": JF to SM, March 27, 1939, NYR 315.

299 "Events seem worsening": JF to SM, April 12 1939, NYR 315.

299 Watching the French and English: FNY, April 8, 1939.

299 She predicted: FNY, March 25, 1939.

299 "Fantastic and unreal": FNY, April 22, 1939.

300 "It seems to me that you": SM to JF, undated, (Spring by context) 1939, NYR 315.

300 "I feel relaxed and more": JF to SM, undated, 1939, NYR 315.

300 "I stepped out a lot": JF to RAH, June 22, 1938, NYR 295.

300 "She feels she can't leave": Murray, *Janet*, 72.

301 Flanner threw out: JF to SM, April 15, 1939, NYR 315.

301 "Maybe the hope": FNY, April 22, 1939.

301 Germany occupied Czechoslovakia: Wineapple, *Genêt*, 157; FNY, March 25, 1939.

301 "A reign of efficiently": JF to SM, undated, (late May by context) 1939, NYR 315.

302 "Rather hysterical": Ross, undated memo, attached to JF to SM cablegram, April 25, 1939, NYR 315.

302 "You've really done": SM to JF, April 29, 1939, NYR 315.

302 She praised those Parisians: FNY, April 1, 1939.

303 It was in the wistful sighs: Flanner, *Paris Was Yesterday*, 218–219.

41: THIS MISERABLE BEAUTIFUL WORLD

304 Now that he'd been: Jardin Birnie, *Cahier*, 227.

305 When Moro tried: Walker, *Outrage*, 109.

305 "I don't want": Lanzalavi, *Vincent*, 121.

306 And so, even while: FNY, July 15, 1939.

307 He saw a page of illustrations: Albert Camus, *Réflexions sur la Guillotine* (Folio, 2008).

307 The literary historian: Kaplan, *Looking*, 50–52.

307 "For everything to be consummated": Albert Camus, *The Stranger*, trans. Matthew Ward (Vintage, 1999), 123.

42: THANKS FOR MONEY. WHAT A STRANGE WAR.

308 Ross and McKelway: SM to JF, January 5, 1939, NYR 315.

309 "There have been money": FNY, July 22, 1939.

309 The cloudless day: FNY, July 29, 1939.

310 "The higher the source": JF to SM, January 7, 1939, NYR 315.

310 They stocked up: Margaret Anderson, *The Fiery Fountains* (Hermitage House, 1951), 172.

310 As the brilliance of July: FNY, August 12, 1939.

311 "Any news dispatched": FNY, April 15, 1939.

311 Alongside her Letters: Flanner, "The Generation That Knows Nothing Else," *Woman's Home Companion*, September 1939, 16–17.

311 "Wonderful country": JF to SM, August 13, 1939, NYR 315.

311 She might just: Craig Seligman, "The Talk of the (Seedy Side of) Town," *New York Times*, March 3, 2010.

311 "Trouble expected": JF to *The New Yorker*, August 24, 1939, NYR 315.

311 "Where's Orgeval?": SM to HR, undated, 1939, NYR 315.

312 The next day: JF to *The New Yorker*, August 25, 1939, NYR 315.

312 And the day after: JF to *The New Yorker*, August 26, 1939, NYR 315.

312 "Diplomatic circles believe": FNY, September 2, 1939.

313 Most of them had already: FNY, September 16, 1939; FNY, October 14, 1939; Kedward, *France*, 253; Amanda Vaill, *Everybody Was So Young* (Broadway Books, 1999), 300; Wineapple, *Genêt*, 159.

313 "It is the evil things": "Great Britain: The Great Change," *Time*, September 11, 1939.

314 Margaret Anderson, listening: Anderson, *Fiery*, 174.

314 Monsieur Louis stood: Solano, "Hotel Bonaparte."

314 On that same Sunday: Hildegarde Flanner to HR, September 3, 1939, NYR 315.

315 She closed her message: JF to *The New Yorker*, September 4, 1939, as translated from French by *New Yorker* staff, NYR 315.

315 "Flanner is in some kind of panic": SM to HR, memo dated only "Monday," but from context likely September 4, 1939, NYR 315.

315 But by then Ross: HR to JF, September 4, 1939, NYR 351.

315 Shortly afterward, Hildegarde: SM to HF, September 5, 1939, NYR 315.

316 Four and a half million: Kedward, *France*, 235.

316 "Censoring and control": JF to SM, September 7, 1939, NYR 315.

317 "American women": FNY, September 16, 1939.

317 Without knowing it: Jeremy D. Popkin, *A History of Modern France*, 2nd ed. (Pearson, 2000), 251.

318 They spent "from the first": FNY, September 16, 1939; Anderson, *Fiery*, 171.

318 "Multitudes of French": FNY, September 23, 1939.

318 The Germans and Italians: FNY, September 23, 1939.

319 "Would the life": Anderson, *Fiery*, 172.

319 "Never have nights": FNY, September 23, 1939.

319 "I cannot compete": Murray, *Janet*, 74.

320 "We were like figures": Anderson, *Fiery*, 176.

320 Soldiers had written: Wineapple, *Genêt*, 160; FNY, September 30, 1939.

320 The women saw artillery: FNY, September 30, 1939.

320 Rejoining the main road: FNY, September 30, 1939.

320 Hemingway had taken: Baker, *Hemingway*, 3.

321 A few weeks earlier: Vaill, *Everybody*, 301.

321 When Sara and Honoria: Vaill, *Everybody*, 301.

321 Any place dealing: Wineapple, *Genêt*, 160.

321 Bordeaux was now: FNY, October 14, 1939.

321 The army had put many: FNY, October 7, 1939.

322 Flanner lauded the staff: FNY, September 30, 1939.

322 She spotted, among: FNY, September 30, 1939.

322 His was a lovely name: FNY, October 7, 1939.

323 After three weeks: William Shawn to New York Custom House, October 11, 1939, NYR 315.

323 Before leaving she'd: HR to JF, September 28, 1939, NYR 23.

323 "This period has brought": FNY, October 14, 1939.

43: PARIS, GERMANY

325 Paris, Germany: I take the chapter title "Paris, Germany" from a Flanner *New Yorker* piece of the same name, FNY, December 7, 1940.

326 Renée Jardin actively collaborated: 1612W 36 dossier 87: (Ministère chargé de l'économie et des finances: dossiers de séquestre de biens après condamnation pour des faits de collaboration); 219W 34 [3], Jardin, Renée: arrêt du 5 juillet 1945 pour Intelligence avec l'ennemi et propagande antinationale, (Cour de Justice); 1081W 180 [10], Jardin, Renée: arrêt du 07 juillet 1945 pour atteinte à la sûreté de l'Etat (groupe "Collaboration").

(Cour de Justice); 1338W 18 [1], Jardin, Renée: arrêt du 3 mars 1946 pour atteinte à la sûreté de l'Etat, (Chambre civique), Archives Départementales des Yvelines; Colombani, *L'Affaire*, 316–317; Jacques Delarue, *Le métier de bourreau* (Fayard, 1989).

CODA: HARSH INTELLIGENCE AND BEAUTIFUL SPOILS

327 Following the liberation: Janet Flanner's *New Yorker* contract, November 1, 1944, LOC.

327 William Shawn threw: Flanner, *Darlinghissima*, 32.

327 She told Ross: HR to "Mr. Cook," October 27, 1944, NYR 44.

328 It was there: Murray, *Janet*, 25.

328 Solano, who despised Murray: SS to Margaret Anderson, undated, 1942, LOC.

330 "She wondered where": Flanner, *Darlinghissima*, 31.

330 Terrified of flying: JF to Esther Traversari, November 8, 1944, LOC.

330 "I am as calm": JF to Natalia Danesi Murray (hereafter NDM), November 9, 1944, LOC.

330 During her stopover: JF to SS, November 15, 1944, LOC.

330 A few months earlier: NC to JF, August 24, 1944, LOC.

330 As soon as Flanner: Judt, *Postwar*, 17.

331 Noël met her at the train: JF to SS, November 22, 1944, LOC.

331 She looked thin and bent: JF to SS, November 22, 1944, LOC; JF to SS, January 3, 1945, LOC; JF to NDM, November 26, 1944, LOC.

331 And yet for someone: JF to SS, November 22, 1944, LOC; JF to SS, January 3, 1945, LOC; JF to NDM, November 26, 1944, LOC.

331 "Noel is incommunicado": NC to JF, September 12 (year undated but 1940 from context), LOC.

331 Murphy had learned: JF to SS, November 22, 1944, LOC. The passage describing Hemingway has been blacked out, almost

certainly by Solano, but not so well that it is entirely indecipherable.

331 She accepted "without question": JF to SS, January 3, 1945, LOC. The passage in question is blacked out but not indecipherable.

331 "How can I hate": JF to NDM, November 26, 1944, LOC.

332 "I am not interested": JF to SS, April 17, 1945, LOC.

332 Canadian soldiers: JF to SS, December 26, 1944, LOC.

332 Much of the Tuileries Gardens: James J. Rorimer, *Monuments Man: The Mission to Save Vermeers, Rembrandts, Da Vincis, and More from the Nazis' Grasp* (Rizzoli Electa, 2022), 93.

332 Flanner found the city: JF to SS, November 22, 1944, LOC.

332 The gossip was: JF to SS, November 22, 1944, LOC; JF to SS, January 3, 1945, LOC.

333 Flanner told Solano: JF to SS, April 17, 1945, LOC; JF to SS, May 17, 1945, LOC.

333 The French friends: Flanner, *Darlinghissima*, 36–37.

333 Flanner saw the whole: JF to NDM, November 27, 1944, LOC.

333 There she and her colleagues: Ronald Weber, *Dateline: Liberated Paris* (Rowman and Littlefield, 2019), 1–2; JF to NDM, November 26, 1944, LOC.

333 She and the few other: JF to NDM, November 9, 1944, LOC.

333 She favored dry martinis: Murray, *Janet*, 129.

333 Hemingway joined her: JF to SS, February 7, 1945, LOC.

333 Sometimes they visited: Flanner, *Paris Was Yesterday*, viii.

333 She thought the poems: Wineapple, *Genêt*, 186.

334 All around her she saw: JF to SS, undated, 1945, LOC.

334 This was the so-called: Julian Jackson, *France: The Dark Years, 1940–1944* (Oxford University Press, 2001), 577–581.

334 "You have no idea": JF to SS, undated, 1945, LOC.

334 Surveying the French capital: Flanner, *Darlinghissima*, 36–37.

335 Even while walking: JF to KSW, February 12, 1946, BM.

335 "I continue to feel": JF to NDM, November 27, 1944, LOC.

335 She covered food rationing: FNY, December 23, 1944.

336 Ross cabled her: HR to JF, December 21, 1944, NYR 44; JF to HR, December 21, 1944, NYR 44; JF to SS, January 22, 1945, LOC; JF to NDM, January 21, 1945, LOC.

336 She was, however: JF to SS, January 22, 1945, LOC; JF to NDM, January 21, 1945, LOC.

336 At the Hotel Scribe: JF to SS, December 26, 1944, LOC.

336 "I do not see": JF to NDM, December 14, 1944, LOC.

336 She said that she had long: JF to NDM, May 29, 1946, LOC.

337 She wondered if she'd lost: JF to SS, February 7–8, 1945, LOC.

337 She arrived wearing: JF to SS, June 5, 1945, LOC; various photographs, LOC; Wineapple, *Genêt*, 184, 189.

337 She told Solano: Wineapple, *Genêt*, 189.

337 She slept in simple: Wineapple, *Genêt*, 191.

337 She tried to manage: JF to SS, undated, 1945, LOC.

338 "During their first": FNY, March 31, 1945.

338 Ross advised Flanner: Yagoda, *About Town*, 181–182.

338 Flanner wrote her piece: JF to SS, April 24, 1945, LOC.

338 Flanner confronted readers: FNY, May 5, 1945.

338 A young survivor: Wineapple, *Genêt*, 192.

339 "I wish nothing": JF to SS, April 24, 1945, LOC.

339 "The news from the concentration camps": JF to NDM, May 19, 1945, LOC.

339 She echoed: FNY, May 19, 1945.

339 Over the following months: JF to SS, undated, 1945, LOC.

339 She'd seen "wicked *proof*": JF to SS, September 25, 1946, LOC.

339 "You'd not know me": JF to NDM, April 24, 1945, LOC.

339 "Death to tyrants": JF to NDM, April 24, 1945, LOC.

339 All she could think: JF to SS, May 17, 1945, LOC.

340 "Physically war stops": JF to NDM, May 15, 1945, LOC.

340 Their time in Italy: JF to NDM, July 20, 1945, LOC.

340 In the fall of 1945: JF to NDM, October 22, 1945, LOC.

340 She'd planned to attend: JF to NDM, December 9, 1945, LOC.

340 The Allied powers: Michael R. Marrus, *The Nuremberg War Crimes Trial, 1945–46* (Bedford/St. Martin's Press, 2017), 2.

341 The tribunal's driving goals: Jack Fairweather, *The Prosecutor: One Man's Battle to Bring Nazis to Justice* (Crown, 2025), 78–80.

341 When the official: Wineapple, *Genêt*, 197.

341 Flanner joked: Flanner, *Darlinghissima*, 73.

341 On the trial's first day: Fairweather, *The Prosecutor*, 81.

341 She turned fifty-four: JF to NDM, March 12, 1946, LOC.

341 Fellow reporters: Wineapple, *Genêt*, 198–199.

341 "I have never worked harder": JF to NDM, June 6, 1946, LOC.

342 "It seemed as if": Wineapple, *Genêt*, 198.

342 She understood how angry: JF to NDM, March 26, 1946, LOC.

342 "Our lawyers have succeeded": Flanner, *Uncollected*, 100.

343 And she didn't flinch: Flanner, *Uncollected*, 108.

343 She quoted a German: Flanner, *Uncollected*, 101.

343 When the last: Wineapple, *Genêt*, 198.

343 Katharine White added: Murray, *Janet*, 125.

344 Most of the criminals: Fulbrook, *Reckonings*, 248.

344 Flanner shot back: Murray, *Janet*, 167.

344 She admitted that her heart: JF to NDM, October 24, 1945, LOC.

344 Murray floated the idea: Wineapple, *Genêt*, 196.

344 "I feel a foreigner": Murray, *Janet*, 167.

345 Flanner wrote back, "I think": Murray, *Janet*, 173.

346 "I do NOT think": JF to SS, September 25, 1946, LOC.

346 She'd earlier received: Wineapple, *Genêt*, 204.

BIBLIOGRAPHY

Anderson, Margaret. *The Fiery Fountains*. Hermitage House, 1951.

Anderson, Margaret. *My Thirty Years' War*. Covici, 1930.

Anthes, Louis. "Publicly Deliberative Drama: The 1934 Mock Trial of Adolf Hitler for 'Crimes against Civilization.'" *The American Journal of Legal History* 42, no. 4 (1998): 391–410.

Bainbridge, John. *Another Way of Living*. Holt, Rinehart, and Winston, 1968.

Baker, Carlos. *Ernest Hemingway: A Life Story*. Collier Books, 1988.

Barnes, Djuna. *Ladies Almanack*. Harper and Row, 1972.

Beevor, Antony. *The Battle for Spain: The Spanish Civil War, 1936–1939*. Penguin Books, 2006.

Belin, Jean. *Trente ans de Surete nationale*. Bibliotheque France-Soir, 1951.

Benstock, Shari. *Women of the Left Bank: Paris, 1900–1940*. University of Texas Press, 1986.

Bourdel, Phillipe. *La Cagoule*. Albin Michel, 1970.

Bower, Tom. *The Pledge Betrayed: America and Britain and the Denazification of Post-War Germany*. Doubleday, 1983.

Burden, Hamilton T. *The Nuremberg Party Rallies: 1923–1939*. Frederick Prager, 1967.

Camus, Albert. *Réflexions sur la Guillotine*. Folio, 2008.

Camus, Albert. *The Stranger*. Translated by Matthew Ward. Vintage, 1999.

Charters, James [Jimmie the Barman], and Morrill Cody. *This Must Be the Place: Memoirs of Montparnasse*. Lee Furman, 1937.

Chisholm, Anne. *Nancy Cunard: A Biography*. Knopf, 1979.

Cohen, Deborah. *Last Call at the Hotel Imperial: The Reporters Who Took On a World at War*. Random House, 2022.

Colombani, Roger. *L'Affaire Weidmann*. Albin Michel, 1989.

Conradi, Peter. *Hitler's Piano Player: The Rise and Fall of Ernst Hanfstaengle, Confidant of Hitler, Ally of FDR*. Carroll and Graf, 2004.

Cowley, Malcolm. *A Second Flowering: Works and Days of the Lost Generation*. Viking, 1973.

Cunard, Nancy. *These Were the Hours*. Southern Illinois University Press, 1969.

Daladier, Édouard. *Journal de captivité: 1940–1945*. Calmann-Lévy, 1991.

De Beauvoir, Simone. *The Prime of Life*. World Publishing, 1962.

De Beauvoir, Simone. *The Second Sex*. Vintage, 2009.

Donovan, James M. *Juries and the Transformation of Criminal Justice in France in the Nineteenth and Twentieth Centuries*. University of North Carolina Press, 2010.

Eksteins, Modris. *Rites of Spring: The Great War and the Birth of the Modern Age*. Mariner Books, 2000.

Ellmann, Richard. *James Joyce*. Oxford University Press, 1982.

Euloge, Georges-André. *Histoire de la Police*. Plon, 1985.

Evans, Richard J. *The Coming of the Third Reich*. Penguin Press, 2005.

Evans, Richard J. *The Third Reich at War: 1939–1945*. Penguin Press, 2008.

Evans, Richard J. *The Third Reich in Power: 1933–1939*. Penguin Books, 2006.

Fahs, Alice. *Out on Assignment: Newspaper Women and the Making of Modern Public Space*. University of North Carolina Press, 2011.

Fest, Joachim. *The Face of the Third Reich*. Pantheon Books, 1970.

Fiss, Karen. *Grand Illusion: The Third Reich, the Paris Exposition, and the Cultural Seduction of France*. University of Chicago Press, 1997.

Fitch, Noel Riley. *Sylvia Beach and the Lost Generation: A History of Literary Paris in the Twenties and Thirties*. Norton, 1985.

Fitzgerald, F. Scott. "My Lost City," in *The Crack-Up*. New Directions, 1945.

Flanner, Janet. *Darlinghissima: Letters to a Friend*. Edited by Natalia Danesi Murray. Random House, 1985.

Flanner, Janet. *Janet Flanner's World: Uncollected Writings, 1932–1975*. Edited by Irving Drutman. Harvest, 1981.

Flanner, Janet. *Paris Journal, 1956–1964*. Edited by William Shawn. Harvest, 1988.

Flanner, Janet. *Paris Was Yesterday 1925–1939*. Edited by Irving Drutman. Harvest, 1988.

François-Poncet, André. *The Fateful Years: Memoirs of a French Ambassador in Berlin, 1931–1938*. Harcourt, Brace, 1949.

Friedman, Alice T. "Queer Old Things: Image, Myth, and Memory in 20th-Century Paris." *Places*, February 2015.

Friedrich, Otto. *Before the Deluge: A Portrait of Berlin in the 1920s*. Harper and Row, 1972.

Fulbrook, Mary. *Reckonings: Legacies of Nazi Persecution and the Quest for Justice*. Oxford University Press, 2018.

Fussell, Paul. *Abroad: British Literary Traveling Between the Wars*. Oxford University Press, 1994.

Fussell, Paul. *The Great War and Modern Memory*. Oxford University Press, 2013.

Gambino, Megan. "When Gertrude Stein Toured America." *Smithsonian*, October 13, 2011.

Gardiner, Juliet. *The Thirties: An Intimate History*. Harper, 2010.

Gay, Peter. *My German Question: Growing Up in Nazi Berlin*. Yale University Press, 1998.

Gemie, Sharif. "The Ballad of Bourg-Madame: Memory, Exile, and the Spanish Republican Refugees of the 'Retirada' of 1939." *International Review of Social History* 51, no. 1 (2006): 1–40.

Gill, Anton. *A Dance Between Flames: Berlin Between the Wars*. John Murray, 1993.

Gill, Brendan. *Here at "The New Yorker."* Random House, 1975.

Golan, Romy. *Modernity and Nostalgia: Art and Politics in France Between the Wars*. Yale University Press, 1995.

Goldensohn, Leon. *The Nuremberg Interviews*. Knopf, 2004.

Gonzalez, Jeffrey. "The Metropolitan as Master Subject: Janet Flanner's 'Paris Letters.'" *Mosaic: A Journal for the Interdisciplinary Study of Literature* 43, no. 1 (2010): 41–56.

Gopnik, Adam, ed. *Americans in Paris: A Literary Anthology*. Library of America, 2004.

Gordon, Lois. *Nancy Cunard: Heiress, Muse, Political Idealist*. Columbia University Press, 2007.

Grant, Jane. *Ross, "The New Yorker," and Me*. Reynal, 1966.

Halttunen, Karen. *Murder Most Foul: The Killer and the Gothic Imagination*. Harvard University Press, 2000.

Hausdorff, Don. "Politics and Economics: The Emergence of a *New Yorker* Tone." *Studies in American Humor* 3, no. 1 (1984): 74–82.

Heinzerling, Larry, and Randy Herschaft, with Ann Cooper. *Newshawks in Berlin: The Associated Press and Nazi Germany*. Columbia University Press, 2024.

Henry, Susan. *Anonymous in Their Own Names: Doris E. Fleischman, Ruth Hale, and Jane Grant*. Vanderbilt University Press, 2012.

Herbert, James D. *Paris 1937: Worlds on Exhibition*. Cornell University Press, 1998.

Hillenbrand, Laura. *Unbroken: A World War II Story of Survival, Resilience, and Redemption*. Random House, 2010.

Hobsbawm, Eric. *Interesting Times: A Twentieth-Century Life*. Pantheon Books, 2002.

Hochschild, Adam. *Spain in Our Hearts: Americans in the Spanish Civil War, 1936–1939*. Mariner Books, 2017.

Hoffmann, Heinrich. *Deutschland in Paris*. Heinrich Hoffmann Verlag, 1937.

Hugo, Victor. *Les Misérables*. 1862.

Hulme, Kathryn C. *Undiscovered Country*. Little, Brown, 1966.

Hussey, Andrew. *Paris: The Secret History*. Bloomsbury, 2008.

Jackson, Julian. *France: The Dark Years, 1940–1944*. Oxford University Press, 2001.

Jackson, Julian. *The Popular Front in France: Defending Democracy, 1934–38*. Cambridge University Press, 1998.

Jardin Birnie, Renée. *Le Cahier Rouge d'Eugène Weidmann*. Gallimard, 1968.

Jesse, F. Tennyson. *Comments on Cain*. Collier Books, 1964.

Jones, Colin. *Paris: Biography of a City*. Penguin Books, 2006.

Judt, Tony. *The Burden of Responsibility: Blum, Camus, Aron, and the French Twentieth Century*. University of Chicago Press, 2008.

Judt, Tony. *Postwar: A History of Europe Since 1945*. Penguin Press, 2005.

Kalifa, Dominique. *L'encre et le sang: Récits de crimes et société à la Belle Époque*. Fayard, 1995.

Kedward, Rod. *France and the French: A Modern History*. Abrams, 2007.

Kershaw, Ian. *Hitler, 1889–1936: Hubris*. Norton, 1998.

Kessler, Harry. *Berlin in Lights: The Diaries of Count Harry Kessler, 1918–1937*. Translated and edited by Charles Kessler. Grove Press, 1999.

Klemperer, Victor. *I Will Bear Witness: A Diary of the Nazi Years, 1933–1941*. Random House, 1998.

Kunkel, Thomas. *Genius in Disguise: Harold Ross of "The New Yorker."* Random House, 1995.

Kunkel, Thomas. *Letters from the Editor: "The New Yorker"'s Harold Ross*. Modern Library, 2000.

Kurth, Peter. *American Cassandra: The Life of Dorothy Thompson*. Little, Brown, 1990.

Lanzalavi, Dominique. *Vincent de Moro Giafferi*. Albiana, 2011.

Lanzmann, Jacques. *Paris des années 30*. Editions de la Martinière, 1992.

Larson, Erik. *In the Garden of Beasts*. Crown, 2011.

Lazareff, Pierre. *Deadline: The Behind-the-Scenes Story of the Last Decade in France*. Random House, 1942.

Lee, Judith Yaross. *Defining "New Yorker" Humor*. University Press of Mississippi, 2000.

Lefranc, Georges. *Histoire du Front populaire, 1934–1938*. Payot, 1965.

Lemke, Ute. "Les touristes allemands du IIIe Reich face à l'autre Allemagne lors de l'Exposition Internationale de Paris (1937)." *Viaggiatori*, September 2018.

Lesinska, Zofia P. *Perspectives of Four Women Writers on the Second World War: Gertrude Stein, Janet Flanner, Kay Boyle, and Rebecca West*. Peter Lang, 2002.

Lipstadt, Deborah E. *Beyond Belief: The American Press and the Coming of the Holocaust 1933–1945*. Free Press, 1986.

Lodge, David Clay. *Between Two Fires: Europe's Path in the 1930s*. Norton, 1990.

Loos, Anita. *A Girl Like I*. Viking, 1966.

Lottman, Herbert. *The Left Bank*. Houghton Mifflin, 1982.

Lottman, Herbert. *Man Ray's Montparnasse*. Abrams, 2001.

Mackrell, Judith. *The Correspondents: Six Women Writers on the Front Lines of World War II*. Doubleday, 2021.

Marrus, Michael R. *The Nuremberg War Crimes Trial, 1945–46*. Bedford/St. Martin's Press, 2017.

Mazower, Mark. *Dark Continent: Europe's Twentieth Century*. Vintage, 1998.

McAuliffe, Mary. *Paris on the Brink*. Rowman and Littlefield, 2018.

McCarthy, Mary. "Conversation Piece." *New York Times*, November 21, 1965.

McKelway, St. Clair. *Reporting at Wit's End: Tales from "The New Yorker."* Introduction by Adam Gopnik. Bloomsbury, 2010.

Miller, Donald. *Supreme City: How Jazz Age Manhattan Gave Birth to Modern America*. Simon and Schuster, 2014.

Miller, Michael B. *Shanghai on the Métro: Spies, Intrigue, and the French Between the Wars*. University of California Press, 1994.

Millington, Chris. *The Invention of Terrorism in France, 1904–1939*. Stanford University Press, 2023.

Millington, Chris. *Le Massacre de Clichy*. Éditions Critique, 2021.

Monk, Craig. *Writing the Lost Generation: Expatriate Autobiography and American Modernism*. University of Iowa Press, 2008.

Montefiore, Janet. *Men and Women Writers of the 1930s: The Dangerous Flood of History*. Routledge, 1996.

Moorehead, Caroline. *Gellhorn: A Twentieth-Century Life*. Henry Holt, 2003.

Morisi, Ève. *Capital Letters: Hugo, Baudelaire, Camus, and the Death Penalty*. Northwestern University Press, 2020.

Morton, Patricia. *Hybrid Modernities: Architecture and Representation at the 1931 Colonial Exposition Paris*. MIT Press, 2000.

Murray, William. *Janet, My Mother, and Me*. Simon and Schuster, 2000.

Nogueres, Henri. *La Vie quotidienne au temps du Front populaire*. Hachette, 1977.

Nye, Robert A. *Crime, Madness, and Politics in Modern France: The Medical Concept of National Decline*. Princeton University Press, 1984.

O'Neal, Hank. *"Life Is Painful, Nasty & Short—In My Case It Has Only Been Painful and Nasty": Djuna Barnes, 1978–1981: An Informal Memoir*. Paragon House, 1990.

Orwell, George. *Homage to Catalonia and Down and Out in Paris And London*. Houghton Mifflin, 2010.

Orwell, George. *Orwell in Spain*. Penguin Books, 2001.

Ory, Pascal. *La Belle Illusion: Culture et politique sous le signe du Front populaire, 1935–1938*. Plon, 1994.

Patterson, Patrick. *Ladies of the Rope: Gurdjieff's Special Left Bank Women's Group*. Arete, 1999.

Paxton, Robert O. *Vichy France: Old Guard and New Order, 1940–1944*. Columbia University Press, 2001.

Pearl, Monica B. "'What Strange Intimacy': Janet Flanner's Letters from Paris." *Journal of European Studies* 32, no. 125–6 (2002).

Peer, Shanny. *France on Display: Peasants, Provincials, and Folklore in the 1937 Paris World's Fair*. State University of New York Press, 1998.

Pellissier, Pierre. *6 Février, 1934*. Perrin, 2000.

Peterson, Rai. "Janet Flanner's *The Cubical City* and the Life She Left Behind," *e-Rea* 16, no. 2 (2019).

Pettegree, Andrew. *The Invention of News: How the World Came to Know About Itself*. Yale University Press, 2015.

Puchner, Martin. *Poetry of the Revolution: Marx, Manifestos, and the Avant-Gardes*. Princeton University Press, 2006.

Randa, Philippe. *L'Affaire Weidmann*. Fleuve, 1992.

Reading, Amy. *The World She Edited: Katharine S. White at "The New Yorker."* Mariner Books, 2024.

Rearick, Charles. *The French in Love and War*. Yale University Press, 1997.

Roberts, Mary-Louise. *Civilization Without Sexes: Reconstructing Gender in Postwar France 1917–1927*. University of Chicago Press, 1994.

Rorimer, James J. *Monuments Man: The Mission to Save Vermeers, Rembrandts, Da Vincis, and More from the Nazis' Grasp*. Rizzoli Electa, 2022.

Rosenberg, Clifford. *Policing Paris: The Origins of Modern Immigration Control Between the Wars*. Cornell University Press, 2006.

Roth, Joseph. *What I Saw: Reports from Berlin, 1920–1933*. Norton, 2003.

Ryback, Timothy W. *Takeover: Hitler's Final Rise to Power*. Knopf, 2024.

Sante, Lucy. *The Other Paris*. Farrar, Straus and Giroux, 2015.

Schwartz, Vanessa, and Jason Hill, eds. *Getting The Picture: The Visual Culture of the News*. Routledge, 2015.

Scutts, Joanna. *Hotbed: Bohemian Greenwich Village and the Secret Club that Sparked Modern Feminism*. Seal Press, 2022.

Sebba, Anne. *Battling for News: Women Reporters from the Risorgimento to Tiananmen Square*. Hodder and Stoughton, 1994.

Sereny, Gitta. *Albert Speer: His Battle With the Truth*. Knopf, 1995.

Sherwill, Ambrose. *A Fair and Honest Book*. Lulu, 2007.

Shirer, William L. *Berlin Diary*. Knopf, 1941.

Shirer, William L. *The Rise and Fall of the Third Reich*. Simon and Schuster, 1990.

Shirer, William L. *Twentieth Century Journey: A Memoir of a Life and the Times*, vol. 2, *The Nightmare Years, 1930–1940*. Little, Brown, 1984.

Sicot, Marcel. *Servitude et grandeur policière. Quarante ans à la Sûreté*. Les Productions de Paris, 1959.

Sorel, Nancy Caldwell. *The Women Who Wrote the War*. Harper, 1999.

Soucy, Robert. *French Fascism: The Second Wave, 1933–1939*. Yale University Press, 1995.

Souhami, Diana. *No Modernism Without Lesbians*. Bloomsbury, 2020.

Spangler, Luita Deane. "On Her Mouth You Kiss Your Own: Lesbian Conversations in Exile, 1924–1936." Unpublished dissertation, University of New Hampshire, 1992.

Speer, Albert. *Inside the Third Reich: Memoirs*. Translated by Richard and Clara Winston. Macmillan, 1970.

Starck, Lindsay. "Janet Flanner's High Class Gossip" and "American Nationalism Between the Wars," *The Journal of Modern Periodical Studies* 7, nos. 1–2, (2016): 1–25.

Sternhell, Zeev. *Neither Right Nor Left: Fascist Ideology in France*. Translated by David Maisel. University of California Press, 1986.

Sudjic, Deyan. *Stalin's Architect: Power and Survival in Moscow*. MIT Press, 2022.

Toulemon, André. *Portraits d'Avocats: Moro-Giafferi, Henri-Robert, Léon Bérard, le Bâtonnier Fourcade, etc.* Dalloz, 1965.

Vaill, Amanda. *Everybody Was So Young*. Broadway Books, 1999.

Vaill, Amanda. *Hotel Florida: Truth, Love, and Death in the Spanish Civil War*. Picador, 2015.

Valéry, Paul. *Variety*. Translated by Malcolm Cowley. Harcourt, Brace, 1927.

Wagner-Martin, Linda. *Favored Strangers: Gertrude Stein and Her Family*. Rutgers University Press, 1995.

Walker, David H. *Outrage and Insight: Modern French Writers and the "Fait Divers."* Berg, 1995.

Wardhaugh, Jessica. *In Pursuit of the People: Political Culture in France, 1934–39*. Palgrave Macmillan, 2009.

Watling, Sarah. *Tomorrow Perhaps the Future: Writers, Outsiders, and the Spanish Civil War*. Knopf, 2023.

Watts, Philip. "Saint Weidmann." *L'Esprit créateur* 35, no. 1 (1995): 11–19.

Weber, Eugen. *Action Francaise: Royalism and Reaction in Twentieth Century France*. Stanford University Press, 1962.

Weber, Eugen. *La France des années 30*. Fayard, 1995.

Weber, Ronald. *Dateline: Liberated Paris*. Rowman and Littlefield, 2019.

Weber, Ronald. *News of Paris: American Journalists in the City of Light Between the Wars*. Ivan R. Dee, 2006.

Weiss, Andrea. *Paris Was a Woman*. Harper San Francisco, 1995.

Werth, Alexander. *The Last Days of Paris: A Journalist's Diary*. Hamish Hamilton, 1940.

Werth, Alexander. *The Twilight of France, 1933–1940*. Howard Fertig, 1966.

Westcott, Glenway. "The Frenchman Six Foot Three." *Harper's*, July 1942.

Williams, William Carlos. *The Autobiography of William Carlos Williams*. New Directions, 1967.

Wineapple, Brenda. *Genêt: A Biography of Janet Flanner*. University of Nebraska Press, 1992.

Wiser, William. *The Twilight Years: Paris in the 20s*. Carroll and Graf, 2000.

Yagoda, Ben. *About Town: The New Yorker and The World It Made*. Da Capo, 2000.

Zox-Weaver, Annalisa. *Women Modernists and Fascism*. Cambridge University Press, 2011.

FILM

Moore, Richard O., dir. *The Writer in America: Janet Flanner*. Perspective Films, 1975.

ABOUT THE AUTHOR

Mark Braude is the author of three books of nonfiction, most recently *Kiki Man Ray: Art, Love, and Rivalry in 1920s Paris*, a *New York Times* Notable Book of 2022 and a *New Yorker* Best Book of the Year. He has been a Postdoctoral Fellow at Stanford University, a Visiting Fellow at the American Library in Paris, and an NEH Public Scholar. He has written for *The New York Times*, *The Los Angeles Times*, and other publications. He lives in Vancouver with his wife and their two daughters.